YOUR KIDS ARE GROWN

Moving on With and Without Them

YOUR KIDS ARE GROWN

Moving on
With and Without Them

FRANCINE A. TODER, Ph. D.

INSIGHT BOOKS

PLENUM PRESS • NEW YORK AND LONDON

Library of Congress Cataloging-in-Publication Data

Toder, Francine, 1940-
    Your kids are grown : moving on with and without them / Francine
A. Toder.
        p.   cm.
    Includes bibliographical references and index.
    ISBN 0-306-44761-4
    1. Parent and adult child.   2. Intergenerational relations.
I. Title.
HQ755.86.T63   1994
306.874--dc20   94-19496
                                                                    CIP

ISBN 0-306-44761-4

Insight Books is a Division of Plenum Publishing Corporation
233 Spring Street, New York, N.Y. 10013-1578

An Insight Book

Printed in the United States of America

For my very dear friend, Claire Ostern,
a natural mother who seemed instinctively to know
how to parent her daughters as children
and then as adults. Loving, honest, and wise,
she will be greatly missed.

Acknowledgments

Thanks first to my son, Matt, now a young adult, for providing the life circumstances that piqued my curiosity and led to the writing of this book. Along the way, in the five years that followed, I spoke with everyone I met about their concerns in parenting adult children.

To the clients in my private practice, and to those who consulted with me at the Student Health Center at California State University, Sacramento, I am grateful for the honest, open expressions of feelings and astute observations about the parent–adult-child interaction.

My university colleagues offered support and allowed me time to collect data from young-adult students. The responses to my questionnaire, focusing on the evolving adult-based relationship with their parents, were candid and thoughtful. Their willingness to share what worked and what didn't greatly increased my knowledge and understanding.

Dr. Carol Schneider, longtime friend and psychologist, read and critiqued the manuscript as it evolved from beginning to end. I very much valued her honest appraisal. I also trusted her to be gentle in her criticism.

Dr. Virginia Kidd provided the perspective of a communication studies professor and mother of a son in his mid-twenties. Her keen eye for editing and her wonderful sense of humor helped make the process of review and revision bearable.

Frank Darmstadt, editor at Insight Books, was always very respectful, taking an almost finished manuscript and shaping it without sacrificing its form or message. His expertise enhanced the book by increasing its clarity and depth. For his help I am extremely grateful.

Finally, my husband, Joe Hustein, deserves much credit for the many hours he spent encouraging, motivating, and always supporting my work, even when it seemed to absorb our family life. Nobody knows me, or understands what I am trying to say, better than Joe. My daughter, Flynne, a creative teenager with great compassion and maturity, intuitively understood my need for space and time to think, and I am very appreciative.

Contents

YOUR KIDS
ARE GROWN

Moving on
With and Without Them

Introduction

Your Kids Are Grown: What's the Problem?

If you are exasperated with your adult-children, this book is for you. When your attempts to communicate are met with distance, deafness, rejection, anger, or misunderstanding, you feel disappointed and hurt. It isn't that any love is lacking between you and your child. Rather, your contact feels like opposite ends of a magnet that just keep repelling one another. You think that there must be some better way to reach them, but you don't know what it is.

Why is it that there's so much tension between you? It wasn't always this way! For years you imagined how lovely it would be when your children were grown and independent. You anticipated a special adult connection, not possible before. You looked forward to sharing their lives, and without the responsibility of a parent. It looked easy to accomplish.

Instead you often feel excluded or misconstrued. When you approach with advice, they bristle. When you show concern about their problems, they say you're intrusive. When you ask about their plans, they're defensive. When you forget something they've told you, it's because you are insensitive and uncaring.

Current struggles may subside, but the underlying pattern of miscommunication is likely to lead to conflict that surfaces again and again. Is it your problem? You can see how your own issues or problems get in the way. Maybe you respond defensively, angrily, or intrusively. You wonder whether your own psychological or emotional traits interfere. Perhaps you are overly sensitive to certain behaviors or attitudes expressed by your adult-children.

Is it their problem? Your grown-up son or daughter may have developed habits, personality traits, behaviors, or ways of communicating that make contact with them painful or impossible. They may overreact (blow up or become enraged) or underreact (show nothing of what they feel or sulk). Their competence to manage an adult life may be in question. Independent functioning may be an issue because of an addiction, a disease, or a developmental delay.

The strife may not be entirely your problem or theirs but an interactive struggle. Such a conflict has no culprits. Both of you are victims.

Once upon a time there would have been no need for this book. Long ago parents did not need to figure out how to redesign a relationship with their adult-children. Life was predictably short, and survival into middle age was not something one could count on. Understanding the process of growth and change in the young adult, the midlife adult, and the senior adult was really not very significant to the average person.

Before the era of self-help books, people learned their parenting skills from their parents, their extended family, and the community at large. Learning to parent was a hands-on experience stemming from what people saw around them plus human instinct in the novel situations that went beyond the limits of their knowledge.

Even a hundred years ago life didn't go much beyond basic survival and spirituality. To live to forty was fortunate.* There was no time or need to learn relationship refinement techniques. By twenty-one you knew all that had to be known. The whole process was complete, only to be played out again and again by succeeding generations.

Until the twentieth century, life centered on learning enough skills to survive childhood and then using those skills to raise the next generation. Religion helped by creating personal meaning to soften the sharp edges of daily life. These were the tools for forging life, but they are no longer sufficient.

With the possibility of a much longer life, it is now relevant to learn what happens to human relationships when adults *do* survive beyond forty, and perhaps beyond ninety.† What happens to your ongoing contact with your children who enter adulthood, when they are twenty, thirty, forty-five? Does a sixty-year-old mother really need to adapt her parenting skills to have a viable relationship with her forty-year-old son or daughter?

When parenting no longer requires day-to-day attention, there is an expectation of a mature relationship with one's adult-kids marked by tranquillity and contentment. The promise of satisfaction is not always fulfilled.

You may be one of the enormous number of midlife parents who wish to have a substantial and loving connection with your grown children but find that something is lacking. Rushed phone

---

*"In ancient Greece the average life expectancy was approximately twenty years. . . . During the Middle Ages a person could expect to live for thirty years if she or he could escape the plague, war or starvation. . . . Our grandparents or great-grandparents, born around 1900, could expect to live fifty years; today we can expect to live seventy-five or more years, an increase of twenty-five years in less than a century!" (Van Hoose, 1985, p. 103).

†According to M. Gerber, the author of *Life Trends: Your Future for the Next 30 Years* (1991), "During the 1990's, the number of Americans in the 35–50 age bracket will grow four times as fast as the number of those in any other. Most of these new middle aged will be baby boomers, the first of whom will turn 50 in 1996" (p. 1).

calls may be a subtle cue. More obvious signals may be anger or accusation. When your adult-children do not feel capable of leading the kind of life you envisioned for them, they may become distant to avoid a sense of guilt. Whatever it is, you feel a knot in your stomach, tension in your shoulders, or sadness in your heart.

Problems come in all sizes and shapes. Some are easy to identify but difficult to address. If your son or daughter marries outside the family faith or chooses a lifestyle unacceptable to you, the source of the conflict is very clear, but emotions may run too high to be communicated effectively. For example, everyone may be aware of your unhappiness about your son's or daughter's choice. Being a sensitive subject, it is avoided verbally. Still, any contact reveals the tension in your voice and body. Your feelings are thinly veiled.

Other problems are easier to work on but more difficult to pinpoint. These are often due to an old misunderstanding or hurt that grows, like a virus, over time. When the issue is finally seen it resolves itself through talk or symbolic gestures. A thoughtless remark or lack of support at a critical point can begin a downward cycle.

I remember a young woman who was convinced that her parents favored her older sister. She recalled, with hurt, her parents' gift of a new car to her sister, which she herself got only after it had been discarded by her sibling. This reinforced her view. For years she tried to please her parents by following in her sister's footsteps. Because she was not following her own talents or inclinations, she never accomplished her goals to her satisfaction. Sadly, she also saw herself as second-rate in her parents' eyes. When her efforts showed little reward, she lost her direction and began to drift. Her worried and confused parents showed their disappointment and again reinforced the young woman's belief that she was less valued than her sister.

Siblings can continue to be rivals as adults. The need for parental approval or support does not end with childhood. Although these issues are quite common, disruptive of communication, and hard to spot, once identified, they are easier to resolve. This book will help you identify the issues and give you help in working on them. You and your adult-children face all kinds of difficulties and conflicts, some quite serious, others simply annoying.

Another goal of this book is to provide the tools for reinforcing shaky relationships once the active struggles with your child and adolescent give way to the more subtle stresses and strains of adult–adult contact. In the best of circumstances, the skills we all learned in parenting young children simply don't apply to adult-children. The skills need to be retooled, abandoned, or otherwise modified for grown-up kids.

The focus of this book includes many serious challenges as well as the petty conflicts of everyday life. In most families, the major issues stand out like a sore thumb and are easy to identify, even if they are not easy to resolve. On the other hand, the petty issues appear minor but build and accumulate gradually over time like a pile of old newspapers. Unnoticed until you begin to trip over it, the pile of small grievances gets in the way of effective communication.

Large or small, family conflicts are inevitable. Unfortunately, the motivation to resolve problems is often higher than the skill levels required. In *Midlife Myths: Issues, Findings, and Practical Implications*, Hunter and Sundel tell us, "The importance of maintaining relationships is attested to by the maneuvers family members use in handling conflicts. They tend to restrict their fights to 'trivial' matters rather than serious ones, to hair length rather than decisions for the future" (p. 218). Serious matters sometimes seem too ominous to confront.

This book will help you resolve a no-win situation without placing blame on either party. The goal is to search for the source of conflict between you and your adult-child and to find ways through or around the wall that has been formed between you.

Another goal of this book is to look at both types of struggles—both major and minor—and to identify the strategies that lead to changes in thinking and behaving. Along the way there will be numerous exercises and examples to reinforce what you learn and give you courage to try out new ideas.

What are the issues that you will learn more about?

Major challenges in coping with an adult-child who
- is physically, mentally, or psychologically disabled.
- has an addiction problem.
- has an alternate lifestyle.
- has conflicting values.
- has difficulty accepting adult responsibility.

Day-to-day matters that undermine communication are
- competition.
- personality and style differences.
- family traditions.
- expectations.

Let's examine an example of a major challenge that comes to mind. One day while working on this book I received a call from a friend who wanted to blow off some steam. She had just finished a conversation with her thirty-two-year-old "adolescent" son. He was planning to move home again after being laid off from his current job of two months. On the surface he seemed no different from many other workers displaced by a sluggish economy. Why was she so angry?

Her son hadn't planned very well, and that was nothing new, according to his mother. She could recall numerous times during his adolescence when he had failed to see the consequences of his actions, for example, buying things that he couldn't quite afford. When his last job had begun he had bought a new car. He had no savings and little skill in managing money. From his mother's vantage point, there was no sign that he could imagine his future or even plan beyond next week.

Her furious reaction seemed excessive. Clearly, some of that anger was directed at a pattern of events that went beyond the loss of a job. How does a parent deal with a thirty-two-year-old adolescent? Supportive structure, discussed in Chapter 4, is one key to change.

While finding a solution is necessary, it is often not enough. In addition, your own culture, family history, and personality play a key role in the way you see and handle the struggles with your adult-children. In the next few chapters you will see how recognizing these contributory factors leads to increased understanding and change.

The remainder of this book will arm you with knowledge and techniques that will help you feel better about yourself. You will experience increased confidence in relating to your adult-children. You will probably try new interventions when tension escalates between you and your adult-children. Most of all, you will have the emotional tools to cope with future distress so that you can move on with and without your adult-children.

Part I

UNDERSTANDING THE TENSION BETWEEN YOU

Chapter 1

What Do They Want from Us? A Survey of Adult-Children

Their Perspective

When I set out to write this book I had my own biases based on a lifetime of being a daughter and a mother. I found it intriguing that what I most wanted from my own parents—respect, support, and interest—were the very things I was sometimes guilty of not showing my own children. To make certain that my personal mistakes and shortcomings didn't interfere with my writing, I did what all psychologists do: I talked with colleagues and friends.

The array of responses was incredible. There is no easy way to summarize a person's relationships with his or her parents. Even so, after speaking with as many people as could tolerate my questioning, I still felt that I had a biased sample. Certainly the experiences of mental health professionals could not be representative of those of others!

I wondered if there really were some communication patterns that characterized satisfactory relationships. I was curious about the existence of some universal standards for parenting that must be met. I questioned whether men or women had different wishes or expectations. I thought about the effect of religion, education, or occupation on how people viewed contact with their parents. It was time to find out.

It is easy to do research at a university because students, faculty, and staff are used to being asked to participate in surveys. This was my starting point, but a university population is not very representative. I found myself distributing questionnaires to friends of friends and cousins of neighbors one thousand miles away. Finally I had collected about one hundred responses from all kinds of people and felt ready to make sense out of a mountain of information.

The participants ranged in age from eighteen to sixty-six, and the average age was about twenty-nine. There was a big group of young adults in their early twenties and another big group of midlife adults in their early to mid-forties. The sixty-six-year-old woman in the sample indicated that she is still negotiating a relationship with her mother and confirmed my belief that at any age there is value in working on and reworking relationships with parents. Incidentally, this same woman reports that her mother is both interested in and capable of changing how she relates to her daughter.

Of those who returned a questionnaire, 58 percent were women. It is not surprising that more women than men responded. Our culture has taught women to be more sensitive to relationships and to be more willing to communicate their feelings in surveys such as this one.

In terms of educational background, the average respondent had had some college experience. The range, however, was broad and included high school graduates as well as people with professional degrees. The occupations included students, businesspeople, professionals, homemakers, and government workers. The group also turned out to be diverse in religious affiliation. While it was not an ethnic mirror of the United States, there was definitely input from most major cultural or racial groups.

I thought that race, religion, and educational level would play a bigger role in determining what kids (whatever their ages) wanted and needed from their parents. To my surprise, these factors did not separate the people who had filled out the questionnaire. Instead, I found a consistency of memories from childhood; most people reported that their growing-up years had been relatively happy and normal. This report pleased me because my goal was to understand what "the average healthy person" felt.

This book is being written for the "average" midlife and later-life parent and not necessarily for the parent who is abusive, alcoholic, or otherwise emotionally unavailable. It is for people like you and me, with the best of intentions, who have fallen short of the mark and wish to learn what we can now do to get closer to the mark.

The beginning of the survey tapped childhood memories and the ways in which parents showed support and love as well as disappointment and disapproval. The survey provided choices including verbal, nonverbal, and physical ways of giving feedback to children. Here are the categories:

Mother/father showed their love and support by
>touching, hugging, and/or kissing _____
>telling me with words _____
>giving me material things or money _____
>facial expressions and other body language _____

Mother/father showed their disappointment or disapproval by
>tone of voice _____
>telling me with words _____
>physical means (hitting, spanking, etc.) _____
>depriving me of material things or activities _____
>withdrawal of their attention or help _____

The point of including childhood memories was to try to determine whether good, healthy parent–child relationships would lend themselves to satisfying parent–adult-child relationships. The outcome does not support this idea. Apparently, even parents who seemed to master childhood parenting skills, according to the recall of their offspring, may not be knowledgeable or effective parents to their adult-children. This book has been developed on that premise.

Before moving on let me share a few interesting observations from the survey:

"I wish that mother/father could have given me . . ." was an open-ended question that produced a number of very similar responses. Out of the entire group only one person indicated a material request, and even this twenty-year-old college student seemed to be demonstrating his wit: "A Ferrari, joke!" Almost all of the other comments focused on intangibles that could have been given to them in childhood.

The pervasive wish included more touching, hugging, affection, support, time, nurturance, and respect. One thirty-year-old attorney said, "Greater respect for my decisions and autonomy (such as I had)." A twenty-year-old bookstore clerk wished for "more attention when I was feeling disappointment." A mid-thirties engineer wished "we could have spent more time doing fun things as a family." A postfifty pharmacist felt he could have used "time to talk out situations. . . . I would have preferred any explanation rather than silence."

A small but convinced group gave responses that should make their parents beam with joy: "They have given me everything I've needed," said a twenty-year-old male student. This was echoed by another student: "Nothing more than they have." A college junior was the only one to wish for "more responsibility and work around the house when I was younger." Clearly, his view represents a minority opinion!

A philosophical forty-nine-year-old woman stated her wish this way: "More positive affirmations than my mother gave, although I realize that one cannot give what one does not have to give." Accepting her mother's limitations helped her soothe her disappointment. All in all, the men and women who participated did not seem very critical of their childhood memories.

Looking at current relationships with their parents, this same group of eighty expressed more dissatisfaction. It's difficult to summarize the feelings without losing their richness. For that reason, I have included the following representative anecdotes in response to the statement: "In my day-to-day relationship with my mother and/or father I wish they would be more sensitive to . . ."

A fortyish college professor from the Midwest captured a general sentiment in describing her father's failure to be sensitive: "I wish he would actually listen to what I say, rather than simply responding that 'Everything will be alright.'" A variation on this idea was offered by a twenty-year-old cashier whose parents were not sensitive to "what I want to do, rather than what they think I should do." Neither of these people felt that they were taken seriously by their parents, and both felt that their worries or views were disregarded. At twenty-two, a college coed echoed this feeling. She wished that her father could be more sensitive to "my age and my ability to live my own life by accepting my decisions whether he agrees with my choices or not."

A sales associate in her early twenties was concerned about "the fact that I control my own life now and they shouldn't treat me like a child." The theme of adult status came up again and again. Somehow, parents who were sensitive to the needs of their children and adolescents had failed to make the transition to their offspring's adulthood.

Some additional comments on "wished-for" qualities are presented in the respondents' own words:

- "See me as an adult; supportive of my judgment."
- "Acknowledge what I'm doing, and what I've achieved."
- "Appreciate my life as an adult, trying to make it in the world, e.g., financially, scholastically, and socially."
- "Notice the ways in which I am a competent and happy

adult rather than showing attention only when there are problems."
- "Understand my responsibilities as a single parent."
- "Accept my maturity, individuality, and separateness."
- "Comprehend that I need a little more space than what they are used to allowing/giving me."
- "Support my search for the meaning of life. Sometimes they feel that I lack a purpose."
- "Be aware of my fear of failure and realize the amount of pressure on today's young adults."

The common thread seems to be the desire to be seen and appreciated as a separate, responsible adult with appropriate judgment and decision-making abilities. The message to parents might be "Back off; give me more space, and see me as I am rather than as you think I am."

Needs at Different Stages

When we talk about the needs of adult-children we do not necessarily mean twenty-year-olds. Each stage of life and decade between twenty and fifty is significant and provides unique challenges and events. The way a parent demonstrates support to a twenty-five-year-old daughter will be markedly different from the caring shown to a forty-five-year-old son.

In this section the distinction is explored. The danger of summarizing a decade in a single brief section is that a composite picture may not capture the variety and richness of the lifestyles available.

The Twenties

At twenty years of age, the will reigns,
at thirty, the wit; and at forty the judgment.
BENJAMIN FRANKLIN, *Poor Richard's Almanac* (May 1733)

The twenties are an unsettling time in a person's life. Pulls come from all directions, and the assurance that comes later in life is still lacking. A fiercely independent and competent young adult becomes a scared child overnight, abandoned by family and institutional support, adrift without a sail on the sea of life. If this sounds dramatic, then it accurately captures the feelings of the "twenties" grown-up. Roger Gould, author of *Transformations* (1978), studied the age-related crises and changes in adulthood. He observed that false assumptions carried over from childhood get us in trouble as adults. The idea that our parents will be there when we can't do something on our own "is most powerfully challenged during our twenties, when we are setting up an independent life and making major decisions that no one else can make for us. . . . When this assumption fails, we drop another piece of illusory safety" (p. 40). Out of this chaos and disappointment emerges new strength and competency.

In my work at the university with young men and women at this stage in life, I am intrigued by how well they can present a veneer of composure and a confident presence that belies the inner fear. The more unstable their lives, the more bravado they present to the outside world.

If "twenties" adults are uncomfortable, they are very anxious to conceal that fact from the outside world, and particularly from their parents. It's not that parents won't be supportive; it's that the new adult-child wants to feel autonomous and in control of her or his life. Any anxiety picked up from the parents in the form of questioning, worrying, wondering, or problem solving evokes self-doubt.

What parents see, and often can't understand, is stubborn independence and rigidly held opinions. These serve, like a suit of armor, to protect feelings of vulnerability and dependence. What twenties adults hate most is a parent's sniffing out a problem that they wish to hide, for example, inquiring about the state of their finances when the parent knows that they are bouncing checks. The parent, of course, has a great deal of experience in recognizing problems and can't easily turn off the process.

What did the survey tell us about this newly freed group and their wishes concerning parental behavior? The themes tended to revolve around independence, separateness, and control. What this group wanted most from their parents was acknowledgment of their adult status and sharing of their experiences without criticism, judgment, or advice. If these young adults' tenuous footing was noticed, they wanted their parents to remain silent until specifically asked for help.

If one could sum up this stage in a single statement, it might be "Listen to me tell you about my life. Care about what I have to say. See me more as an equal than as a child. Appreciate what I'm doing rather than point out what I'm not doing. Follow my lead and try not to catch me in my inexperience by using the advantage of your years."

The Thirties

> You must be free to take a path
> Whose end I feel no need to know,
> No irking fever to be sure
> You went where I would have you go . . .
> So you can go without regret
> Away from this familiar land,
> Leaving your kiss upon my hair
> And all the future in your hands.
>
> MARGARET MEAD, *Blackberry Winter* (1972)

The thirties are a time of great stress. "Thirties" adults are typically overburdened and overextended. They "want their piece of the rock, and they feel an urgency about reaching their goals. Forty is an approximate deadline that many young adults unconsciously set for reaching the goals that so often constitute 'making it'" (Hudson, 1991, p. 145).

The fast track that characterizes the thirties has an urgency about it. Anything or anyone imposing additional demands on the thirties adult will be distanced or avoided. This is one way to cope with a "too busy" life. At this stage there is the building of attachments to a partner (if it hasn't happened in the previous decade), a family, and a community. Career and/or family development demands endless attention. The thirties man or woman doesn't like to be sidetracked from achievement.

At this age, people tend to be removed from their parents more than ever but usually don't take the time to notice. We as parents, however, are keenly aware of their distance. The need may be disguised, but they do still need us, though not in the same ways as before.

The thirties group made this point in the survey: They wanted to share what was happening in their lives but often from a distance. They didn't have time to see their parents. They liked checking in with their parents in a once-weekly phone call, but they resented being badgered to visit. If the thirties adult had children they saw the grandparents as helpers, baby-sitters, and "support staff." They felt far too busy to interact directly.

The harried existence of average adults in this decade requires their parents to function behind the scenes. Acceptance and support are required but should be indirectly given. Visiting for the winter or summer vacation may seem overwhelming to your child, which may feel rejecting to you. However, communicating your feelings of rejection may be perceived as stifling and may lead to a further push away. The reverse may also be true. Ironically, if you can maintain your distance and remain respectful of your children's need to set the distance, they may see you as more approachable.

A composite picture of the thirties would show an intensely busy life pushing the limits of time, holding itself together by sheer energy. If your relationship with your adult-child is perceived as another demand, you are likely to be shut out for a while. They need you primarily for support, from a distance. What specifically do they need you to support? This is a good question. Ask them!

The Forties

To hold the same views at forty as we held
at twenty is to have been stupefied for a score
of years, and take rank, not as a prophet, but
as an unteachable brat, well birched and none
the wiser.

ROBERT LOUIS STEVENSON (1881)

Between forty and fifty the pace of life usually settles down. Initial goals for work and marriage have probably been attained. The achievement demands of the last decade tend to have leveled out. The climb is often over as careers peak:

> Forty is a symbolically powerful age for Americans. . . . The forties is the decade when almost all will reach their plateaus at work. For the majority, work will be mastered, promotions will end, and the responsibilities of child rearing will be over; thus the commitments made in the past no longer provide satisfaction in the present or guidelines for the future. (Bardwick, 1990, p. 202)

Fortyish persons experience their maturity as parents, as workers, and as community members. During this decade there tends to be increased introspection, both looking inward at oneself and looking outward at life more philosophically. There is a "dawning of wisdom in middle age, the beginning of a new developmental era" (Colarusso and Namiroff, 1981, p. 169).

This information may give you, as a parent to the "forties" adult, hope for more contact. After all, life has slowed down for those in their forties. You imagine more shared time together, but you are likely to be disappointed. This decade is filled with its own distractions.

The struggles of midlife are certainly familiar to you and may be part of your own current or recent past experience. The forties are the generation in the middle, surrounded by children on one side and parents on the other. They are also the generation in the middle of life, with youth in the past and old age still to come. This is a time to take stock, to notice lost opportunity, and to feel the disappointment of what "could have been." Midlife crises or changes are fueled by the desire to fill the significant voids in relationships, work, education, spirituality, and so on, before it's too late.

Midlife people have a new concern: the well-being of their parents. There is a realization that their parents are aging, losing their strength, and becoming more vulnerable. This change evokes an awareness of their own sense of mortality. For the first time, they may see the finiteness of life: "During this stage several internal and external events send some clear messages that the ultimate outcome of life is death. These messages come in the form of changes in our own body, grown-up children recording the passage of years, and illness and death of our friends and parents. These events break through our illusions of immortality and heighten our awareness that there is an end to life's story" (Van Hoose, 1985, p. 91).

What does this generation need or want from their parents? The survey showed that, besides continuing to want support and caring for themselves, the forties group wanted their parents to achieve comfort, contentment, and fulfillment in their own lives. Perhaps this wish represents the younger generation's fear of carrying the burden of their parents' unhappiness or disappointment.

Forties individuals who responded to the survey provided the following representative statements about wished-for kinds of attention from their older parents:

- "Learn to say supportive and affectionate things."
- "Be on my side no matter what."
- "Give me their respect."
- "Love me regardless."
- "Find some contentment in life. Like herself better and have some fun before she dies."
- "Love my father despite the superficial nature of my rela-

tionship with him. I owe him a great deal and no longer really expect any more from him other than to enjoy the rest of his life."

• "Be valuable in her life in more than an instrumental sense (buying groceries, running errands, listening to her disagreements with friends)."

Forties adults still want to be loved and understood. Even more pressing is their desire for their aging parents to be satisfied with their own lives. A signal that your life is OK would offer reassurance. Your acceptance of them as they are would provide comfort. They wish you could accept yourself as well. A "friendship" based on mutual respect and meaningful sharing is their wish. There is a fear of responsibility for your life or guilt about your discontent. All this is a tall order, but it is possible to achieve.

The Fifties

> Backward, turn backward, O Time, in your flight,
> Make me a child again, just for to-night!
> Mother, come back from the echoless shore,
> Take me again to your heart, as of yore;
> Kiss from my forehead the furrows of care,
> Smooth the few silver threads out of my hair,
> Over my slumbers your loving watch keep,—
> Rock me to sleep, mother, rock me to sleep.
>
> ELIZABETH AKERS ALLEN (1860)

If your child is in his or her fifties as you are reading this book, you then have the wisdom that advanced years provide as well as the openness to explore new ways to maintain satisfying relationships. You also have an elder's perspective that allows you to see the richness of life. Your "fifties" children have less experience but a similar perspective.

What are their life issues and what do they still need from you? The little that is known about this stage of life suggests that it is a time for reflection and self-assessment. It is also a time for providing guidance to others. Fifties people are coming to terms with the loss of their youth and the changes in their bodies that signal some real limitations. At the same time, they are freed from many of the traditional rules related to work or family life.

As the generation just ahead of them begins to die, the issues of mortality—their own and their parents'—loom large and are sometimes frightening. This is a time for making peace. Whatever the conflict and competition of the past, this is a time for accepting each other "as is." There is a realization that Mom and Dad did the best they could. This generation has the benefit of hindsight and better understands the limitations of relationships. For the first time, your ages are more similar than different. You are more like peers and less like parent and child.

You extend to them the hand of loving friendship. You can both look back over a long life of shared experience. The history between you provides a very solid bond, and you know the other's idiosyncrasies well enough to avoid them—rather than engage them as you would have in decades past. What the younger generation now want from their parents is a sign of independent life lasting as long as possible. This wish is echoed by Donald Donohugh, a psychiatrist who authored *The Middle Years* (1981). Continued activity and autonomy are the themes he developed in guidelines for adults relating to their aged parents.

A fifty-four-year-old psychotherapist commented on his eighty-two-year-old mother, whom he described as "stoic, tough, quiet, and tolerant." A few years before, she had lost her sight and with it some independence. His wish was for her to "regain some independence, to adjust to blindness and not fight it, to have friends and be happy." It's clear that he wanted her to maintain as much autonomy as possible in spite of her advancing years. He still needed her respect, but at this point in life, he would have been happy and relieved to see her maintaining herself. Little else was wished for.

Hearing Their Concerns

What more can be learned from these adult-children? Perhaps through their disappointment and the "wished-for" relationships that never came to pass, we have a chance to self-correct with our own progeny. Their perceptions give us an opportunity to observe our interactions from a vantage point that is seldom available and that provides us with fresh insight and an impetus for change.

As I look back over all of the data I collected, whether through the survey or through the comments given to me in person, I am struck by a number of common themes. Without exception, these adults could point to changes that would have enhanced the relations between them and their parents.

It was not difficult to narrow down the focus to a few key ideas. The younger adults tended to echo the need to be accepted as equals and to be respected for independent decision making, whatever the choices. In the words of a twenty-four-year-old male: "I want them to give support for what I do and not to downplay what I do as insignificant, to treat me as an adult and listen to what I have to say with an open mind." A twenty-year-old assistant accountant detailed her current needs for "an open communication without fear of disapproval or rejection because of my present beliefs. They need to respect the decisions I make in accordance with *my* life's needs and wants and become more open-minded about changes and evolutions of beliefs—*my* beliefs." A woman in her early twenties wanted her parents to "understand and remember what it's like to be young." In response to the query about what would improve the relationship, another twentyish woman said, "Time—maybe in a few years it will improve."

These young people were hopeful and believed change was possible. They wished to be seen and respected as adults, but adults with views and behaviors different from those of their parents. In the wish most frequently expressed, they wanted to keep "the lines of communication open." They felt that any conflict could be talked about. Only silence was viewed as dangerous.

By the middle years (thirty-five to fifty), those surveyed still displayed energy for changing the problem aspects of the relationship. A thirty-six-year-old electronics engineer wanted "less criticism from mother (doubts my goals)—greater interest in what I am doing shown by father." On a similar note, a thirty-seven-year-old counselor gave his ideas about improving the communication process with his father: "He needs to listen more carefully before my ideas are rejected." A government worker in her late thirties wanted "friendship, support, not advice."

A woman psychologist of forty-three said, "I would like a sense of having fun together or finding pleasure together rather than simply fulfilling a goal. . . . Too much of our relationship centers on duty and fulfilling appropriate roles." Her point was implied by others who wished that their interactions were less serious and more lightened up. There was a sense that the business of parenting was taken much too seriously at this stage. There was a wish to get beyond the work.

The quotes above don't summarize the wants and needs of this middle-aged group but are representative of their concerns. Parents who are still trying to shape, influence, and direct their midlife children are perceived as interfering. This level of involvement is viewed as a sign of dissatisfaction and disappointment. Instead, there is a wish for genuine interest, acknowledgment, appreciation, and *fun*.

The oldest group surveyed were less interested in changing things and more accepting of the limitations. One person suggested that time was running out and that the satisfaction of remaining needs could not be expected of aging parents. The most commonly expressed wish was for parents to enjoy the remainder of their lives. It was said in a variety of ways, but the message was the same: "What I need from you now is to see that you are satisfied, happy, and as healthy as possible."

There was much less emphasis on smoothing out troubled

relationships. The conflict remaining between the two generations was minimized. The goal was transformed into mutual acceptance. Perhaps it can be assumed that if the struggles and misunderstandings between parents and adult-children have not been worked out by the time the younger generation turns fifty, it is probably not going to happen. For most of us, that's plenty of time.

"At the turn of the century, the average infant born in the United States was expected to live to age 47. Today that figure is 75. Even more striking is the fact that when Americans reach age 65, they can now expect to live another seventeen years, to age 82" (Neugarten and Neugarten, 1989, p. 148). This is a happy fact of the 1990s. When your kids are grown, you still have about thirty years to develop, negotiate, and refine a relationship!

Chapter 2

How Did It Get to Be This Way?

You may wonder about the source of conflict that permeates the interactions with your adult-children. Sometimes the arguments don't even make sense. How do you get hung up on the issues that you fight about? Why is it that you and your adult-children are extremely sensitive to certain comments or innuendos?

Strained relationships often come from differences between parents and adult-children in the way life is experienced. Usually there are no culprits, and seldom is hurt intentional. Nevertheless, you both may feel threatened, misunderstood, and frustrated.

Your adult-child may have an addiction to alcohol, drugs, or gambling. On the other hand, he or she may be a thirty-year-old adolescent. In either case there are some common threads that underpin the conflict and help to explain it. Whether the struggle is over holiday visitation or money management, it isn't just a struggle between parent and child. What you may have thought was an interaction between you and your children turns out to be a stage play with a very large cast.

Numerous influences play a role in shaping your relationship with your children. Your own culture (or ethnic group), family history, and personality are uninvited guests in your family interactions. This is especially noticeable when a family is transplanted to the United States and tries to continue living according to the cultural rules of its homeland.

A nineteen-year-old college student complained to me about the restrictiveness of her parents, who had moved to California from Eastern Europe when she was eight. She spoke English with barely a trace of an accent, and in most outward respects she resembled her peers. Yet at home she felt trapped by family demands and a standard of behavior that required an obedient and demure response that conflicted with her acculturation to the outside world.

In this family the conflicts were obvious. Often they are less apparent because the cultural or ethnic influences are no longer observable. Over time the "melting pot" obscures many differences, but underlying traditions and values continue to exert a subtle influence. Just as powerful, but harder to spot, the family problem becomes more difficult to identify and resolve.

Carrying out the business of everyday family life demands simple here-and-now solutions. Most of us don't stop to consider the role of long-ago events in current interactions. When we do so, it is more often for the purpose of reinforcing an old wound than of understanding the hurt. Most of the time, family disagreements are ironed out or covered over for expediency. The term *demilitarized zone* is used "to describe the way families try to avoid discussing sensitive issues that would endanger ongoing relationships" (Hunter and Sundel, 1989, p. 218).

Parents survive these times, and youngsters grow up in spite of them. The need to coexist in the same household is the glue that keeps conflict from escalating. But once your children reach adulthood, conflicts may result in pain and confusion that are not dealt with directly because coexistence is no longer a financial or legal necessity.

There is a need to examine the conflict and learn to deal

with it because the alternative is to tolerate contact that is superficial, brief, and/or unsatisfying. Even then, there is an increased possibility of flare-ups in tension when contact becomes extended, such as during a long holiday weekend.

In examining and learning how to deal with conflict, the first step is to identify its source, and then to search for the underlying patterns. This chapter explores the outside factors that contribute to the way you see and handle the struggles with your adult-children. At this point it's necessary to expand the picture of family life to see some new facets, to get a bird's-eye view. First, we will explore a number of these facets and then, armed with new information, search for previously hidden directions and new solutions.

Mistakes from the Past

Annoyance is a tolerable feeling. Children and adolescents learn to tune out annoying reminders that parents insist on giving. Much of how and what our children have learned from us was borrowed from the preceding generation. According to Monica McGoldrick and Randy Gerson (1985), who have researched multigenerational families, "Families repeat themselves. What happens in one generation will often repeat itself in the next, i.e. the same issues tend to be played out from generation to generation" (p. 5).

These messages seem to be relayed and transmitted as if written in stone. But a time comes when our children tend to be less tolerant of what we say. This is a normal part of the developmental process characterized by pulling away physically as well as intellectually.

As adults they may challenge what they don't want to hear (active conflict), or they may gloss over it (passive conflict). They may tell you about it or they may not. When annoyance builds to a sufficient level, listening and sharing cease to be genuine. This is understandable when you recognize that, for discomfort to be kept under control and manageable, it must be stopped from building. It's like putting a video on pause, which stops the live action. What remains is a static picture. To keep the annoyance from exploding, the whole communication process is stifled. The remainder has little vitality.

These annoying messages often have roots deep in the past. The subjects may be explosive or they may be trivial. Sadly, they may serve to undermine your adult-child's confidence. The expression that describes this process is *shining on*, an attempt to psychologically leave the scene.

Adele had twin daughters, one of whom suffered throughout her childhood from many illnesses. None were life-threatening, but this was a time before regular inoculations were available to combat childhood diseases. The sickly child was worried about and fussed over, for good reason. She received more than her share of parental attention and came to associate getting attention with being sick. Fortunately, she outgrew her health problems and lived a normal adult life. However, when she had a child of her own, she tended to be especially concerned about his health. She had learned that pattern from her own mother. The worry, attention, and care she lavished on her son was unnecessary and annoying to him. As a child and adolescent he tended to ignore her concern about his health. In fact, he was quite healthy. As an adult he found her apprehension annoying.

The contact between mother and son grew more perfunctory as she worried more about his health and safety. Here was a strong, competent man, unnecessarily cautioned about minimal risk taking such as flying, freeway driving, sports participation, and eating certain foods. His conversations with his mother grew increasingly frustrating until contact became very limited. The young man found himself listening to his mother on the phone while reading the newspaper or paying bills. He couldn't stand to listen to her irrelevant ideas. How did Grandmother's fears about her sick child creep into the life of the next generation?

In the above example, fear and cautiousness didn't make sense for this young man, though they had applied to his mother.

When behavior patterns become automatic they are acted out without much conscious thought. Becoming conscious of the patterns enables people to make changes in the way they see or respond to things.

Psychologists would say that behavior patterns are learned over time and eventually become automatic; for example, a child learns that her mother will listen and respond to some, but not all, of the things she says. The child finds she gets a great deal of attention when she is worried, upset, or hurt. As time goes on, she knows how to get her mother's attention: by behaving in a "troubled" way. Neither may be aware that the mother is soliciting this painful behavior or that the daughter is producing it to receive attention. What once was an effective behavior may become useless, unnecessary, and even destructive at a later time.

Sometimes the annoyances seem trivial, but over time they build and grow out of proportion to the original problem. Sadly, much of the conflict between parents and adult-children begins, and is reinforced, by seemingly minor annoyances.

My grandparents were in their sixties when my mother was forty. As a middle-aged woman with a family of her own, she recalled her mother always ending her good-bye with the caution "Be careful crossing the street." The advice wasn't useful or valued, but to my grandmother it was the appropriate thing to say to a daughter as she left the house. While my mother didn't waste much energy conveying her annoyance, it must have been important enough for her to recall that tale for me at least 150 times. Interestingly enough, she used that story to justify her own behavior. Today, when she reminds her own past-forty-year-old daughter to wear a sweater on "such a cool day," her reaction to my annoyance is a retelling of this story. Her automatic response was learned from her own mother—though it was not appreciated then either.

Many seemingly useless ideas from my mother's collection of parenting stories were handed down to me simply because they had been presented to her by her mother. Though I sometimes recognized their absurdity, I was occasionally surprised to hear an annoying reminder from the past coming out of my own mouth, aimed at my adult-child, and received, not surprisingly, with disgust. When I hear myself advising my twenty-two-year-old son to "eat all your food," I'm appalled. But old habits, learned without much conscious thought, die hard.

The following exercise is designed to help you see how some interactions with your grown kids have roots deep in the past.

Let your mind wander back over the years to something "childish" suggested to you by your parent or someone of your parent's generation. You may recall feeling annoyed or amused, or you may have long since stopped responding emotionally to such advice. Try to gather a few of these "reminders." Perhaps you can note the similarities. Do they all have to do with safety or eating or cleanliness? When you have made your list of statements or anecdotes, stop and examine how many of these you throw out to your own adult-children. If you seldom do, then one of two possibilities exists. One is that you probably had exceptional parents who somehow learned to make age-appropriate comments. If this wasn't so, you have probably made a conscious effort to watch what you say—a very difficult process. Either way you have managed to correct the errors of history.

Parents and adult-children tend to be made insecure by new roles and expectations during the first decade following adolescence. There are new rules to be learned and old ones to be unlearned, according to Roger Gould (1978), a psychiatrist who closely studied life transitions for five years. He says that during this period "our parents are always looking over our shoulder, ready to point out failures that occurred because we broke some rule or program or because we abandoned the 'one right way'" (p. 91).

If you are now aware of transmitting to your adult-children "child-care" statements that come directly from your adult experiences with your own parents, then you've already made the first step toward change: awareness. Now you can watch yourself and observe how often you catch yourself giving advice more suited to children or adolescents. Later in the book, you will learn a new, more adaptive dialogue to fill in the void.

There isn't anything terribly wrong when there are relatively few remarks to adult-children that have outlived their usefulness, but when the communication pattern itself is outdated, major problems can occur. Keep in mind that parenting skills were never designed to work for parents with grown children. Less than one hundred years ago, the parent–child relationship was often terminated by the death of the parent in midlife: "In 1900, the average life expectancy was 49 years. Women barely lived long enough to see all their children leave home" (Fodor and Franks, 1990, p. 445).

The parent role was designed to ensure the survival of children but did not reach much beyond. Skills refined from generation to generation were ultimately limited not in depth, but in scope. Increasing the scope of communication skills is the focus of Part II of this book.

Mistakes from the past are only one kind of intergenerational troublemaker. Seeing the traps that lead to conflict makes it easier to avoid them. Let's explore some additional sources of friction.

Cultural Roots

Did you have an Italian or Jewish grandmother who stuffed you with food, and for whom food preparation and eating were an important part of your relationship? Did the work ethic of your northern European ancestors rub off on you and then get rubbed off on your children? Did your fierce family loyalty and protectiveness grow out of an Asian tradition of the past?

The culture that surrounded you in your formative years probably made a significant contribution to your parenting style and skills. Each culture has its own unique stamp and set of expectations for raising its young. R. Thomas discusses the influence of cultural differences and expectations in his book *Counseling and Life-Span Development* (1990). He considers the roles and rules that affect child and adult development: "Each position is marked by expectations about how the individual will act and about what privileges and responsibilities accompany the role" (p. 230). If your family had its roots in Asia, the Middle East, or the Mediterranean, how is your parenting different from that of friends, neighbors, or even spouses from other cultures?

Think for a moment about someone raised with a different cultural orientation and the ways in which your parenting styles are different from theirs. You may notice a difference in the rules that apply to respect, privacy, work ethics, and the display of feelings. These are learned through day-to-day living in nuclear families that are tied together by the larger culture. Cultural rules help to give some direction to individual families. They also offer guidelines for behavior and expectations so that each new interaction doesn't have to be thought out individually.

Some cultural groups place a premium on education and particularly on the attainment of professional status. If this perspective is part of your history, then your parenting style is bound to reflect these values. You will make certain assumptions about the role of education in your child's life and will do everything possible to provide opportunities and resources for enriched learning. While you may be a generally supportive parent, you may be aware that you have no tolerance of poor school performance. For example, educational achievement is nonnegotiable to you because it has always been a given for your cultural subgroup. Adhering to this value helps to maintain a good connection between your family and the culture at large. This implicit rule is useful in guiding the earlier stages of parenting but is a definite stumbling block later on.

It may surprise you that parents' relationships with grown children outlive the cultural rules. The safety and security provided by cultural standards does not carry over when kids are grown, and a void is created. When adult-kids don't conform to the old cultural standards, great stress may be experienced by everyone involved. Yet the source of the stress may not be obvious. What specifically causes the stress? Here's an example.

A family crisis was brewing. A twenty-six-year-old man from a traditional Mediterranean family married a twenty-eight-year-old woman of northern European extraction. While their relationship with each other was not a problem, their interaction with his parents and his extended family was tense and uncomfortable.

In social situations, the young woman was quiet and reserved. Her style made her mother-in-law uncomfortable since the older woman misinterpreted the meaning of the young wife's body language, that is, the way in which she communicated without words. At family events, the young couple was increasingly bypassed by relatives who saw the young woman as standoffish and cold. Her reaction was to be polite but guarded, gestures further fueling the fire of misunderstanding. Soon the couple declined invitations from the young man's extended family, and this insulted his mother.

This conflict, built on cultural styles and differences, reached an impasse. Hurt was experienced but not acknowledged. The couple felt isolated and punished, and because there was no formal way to respond, they continued to retreat. Distance was created and only lengthened by time. When conflict is based on cultural standards that become exclusive, there is no room for growth, new ways, or new members.

Your adult-child is bound to challenge at least some of the family ways through marriage outside the culture, lifestyle choice, career decisions, holiday celebrations, and so on. Research tends to support the "developmental-stake" hypothesis at work between parents and their adult children: "Middle-aged parents consistently overestimated the degree of similarity between themselves and their children, whereas their children overestimated the degrees of difference. It is presumed that the parents are motivated by a desire to see their work of socializing having a lasting effect, that their children will 'carry the torch' so to speak, whereas their children are motivated by a desire to show that they are unique unto themselves and not duplicates of their parents" (Hunter and Sundel, 1989, p. 218). The clashes that result signal the need for more dialogue and a greater acceptance of differences. These are seldom easy.

Family Ties That Strangle

The family tree has been around for a long time. Recently there has been a rekindling of interest in family genealogy as a way of studying and making sense of family characteristics that wind their way through the generations. Family therapists have been using genograms for years to understand how

> family members, patterns and events may have recurring significance. . . . Family diagrams which map relationships and patterns of functioning may help clinicians think systematically about how events and relationships in their clients' lives are related to patterns of health and illness. (McGoldrick and Gerson, 1985, p. 2)

Understanding the specific meaning of the facts of your family history might help explain how certain patterns play themselves out generation after generation. Even more important, you can see where you learned some of the ideas, issues, and myths that guide your current day-to-day living and your child-raising style. Seeing the family patterns may help you understand why you boil inside (and maybe outside) when son John demonstrates the annoying irresponsibility of his great-uncle Harry. (Remember the example of my friend and her unemployed son in the Introduction.)

In her book *Intimate Partners* (1987), Maggie Scarf explored family genealogy in relation to marital relationships:

> Whom we become as adult persons has to do with the environment in which our development takes place, i.e., the social world we inhabit in childhood. Whom we become is profoundly influenced by those people with whom we inter-

act on a daily basis, the significant persons linked to us by blood or by choice. On a genogram, the interplay of generations within a family is carefully graphed, so that the psychological legacies of past generations can be readily identified. (p. 41)

Much of the way in which we learn how to make sense of the world comes from family rules or traits from the past. It is only when the family tree is constructed, and information is collected about the people themselves, that we learn something of our own unique strengths and weaknesses, as well as our family origins. As the family tree grows, it produces shade that may inhibit growth.

Of course there are limitations in looking to the past. How accurate are our memories or those of a grandparent or a great-aunt? More important than gathering the "true facts" is the process of listening to older generations explain how the family affected their development and their role as parents.

Constructing a family genealogy requires a fair amount of work. It helps to have a sense of curiosity and the determination of Sherlock Holmes. Not only do you collect demographic information, such as dates of birth and death, occupations, and geographic locations, but you identify less objective data related to emotions, medical problems, and the behavior of family members. Noting specific tendencies, such as how illness or alcoholism affected work habits, is useful in understanding patterns. Significant family events—for example, losses, migrations, and transitions—add richness to the picture. Searching for these data is a challenge.

You may find, after going through this process, that you can finally understand the peculiar ways in which some things are done in your family. Looking at family styles will also help you see why certain behaviors and traits observed in your adult-kids will make you angry, intolerant, or fearful.

Bob's conflict with his father actually had its source in the family history. Bob had some extra money after his bills were paid each month. As a child he had been taught to put some money away each month for savings. At twenty-eight his ideas about saving were quite different from those of the family. When his father learned about Bob's "playing the stock market," instead of saving in the bank, he reacted angrily. None of the ensuing conflict made any sense until a family genogram turned up a great-grandfather who had squandered the family money on poor, risky investments. This ancestor was remembered in the family with derision and had been dismissed as a ne'er-do-well. Bob's father, understandably, could not tolerate seeing his son in this light. Establishing the connection made the conflict between them a manageable matter that did not involve ghosts of the past.

Family dilemmas that are not resolved in one generation tend to emerge in the next, or even to skip a generation to surface later. Idiosyncrasies that make no sense whatsoever may be traced to a previous generation. For example, a young man tends to drift. He seems to be unable to settle down like others in his family. In developing the family genogram, it is noticed that his great-uncles were highly successful but geographically very unstable. The young man's drifting may now make more sense or may be more readily accepted by his family. Other, more significant treasures may be unearthed as well.

When you and your spouse joined together, a family nucleus was formed that seemed like a fresh beginning. You imagined building a family different from all other families. When you complete the genogram, you will observe that your own role in the development of family character is actually quite limited. The influence of past generations is very real and sometimes dramatic.

In building your genogram (follow the directions below) start with yourself and your partner; then move upward to fill in the boxes and circles of your parents', grandparents', and great-grandparents' generations. Go as far as you can until you reach the limit of your knowledge about your predecessors.

In putting this puzzle together, you will want to fill in the gaps in your knowledge by talking to as many family members as possible. Stories and themes will come to life and may surprisingly transform this tedious task into an exciting and interesting process. You may discover that some of your own "strange" ideas or habits are directly traceable to a long-forgotten relative. This awareness will keep you from dumping these items on your grown kids.

There is a wonderful by-product in going through this process. Simply exploring the past, as your *own* parents recalled it, provides a new link in your relationship with them, a new way of connecting with them, and a new way of understanding them. If your parents are deceased, talk to others who might remember, such as cousins, aunts, or uncles.

Constructing a lifelike genogram depends on your ability to discover many of the following characteristics for each individual placed on the graph:

1. *Name, formal or informal.* Names have meaning. Was your name created for you or borrowed from the past and the qualities, characteristics, or roles of another person? If you were named after your "rebellious" aunt, did this name create expectations of you that really had nothing to do with your own life? Were you expected to behave in some of the outlandish ways she was remembered for? Think about the names given to other members of your family. Is there a pattern? Do you know what it is? Think about the names you gave your children. As adults will they have to live down the reputation of the name?

2. *Personality or traits.* Are you likened to someone who is remembered as impulsive, reckless, stupid, driven, or saintly? The list goes on and on, but each quality can become a cross to bear in subsequent generations. Do you tend to see some of these family traits in yourself, your children, your grandparents, and so on? Do you look for a family history of depression or alcoholism in your adult-children—and tend to find it?

3. *Occupations.* How has the past shaped your choice of work? Is there a family tradition or business that guides you or gets in your way? Do your children need to be lawyers, or must they avoid certain trades? Are the musicians in your family, for example, admired or thought of as frivolous? Are serious hard

workers valued more than others? Whom do you take after in your work ethics? How do you transmit your work values to your adult children?

4. *Lifestyle.* Are there family rules about where to live, how to live, and which lifestyles to maintain? Do you come from a clan of city-dwellers that shows great disdain for rural ways or vice versa? Was someone in your family a scholar and out of place in a long line of fishermen? Does the lifestyle that you envision for your own children fit with (or defy) any family patterns?

5. *Relationships.* Some families send very clear messages about suitable work partners, marriage partners, and friends. Violating these traditions can make you a hero or a villain. In either case, if you depart from the rule you will stand out and be remembered. How did you follow or challenge these rules in your own family? How are your ideas communicated to your grown kids?

6. *Family tales, myths, and themes.* Stories tend to evolve as a way of explaining deviant behavior or events. The family members who didn't fit, chose different paths, or had colorful lives tend to be remembered as characters or, even more, caricatures. Tales told and kept alive through an oral history often become more dramatic over time. When Great-Aunt Mae ran off with the traveling salesman, it may simply have been an elopement. Over time she became characterized as a wild and unstable woman. Who else in your family is seen in that light? Does this make you less tolerant of your own adult-child's different behavior? Think about it.

The Kennedy family genogram on the facing page has been provided to give you a visual picture of a family with which you very likely already have some familiarity. The Kennedy family is well known for the number of highly successful politicians it has produced across the generations. For all its fame and power, the Kennedy family has had a significant number of tragedies and traumas. These patterns may well cause shock waves to the family system. The awareness of so many life crises, especially to

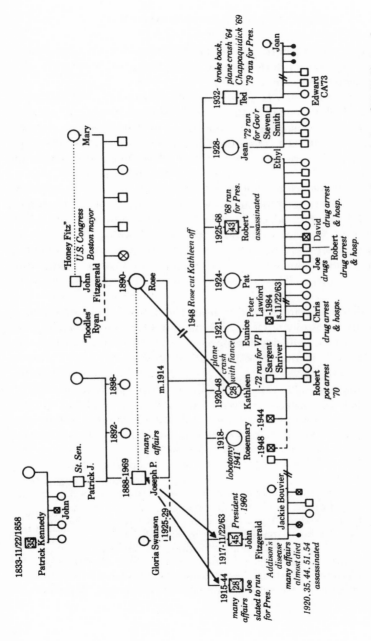

The Kennedy family genogram. Reprinted from McGoldrick and Gerson [1986], p. 89, with the permission of W. W. Norton & Company, Inc. Copyright © 1986 by Monica McGoldrick and Randy Geison.

relatively young men, may lead to fearfulness, tension, or a sense of cautiousness interfering with daily living.

Notice the symbols used in the Kennedy family genogram. Feel free to use this style, but be more creative if you wish. Remember, the goal of this activity is to help you understand one important source of your own thoughts, feelings, and actions: your lineage. The information you uncover will help you to make sense of one more source of conflict with your adult-children.

After exploring your own genealogy it may now be easier to see how previous generations in your family played a key role in "raising" your children. "Mother (or Father) did it that way" is often the rationale for guiding our own parenting. The value of a particular rule is not often questioned. Some ways of doing things continue from one generation to the next, and while they are sometimes called family traditions, the original intent may be lost.

Many examples can be found in the teaching of practical skills in the family, such as cooking, repairing, housekeeping jobs, and physical skill development. Nancy Friday makes this point humorously in her book *My Mother Myself* (1976):

> Peggy is cooking her first big meal for her parents since her marriage—a glorious Virginia ham. Standing up to carve, her new husband asks Peggy why she sliced off three or four inches from the shank end before baking. Peggy looks surprised. "Mother always does it that way."
>
> Everyone at the table looks at Peggy's mother. "That's how my mother did it too," she says, a bit puzzled. "Doesn't everyone?"
>
> Peggy phones her grandmother the next day and asks why, in their family, has the shank end always been cut off before baking. "I've always done it that say," grandmother says, "because that is how my mother did it."
>
> It happens that four generations of women are still alive in this family. A call is put in to great grandmother, and the mystery is solved. Once when her daughter—Peggy's grandmother—was a little girl and learning to cook, they

were baking a large ham. The family roasting pan was small, and so the shank end had been cut off to make it fit. (p. 430)

This anecdote relates to cooking. Most of the time, family patterns have more negative and serious consequences, when a career, life partner, or lifestyle ignores or clearly conflicts with family expectations or mythology. The following story illustrates a more serious family issue.

Grace wouldn't fly and couldn't fly. Nobody, including Grace, knew exactly why this was true. It had never really been a problem before. Grace simply drove or took the train wherever she needed to go, but in the past year her employer had expected her to travel more, and the distances made ground travel impractical. She sensed that, if she didn't adapt, her job might be in jeopardy.

Her friends were sympathetic but were getting tired of hearing about Grace's plight. They tried to reassure her and offered statistics about the safety of air travel. But Grace wasn't afraid to fly. When she thought about her discomfort and aversion to flying, she realized that she wasn't the only one in her family who felt this way. She observed that no one on her mother's side of the family flew—a thought that had not occurred to her before. This was a startling discovery but one that made little sense.

Grace's mother seemed to sidestep the issue: "Grace, honey, there's no place I've ever needed to go that I had to get to that fast, so it doesn't make sense for me to fly." "Mom," Grace replied with a mixture of annoyance and curiosity, "why doesn't anyone else in the family fly?" The response was not satisfying, but it was so final that she knew she would not find the answer here.

Aunt Cindy had a reputation in the family for being straightforward and honest. She summed up her experience after minimal thinking time: "I like to see things, and you can't when you fly. I guess if it had been necessary for me to fly, I might have, but I always had a choice, and it just seemed like a very uninteresting way to spend time." Another dead end!

More conversations took place with other family members, and the following picture was pieced together. It seems that her great-uncle Paul had been a pilot during World War II, and when he returned to civilian life, he had continued flying small charter planes. On a flight during bad weather, his plane was lost, and he was never found. He was presumed dead, but no ceremony or memorial service had ever been held. He had disappeared, but he had left behind a legacy of fear of air travel. A deep sense of worry about flying had rippled through this family and filtered into the life experience of those who had never even known Uncle Paul or heard about his life.

"Family history" helps to make sense of traditions and practices, but it offers no strategies for increasing understanding between you and your adult-kids. When we peel away all the structure and guidance provided by past generations, your specific culture, and the extended family, what's left? Underneath it all is the unique interaction between you and your children. It includes the novel situations that can't be answered by the encyclopedias filled with traditional solutions to life problems. It means that you and your daughter or son must struggle to find a way of proceeding that's new, that's timely, and that meets both of your needs reasonably well. Your current struggles need fresh solutions.

Sadly, most of the accumulated knowledge about how we communicate with our kids is reserved for the years when they live at home and are dependent on us for survival and basic needs. When our offspring reach adulthood, have we finished our job? Is there anything else to offer our eighteen- or twenty-three-year-old?

Historically, parents have been the teachers and children the learners. This tends to be a hierarchical arrangement, with parents having a much larger share of power, control, and also responsibility. As time goes by, your responsibility lessens, and so does your ability to set limits and set examples. If there is still something for you to teach, you will need to find new ways to do it. What once worked is now a highly inflammatory process.

Do your adult-kids need something else from you now? Is it possible for you to become a learner or a peer? Again, this is all uncharted territory. There is little research on the subject. How and what you teach or learn is dependent on your adult-child's specific needs. The conflict resolution process needs to be tailored to fit the situation as well. For example, is the problem caused by expectations that can't be met? Or is the problem caused by an underresponsible adult-child or an overinvolved parent?

Sociologist Lucy Fischer describes changing relationships between adult-daughters and their mothers in her book *Linked Lives* (1986): "As children grow older the nature of the maternal or paternal responsibility changes—until, at some point, parents launch their children and surrender day-to-day responsibility for their care" (p. 9). Fischer goes on to talk about the "continuity of parental responsibility—at least in the symbolic and emotional sense" (p. 9).

Fischer's point is insightful because it makes the distinction between the "day-to-day responsibility," which is characteristic of the teacher–student model, and the "symbolic and emotional" ties that presumably continue when our children reach adulthood. However, the author, being a sociologist, is not especially concerned about how to make that transition come about or how to create new guidelines for this last stage of parenting.

It isn't just our adult-kids who change. We, as parents, continue to grow and change throughout our lives; we don't stop at adulthood. To complicate matters, our adult-children continue to grow and change during *their* adult lives. At any moment in time, when we wish to communicate with them, we are all in a unique, dynamic state that differs from any other point in time. How terribly complicated and confusing this all gets!

Coming to terms with your adult-child requires a flexible process. It means experimenting with new ways to fill the gap when the old ways no longer work. This involves a fair amount of risk taking because trying out alternative ways of approaching another person may not be immediately well received. Changing the way we behave and respond is often initially experienced as threatening. Fortunately, it has wonderful long-term benefits.

Think about the anecdote presented in the Part I introduction. A mother is exasperated with her thirty-two-year-old "adolescent" son. The old ways of guiding him toward responsibility won't work any longer. She must learn to approach him in a way that will be effective but not punitive. If he feels demeaned, he will be defensive and will be closed to growth. A sensitive balance is necessary. The following example makes use of a metaphor to describe a flexible and dynamic process.

When we talk about "flexible and dynamic," we can imagine movement. Partners dancing might be a good metaphor to describe such a process. Imagine that you are dancing with someone you know rather well. You can anticipate, to some extent, the dance scenario. You know enough about your partner's style to anticipate certain steps and routines, and you are likely to know how to respond. But if he or she changes the pattern or tries something new, a new response is required on your part. Responding in any of your former ways could result in one or both of you losing your balance or being in disharmony. Of course, in this situation you wouldn't think twice about adapting your dance steps to fit better. But looking for fresh, creative ways of communicating, when the old patterns no longer fit, somehow seems dangerous. Adapting the family dance is what your relationship requires. Developing new "steps" is the challenge.

Child Development Recapped

"After all I've done, she treats me like this?" A disappointed and hurt mother pulls away to lick her wounds. This response feels like rejection to her twenty-six-year-old daughter. A mother feels unappreciated; a daughter feels guilty. What this mother "did" for eighteen years is significant but in itself does not ensure satisfying contact with her daughter when she reaches adulthood.

This is a reminder of a weary process with a payoff that may seem minimal. But seeing your resentment and your daughter's ingratitude up front is an important step toward the changes that are possible.

The next few pages provide a very brief review of the child development issues you may have struggled with for eighteen or more years. Looking back will help you understand why it's so difficult to leave these ideas behind. You invested so much in your child's growth, but now the burdens of communication far outweigh the joys.

Can you remember the experience of being a new parent? Suddenly, life took a very different direction. Before that time your goal setting and responsibility were focused on yourself or on you and your partner, both adults. When you became a new parent, there was a shift toward caring for someone who was very dependent and vulnerable, which may have required you to hide these same qualities when you saw them in yourself.

Suddenly, you had to put away all of the unfinished business of running your own life. You had to shelve your own feelings and needs. Here was your child, so much a part of you and yet a new person with infinite potential. It was tempting to want to give her or him every opportunity possible—or maybe every opportunity you didn't have. In either case, your child often becomes an extension of who you were or who you could have been.

It need not be embarrassing to realize that many of your motives in child raising were not pure. Ideally, parenting styles are patterned to best meet the needs of the children. Yet inevitably your own childhood experiences and unmet needs poked through and played out old familiar scenarios. It's a different stage, twenty years later, and there's a somewhat different cast of players. Seeing yourself as a separate person from your child is a healthy and significant realization but a job easier said than done.

From the very beginning of their lives, you were shaping, molding, and guiding your children to be the good human beings you thought they were able to become. You modeled good manners, fair play, and problem solving. You rewarded their efforts, gave them encouragement, and allowed them room to explore. What an incredible responsibility! Surprisingly, for the most part, you took this awesome job in stride.

The initial bonding that takes place with mothers and increasingly with fathers is necessary for a baby's survival, both physical and psychological. Bonding is, to a great extent, instinctive. You can see it in human interactions as well as in other high-level mammals. Attachment thrives when the parent is affectionate, attentive, and responsive to the baby's signals. It includes the comfort provided by close bodily contact.

According to Desmond Morris, a well-regarded anthropologist and author of *The Human Zoo* (1969):

> Becoming attached to a mother, a child, or a mate are three of the most vital bits of learning that we can undergo in our entire lives and it is these that have been singled out for the special assistance that the phenomenon of imprinting gives. The word "love" is, in fact, the way we commonly describe the emotional feelings that accompany the imprinting process. (p. 158)

Animals don't need to consult child development books to understand their role in parenting their young. Neither did you. From birth, the strong attachment that took place between the two of you was marked by a fine-tuning of your sensitivity to your baby's needs. You learned how to anticipate your baby's needs, and your baby learned how to please you, another instinctual way of ensuring that its needs would continue to be met.

During the course of the first year, your attachment to each other grew, and both of you learned how to recognize each other's needs and meet them better and better. Then, just as this process was becoming comfortable, it began to change. The safety and security of this very close, mutually dependent relationship began to give way to the changing needs of your child.

As a caring adult you provided a secure environment in which trust could be developed. Through love and the satisfaction of your baby's dependency needs, he or she became secure enough to let you out of sight and to try out some new independent behavior.

With the development of the first physical and vocal skills, what does the healthy baby do but begin to create distance? What a shock! The struggle for separation began just as you were beginning to accept the heavy responsibility for, and the concomitant authority in, giving shape and meaning to your baby's existence. The sense of importance and flattery that Mother Nature bestowed on you was quickly wrenched away. If you did a good job, the process of "moving away" was natural and simply the consequence of maturation and the passage of time.

Erik Erikson, whose psychological theories of child development depend to a great extent on cultural and societal factors, discussed the movement from the first developmental stage to the next in his classic book *Childhood and Society* (1950). He says that a trusting child is ready to move away from his or her mother, or other caring person, "because she has become an inner certainty, as well as an outer predictability" (p. 219).

Erikson embellishes this idea and points out the ambivalence inherent in the process: "As his environment encourages him to 'stand on his own feet,' it must protect him against meaningless and arbitrary experiences of shame and of early doubt" (p. 223). In other words, this stage presents the first confusing message to parents. It says, "Back off and give your baby space to experiment, but don't go too far." It asked you to be prepared to hear the word "no" one hundred times a day, since it symbolized your toddler's new sense of independence and power. At the same time, you were asked to provide a safe harbor for your child to return to, again and again.

Learning to step back, but to step in when needed, was a very difficult task. In a way, this is a developmental task for adults. Your success and sanity as a parent depended on its mastery. Having survived this first developmental crisis, you entered a prolonged stage called separation-individuation. This phase lasted, in one form or another, for the remainder of your live-in relationship with your child.

The struggle for independence and separation (from eighteen months on) reached a crescendo in adolescence, as you well know, when feelings between you and your child intensified in a dance that required extraordinary balance and sensitivity. As parents, we can be fooled by our kids' behavior. They are physically mature and appear to be adults. But emotional dependence lasts much longer than physical dependence, and while they wanted to be separate, seek autonomy, and create distance from us, they still required us to patiently wait in the wings for their distress calls.

No wonder you were so confused and even disappointed when you couldn't be "superparents" by anticipating their needs perfectly. To complicate matters, you may have had your own problems. Perhaps they were related to your own stage in life or to pieces of unfinished business from your own less-than-perfect childhood.

Howard Halpern, author of *Cutting Loose: An Adult Guide to Coming to Terms with Your Parents* (1976), says that

> the parental job is to help their offspring to develop into autonomous self sufficient people and if they (parents) have enough maturity to act on this understanding, they will function in a way that will support our individuation. (p. 15)

Halpern's book is oriented toward the young adult. For the parent, this responsibility may seem immense. No wonder we feel so guilty when our adult-kids are slow to develop. Parenting grown kids can be dangerous to your health!

Legal Issues

The complexity of intergenerational family relationships is now more understandable. Every interaction is built on and around psychological, familial, cultural, and historical factors. Each interaction is potentially like an archaeological dig. Each layer adds new information and an awareness of significant influences. The baggage that both parents drag from their own childhood compounds issues still more. If this were not enough to make communication totally impossible, consider one additional factor: the law.

There was a time long ago when the relationships within a family were private affairs. The law had no role in determining the nature of the parent–child relationship. Then, as society evolved and became more complex, a need arose to codify the system for inheriting family wealth. The law spelled out how money was to move from parent to child and, more specifically, how property would move from father to son(s). Clearly this law established a power base for the relationship. The parent could reward or punish (disinherit) the child.

Children, on the other hand, had no rights until rather recently. They were considered chattel, like animals and other property. The twentieth century brought needed reforms and protection for children. Child labor laws were followed only recently by laws on child abuse and neglect. The move toward expanding children's rights continues. At the same time, adults continue to be seen as having the primary power and responsibility to manage their children's lives. Again, since law follows custom, it's fairly clear that parents are still in control. In most cases, legal parental responsibility is terminated when children turn eighteen and are viewed as adults by society. This doesn't mean that parents can't assume responsibility for their college-aged children. At least financially, this is often the case.

What is significant about all of this is that the role of parent as "powerful authority" and child as "dependent," reinforced by the legal system, is not easily modified when adulthood is reached. Shedding the old roles is difficult for parent as well as for adult-child. This is particularly true when your adult-children still live at home or return home following unsuccessful attempts to manage on their own. The law offers little guidance in building more flexible styles of relating to a dependent adult-child. On the one hand, you are financially responsible; on the other, you may feel manipulated by a less-than-responsible adult-child. The confusion created is intense.

Alice Rossi (1980) writes about the confusion experienced when chronologically adult-children remain dependent:

> One might also question whether and when any parent becomes post-parental. The label itself suggests the termination of a role, when what may transpire is better described as a transition to a new phase of parenting. The lengthened period of time for advanced schooling means economic responsibility for children until they reach the early twenties, and the high unemployment rate among young people under 25 often means economic responsibility for children over 18 who are neither working nor attending school. (p. 141)

Any time that an adult-child returns home, or fails to leave, there is going to be tension because the old roles defining parent and child behavior will no longer fit. The only "postparental" roles are the ones that you must now create for yourself.

The law says an eighteen-year-old is an adult. Lots of people wouldn't agree. A friend just reminded me that, despite his age, her late-twenties son may not be an adult. She observes that chronological age is increasingly not valid as an indicator of adulthood. She is a college professor who believes that the current generation of kids are often not really on their own until twenty-five or twenty-six. Even then, they may not be competent adults. She wonders, "Am I abandoning a lost child in the wilderness when he needs my help? If he doesn't get a job, is it because I am coddling him or because he is so overwhelmed by rejection after rejection when he applies that he gives up in advance? Does this reflect the parents' uncertainty or the adult-child's slow maturity? Perhaps it's because of my job, but I see so many adult-kids who simply don't know how to be grown up. They don't have a clue."

The management of money causes another pivotal struggle between generations. Money and judgment about money are most delicate subjects. Cosigning or underwriting loans seems unsettling when you are not confident in your son's or daughter's ability to manage fiscal affairs. These issues tend to cause great friction between parents and adult-children.

There are no simple answers or remedies. "Difficulties with personal finances are an intimate part of the troubles that many clients suffer in early adulthood," according to Robert Thomas (1990), who offers strategies for counseling adults across the life span. "Money matters are only one part of the distress suffered by young people, since issues of personal finance are linked into a network of other troubles, including their job, marital condition, social life, relations with their parents, and more" (p. 257). Money management is an issue that really encompasses much more than financial concerns.

Creating Awareness

Where can you go to create a new and meaningful relationship, one that works now that your children are adults themselves and need you, but in very different ways from before? Below is an exercise designed to give you confidence in your problem-solving strategies. When you feel that you are lost and frustrated in your attempts to communicate effectively with your adult-children, it is helpful to know that you have an intuitive capacity to build on.

For the next few minutes let yourself think about the following situation:

You are lost on your way from one place to another. You definitely know where you want to be, and you may even have a vague idea of where you are now. You move rather naturally into a problem-solving mode as you have many times before. You begin to think about the aids you may have available to help you get your bearing and direction.

If you are in your car you may look for a map. But imagine that the map you need is missing or outdated. What do you consider next? As you think, you will discover that you know more about problem solving than you ever suspected.

Use your imagination to create a scenario (or use one of the suggested ones below). Then design a problem-solving strategy and follow it to a conclusion. When you are finished, you will have found a *method* for finding your way and a *route* for getting there.

Here are some familiar scenarios to get you started:

- You took the wrong exit off the freeway.
- You copied down the wrong address.
- You thought you would remember the place when you got to the neighborhood, but you didn't.
- You were given the wrong directions.
- You took the wrong map.

Take a minute to answer these questions:

1. How did you find out where you were? Did you ask some-one? Did you recognize a familiar signpost? Did you wander around and accidentally discover where you were? What did you do?
2. How did you get directions? Did you use a trial and error approach? Did you call the American Automobile Association? Did you use logic or natural signs? What did you do?
3. How did you feel while you went through this process? Did you feel anxious or afraid? Did you feel excited by the challenge? A spirit of adventure? Were there other feelings?

Your solution to the problem depended to some extent on the availability of useful information and on your own creativity or problem-solving ability. Probably, you looked for useful information first: signs, guideposts, or rules that you learned in your family, or in your culture, or from past experience. If these didn't offer much help, then you turned to your intuitive processes, those creative ways of understanding and making sense out of things that don't follow logic or available knowledge. You then tailored a custom solution that was very satisfying, if it worked.

Finally, you examined your own feelings because your unique personality plays a significant role in how things turn out and how you feel about yourself.

Tailoring a custom relationship with your adult-child is a process similar to the one described above. All of the information and strategies that you learned as a parent were specific to the needs of children and adolescents. Something new is needed when you are building a path to effective relationships with your adult-children. The good news is that you still know *how* to problem-solve. Whatever stumbling blocks exist between you and them, the solutions will follow from understanding the problems and retailoring the communication process.

The task of the remainder of this book is to identify the issues and to create workable strategies for facilitating the adult–adult family dance of life. The chapters that follow will offer you an opportunity to observe others' experiences, develop new skills, and continue your own journey toward greater self-development. After all, when your kids are grown, it's time to move on—with them and without them.

Chapter 3

Old Rules Die Hard

A good friend of mine is expecting her first child in a month. She is a well-educated professional woman in her mid-thirties. Her husband is similarly well educated and motivated to provide the most loving home and best environment to encourage the development of a happy, healthy child and an ideal parent–child relationship. These people have chosen to be parents and have taken the time to think about their family's future. In short, these are the ideal preconditions on which to build an "ideal" parent–child relationship.

My friends are in the process of collecting ideas about child rearing and child development from others. Their peers with children share current experiences. Their parents' generation share anecdotes, styles, and critical incidents and offer the benefits of past experience, tried and evaluated. The current literature by child development experts and family therapists is read eagerly by this young couple in search of some ideas that may be useful. In the final analysis, this soon-to-be family of three will use any and all of the sources of help they have identified to approximate their ideal family.

If we could check back with them eighteen years from now,

we might have some useful hindsight. By that time, of course, the promise and wish for an ideal parent–child relationship will have become a tarnished memory. Whatever else has transpired, these parents will sense that they could have done better. This is a universally agreed-upon phenomenon. Comparing hopes with reality always results in some letdown.

As new or expectant parents, we all had some ideals and expectations or a set of hopes to guide our parenting. Only in retrospect can we see that we landed quite short of our ideals. The last chapter gave you some ideas about the parenting assumptions you learned before your own life experience. Now we'll explore some of the specific rules you may have developed yourself as a parent, and where they came from. Only when the rules are clear can you modify them for your current needs—as parents of adult-children.

Say Goodbye to Webster and the Golden Rules

The dictionary gives one definition of *rule* as "an established guide or regulation for action, conduct, method, arrangement, etc." You already knew that, and you also knew that having rules would be an aid in problem solving as a parent. It made sense that situations could be grouped so that each new question wouldn't require a novel answer. For example, the idea of establishing a curfew was probably not new to you. How you arrived at a time and how you communicated that time may have been unique to your home, but most families do give some thought to a curfew rule because it sets some limits on the comings and goings of children in a general way and addresses, in advance, many anticipated problems.

The dictionary, in another definition of *rule*, also makes it clear why there is at least one inherent weakness in rule making. This definition focuses on parental power, which is, in the average democratic American family, bound to be challenged. "To have authority over; govern; direct: as, the king *ruled* the country" (Webster's New World Dictionary) offers a hard line bound to be disputed. Here's where the major conflict lies in developing and using rules for guiding parent–child relationships. As if this authoritarian position weren't hard enough to enforce, we often try to impose rules on our adult-children.

Conceptually, it seems so simple to establish rules for family behavior, and it's so disappointing when they don't work, aren't followed, or aren't respected. Yet even the experts in child development seem confused and confusing when they discuss how parents "ought" to be.

You already know, because of your retrospective perch, that many of your ideals were not workable, and that some of the best books were only marginally helpful in your development of your parenting skills. In many situations, trial and error or accident seemed to determine strategy. You may even feel guilty about this since you didn't do the parenting job the way you "should" have. To magnify your guilt, you may believe that the parent–child problems that came about were caused by "incorrect" parenting. The Monday morning quarterback does have a certain advantage in viewing things! If only you had found the right child-raising system, approach, expert, book, and so on, then you could have done it right. For example, you may wish that the "Parent Effectiveness Training" or "Tough Love" programs had been known to you at the time.

There is a very strong need in us to assume that there is a right way to parent. In the pages that follow I will offer you some of the rationale that have served as a guide to parents for generations, and you'll see why they haven't always worked. Beyond that, even if it helped you navigate through childhood and adolescence, you will see how it leads to rough sailing in Phase 2 parenting, that is, the parenting of adult-children.

We are all familiar with the old adages for guiding the parents of past generations. Tried and true for some, but mostly outdated, here are a few of the most common ones and, in some cases, their sources:

1. Spare the rod and spoil the child (Samuel Butler, 1600s).
2. Children should be seen but not heard.

3. Early to bed, early to rise, makes a man healthy, wealthy and wise (Benjamin Franklin).
4. Do as I say, not as I do.
5. If at once you don't succeed, try, try again.
6. A child should always say what's true, and speak when he is spoken to (Robert Louis Stevenson, 1885).
7. Do not consider painful what is good for you (Euripides).
8. Never mind your happiness; do your duty (Will Durant).
9. A person should do one unpleasant duty a day just to keep himself in moral trim (William James).
10. Train up a child in the way he should go: and when he is old, he will not depart from it (Old Testament).
11. Where parents do too much for their children, the children will not do much for themselves (Elbert Hubbard, 1927).

If reading these well-intended morality lessons made you cringe, you are in good company. These ideas, and their variations, represented the best thinking about child rearing for hundreds of years. Yet you can see that styles and trends change even in parenting. These very general notions were taken seriously during a time when parental philosophy had a decidedly authoritarian flavor. While they may have succeeded in developing obedient or compliant children who behaved respectfully to their parents, these narrow ideas don't pave the way for the comfortable, flexible role relationships that work best for Phase 2 parenting. Even if you were able to instill these ideas in your youngster, which is unlikely, your adult-child would never tolerate a concept such as "Do as I say, not as I do."

It is more difficult to explore contemporary proverbs because current parenting philosophies reflect a much broader base of values and cultures than ever before. As in other life arenas, there is a continuum from extremely liberal to extremely conservative, with a thousand steps in between. A few ideas, however, appear to cut across philosophical lines, and some of these are presented for you below. Because old rules die hard, you will see how difficult it is to abandon these myths even when your adult-child has outgrown them.

Myth 1

"Limit setting" is important to help a child become socialized and to fit into a family. Parents need to let their child know which behaviors are appropriate and which are not acceptable. Parents need to reinforce acceptable behaviors and somehow reduce or eliminate the others.

This is a huge general concept that assumes that parents know where to place limits, how to enforce them, and when to make exceptions or give up the limits. The fine art of limit setting may no longer be relevant. You are at a point in parenting beyond the scope of most parent–child self-help books. After setting aside those outdated methods, there may be a lack of useful concepts for clarifying the relationship with your *adult*-child.

On a superficial level, you will probably acknowledge that there is no place for "limit setting" in your current family life. Yet, a concept that was so useful for so long will probably not be laid to rest without a struggle. You may find, through some honest soul searching, that this maxim is still at work when you communicate with your adult-children. It's subtle, so you'll need to pay close attention. This method, except when we discuss mutual limit setting, should move aside when you've learned some new skills.

Mike moved back home in his late twenties. The economy had been bad for some time, and four years after he had gotten his bachelor's degree, he was still in an entry-level job. Mike's optimism was beginning to fade in spite of encouragement from friends and family. He began to feel bad about himself, sensing that he would not achieve the success he had once thought possible.

During the four years, he had virtually put his life on hold. He had avoided committed relationships. He felt undeserving because he hadn't amounted to much. As his confidence began to wane, a friend suggested that he go to graduate school. This suggestion was full of possibilities. He would definitely be on a road somewhere. Surely a master's degree would help him with job prospects and also with self-confidence. He could feel the excitement grow as he thought out the details of his plan more concretely. He experienced growing hopefulness and energy.

With student loans and part-time work, he could pay his tuition and stay ahead of his debt for two years. Affordable housing remained a problem but seemed manageable when he thought about home.

Mike had not lived at home since he left for college, more than eight years before. Still, he felt he had a reasonable relationship with his parents, and since they were so supportive of his returning to school, he knew that living with them was the right decision. Without even a second thought, Mike's parents agreed to let him move back into his old room. So much relief was experienced by everyone that very little thought had been given to the potential problems that would come up as soon as Mike moved back home.

Almost immediately, there was conflict over Mike's coming and going and family rules that didn't make sense to a twenty-seven-year-old. Being punctual for meals and coming home on time were rules that seemed out of place now. Clearly, some new ways were needed for this threesome to relate to one another.

Myth 2

It is the parents' job to provide good role models. Children learn by observing what we do, not what we say. This is called *social learning* and begins soon after birth. Your children closely watched your interaction with the world at large. Though it is amusing to observe a two-year-old imitate us when we're angry, and to see how close they come to expressing our feelings with the correct body language, tone of voice, and even specific language, it is also awesome. How powerful we are in shaping their awareness and their coping strategies! It should not come as a surprise that when they become angry at us they use the behavior they learned from us to express their anger. How annoying to see our own negative behavior mirrored in them!

Clearly, our children also model our strengths and positive attributes, which is what we wish to happen. Actually, if we could have our way, the only behavior that would be emulated would be the kind we value. Then our children would grow to adulthood reflecting the best that we, as parents, are capable of being. So much for wish and fantasy!

I watch my teen-aged daughter react to the frustration of everyday life such as time pressures or projects or plans that don't work out. When I see her impatience or visible annoyance and hear her sharp-edged words, I see myself—my own style and imperfections. This kind of feedback is helpful if I wish to learn some new ways of managing my frustration. But, alas, even if I model new, more adaptive ways, these may or may not be learned by her. As essential as parental role modeling is to children, it becomes less and less relevant as children are exposed to more and more role models throughout the school years and adolescence. By the time your children reach adulthood, they no longer see you as a role model. You have been replaced by a dozen that seem more viable—including media personalities, teachers, bosses and mentors.

Do you find yourself still modeling behavior for your adult children? You may notice that, in the absence of other ways to engage them, you tell them and show them what you are doing in the hope that they will follow in your best footsteps. More than likely, they will experience this as lecturing and tune out.

A father who prided himself on his skill in managing and investing money was anxious for his adult-kids to follow in his footsteps. He noticed that his middle son, Andy, was rather uninterested in discussion that included the stock and bond market as well as other capital-building ideas. Since the subtle modeling methods hadn't worked, this father intensified his efforts by buying his son subscriptions to *Money* and *Forbes*. Still, Andy spent his money rather frivolously, according to Dad. The more this father demonstrated his skill and interest in and appreciation of money matters, the more Andy withdrew from any financial talk. Unfortunately, for Dad this was the single most important avenue for the relationship between him and his son. When modeling gave way to more respectful ways of relating, their interactions began to improve.

Myth 3

Parents should do everything possible to help develop their child's potential. The parents' job is to pave the way for the child's growth, which means providing the resources, financial and otherwise, and clearing away the stumbling blocks. It means stimulating the child's interests and talents. It also means being a source of encouragement—a cheering section, even when the parent isn't up to it. No stone should be left unturned on the road to maximizing promise in the children. In return, all that the parents ask is that the children fulfill their potential!

This idea is certainly reinforced in the child development literature. The question is "Should we keep doing this throughout our offspring's adulthood?" Will it be appreciated or even tolerated? Is this an appropriate way to interact with adult-children, or does it, in fact, backfire and create resentment or a sense of inadequacy in our adult-kids? This mode should probably be retired on the threshold of their adulthood. Pinpointing the threshold may not be easy, but it is probably somewhere between eighteen and twenty-eight.

I am reminded of a young man whose moderate interest in sports helped him achieve attention and satisfaction in high school and college. Todd's physical development had always been way ahead of his social and academic skills. He could depend on his body to perform well, and he could move fast, so he had an edge on the track field and also as a wide receiver in football.

Todd was a mediocre student in college, perhaps because of the time demanded by his sports. Maybe he chose to put energy into the activities that were most rewarding. In any case, by graduation, the other aspects of his life had become sufficiently developed to make him more well rounded. Feeling more comfortable with his peers, he gained confidence in social situations.

Now he is an adult, but his parents are unhappy to see his interest in sports waning. Actually, for Todd, the involvement in sports became less important as other aspects of his life took on more value. It was a natural and comfortable shift for him that somehow went unnoticed by his parents, who were forever sending him sports equipment and expressing verbal support for his athletic abilities. Todd felt annoyed at his parents and also ungrateful. Confusion and guilt made his protests weak and therefore unnoticed. Mom and Dad were still working to develop Todd's potential—a job that they did not realize was finished.

Myth 4

Harmony within the family should be maintained at all costs. Fighting, arguing, jealousy, and other negative ways of expressing oneself ought to be discarded. Establishing and maintaining peace is crucial. Negative feelings or behavior is not tolerable and is either denied, transformed, or punished.

This approach helps to preserve the image of a positive environment. While it helps to paint a pretty and pleasant picture, it is as lopsided as day without night and summer without winter. The normal spectrum of human emotions includes negative feelings, and suppressing them only serves to disguise them. As Haim Ginott suggested in *Between Parent and Child* (1965), his very popular child management book, "When a child is forbidden to have negative feelings or 'nasty' thoughts, he will inevitably have too much guilt and anxiety" (p. 139).

The denial pattern carries over to adulthood. Difficulty in expressing anger, annoyance, frustration, disdain, and other negative feelings leads to communication problems and is one of the leading reasons why people consult professional helpers.

Your family was probably influenced by the harmony and

tranquillity portrayed on TV family situation shows in the 1960s, 1970s, and 1980s. The effect was to make us feel guilty and anxious when turmoil and conflict reared their ugly heads in our homes. The guilt and anxiety were transmitted to our kids, and as an aid to feeling OK about themselves, they may have learned over time to discuss only those feelings that would make us feel comfortable. In the 1990s the TV model families are equally unrealistic.

According to Virginia Kidd, a communication studies professor at California State University, Sacramento, "Current models on TV tell us how families ought to be. We may all realize that 'Beaver' and 'Father Knows Best' are not real, but I think we harbor a longing for 'Mayberry' and the Cosby clan and various other programs where everybody communicates." Working out conflict looks so easy on TV. It's disappointing when real-life efforts fall short.

Even if these models worked for your family when your children were young, you may find that they will be a hindrance in relating to your adult-children. Very often our young adults are in transitional life spaces and don't have a preponderance of good feelings. They may want to talk about confusion, frustration, relationships that don't seem to be working, or job insecurity. They may want to share their fears or anger. If you are not able to hear these negative emotions, you may be left out of any but the most superficial dialogue.

Maya called her twenty-five-year-old daughter, Sally, whom she had not heard from in a few weeks. After the initial greetings, Maya sensed that her daughter was not as responsive as usual. She asked about Sally's work, her friends, managing money, and so on. After a few tense minutes, Sally volunteered that she was confused and disappointed about work since her year-old job was neither satisfying nor leading anywhere. There were some typical self-questioning statements, and a bit of discouragement was expressed. All in all, Sally was wrestling with some very age-appropriate life issues.

Hearing this, however, was upsetting and unsettling to Maya, who wanted reassurance that every thing was OK and tried to gloss over the rough edges of Sally's feelings. Predictably, as Sally became annoyed by her mother's insensitivity to her needs, Maya became more anxious and uncomfortable.

Myth 5

A parent is responsible for the success of his or her child. The thinking goes like this: "I must be perfect, or I will have failed." This logic makes the job of parenting seem even more serious than it already is.

The dreadful responsibility that is felt has more often been assumed by mothers than by fathers in the past. If you are a woman who has chosen parenting as the only or primary career of your life, you probably understand that success in parenting is very much tied to your own self-worth. After all, you worked so hard and invested so much energy, you would like the satisfaction of a job well done. Unfortunately, your success depends on many factors outside your control, some of which are biological or genetic. Environmental influences go only so far. It may be comforting to think that some characteristics are genetic, which translates into "not my fault."

Parents of either gender who believe that the success of their children is a reflection of their own success as parents are bound to experience disappointment. Discussing the cautious parent in his book *The Responsive Parent* (1972), M. Hoover says, "They worry about every move they make, every frustration that their child is forced to endure, fearful that one false step or trying event might somehow spell disaster" (p. 81). These caring parents are deeply involved in their children's day-to-day lives, helping to pave the way by removing stress.

To the extent that this approach worked once-upon-a-time, when the children were young, it is bound to be seen as a useful way of relating to children of any age. Ironically, the day-to-day involvement with your children that helped to contain their stress, and yours, is often experienced by your adult-children as overinvolvement, meddling, and a lack of confidence in them. Here, then, is another idea that has outlived its usefulness!

The interaction of Sally and her mother, just discussed, illustrates this myth very nicely. For Maya, watching Sally flounder and seeing her unable to exhibit her usual self-confidence and spirit were a sign that Maya may have failed somewhere. Specifically, she was currently failing to take away Sally's hurt as she had done so many times in the past.

This inability to "help" activated Maya's sense of helplessness, which affected her feeling of competency. She wanted so badly to help but really didn't know what to do. Wanting to give advice was ruled out in favor of changing the subject. This option was more face-saving. Maya was embarrassed by not having any helpful remedies or solutions for Sally. She really had no idea how to act and was made intensely uncomfortable by the limits of her ability to make things OK. Of course, all that was really needed or desired was an attentive, tolerant listener and a non-judgmental sounding board. But how was Maya to know?

At least part of the problem was that both mother and daughter were going through a period of "separation and self-definition" (LaSorsa and Fodor, 1990). Sally's independence was marked by self-doubt and a wished-for dependence. This was consistent with the development of young adults. LaSorsa and Fodor focus on the similarity of the struggles of young women with those of their mothers. In their research they found that many of the "mothers themselves are confronting their own developmental issues at this time. . . . Like her adolescent daughter, the midlife mother also faces the challenges of separation, autonomy and loss" (p. 594).

Myth 6

The family conference should be the forum for the discussion of family problems and conflicts. This is a good idea borrowed from family system theory, but it is not widely followed. In families that do use this format, the meeting takes place with the entire family together. Parents see this format as egalitarian since it gives an opportunity for even young children to say what they think or feel about a particular situation. The family conference promises a "let's discuss it" problem-solving atmosphere. It assumes that the parents will take a more passive, receptive, listening stance, while the children will be more active and assertive. Sometimes the family forum serves as an effective first step in the development of children's self-advocacy, and for that reason, it is a useful family tool.

Parents feel good about their role in this process. They are giving permission to their children to express themselves and allowing an unstructured dialogue to take place, which may even challenge their parental authority! Yet if you talk to countless young people, or to adults who remember this process from their childhood, they remember parent-centered sessions during which preaching sometimes took place. Solutions were presented by the parents, and preconceived answers, thought up by the parents, were allowed to surface.

This medium for intergenerational discussion certainly has its merits, but it has no place in the relationship with your adult-child, partly because of the difficulty of getting together a "family of origin" after the adult-children disperse and have families of their own. Also, the affairs of one child may be unrelated to the other children and may very likely be private.

Parents remembering the usefulness of the family conference in the past may attempt to keep it alive by consulting by phone or letter with one daughter or son about the problems of a sibling. It is not unusual for a parent to garner support from siblings by lobbying them to oppose a plan, such as a move away, desired by an adult-child. This is never seen as helpful and at worst may seem like a violation of trust. The family conference needs to become an artifact of the past, remembered the way family pictures are—in a photo album.

Janet, a single parent with a six-year-old son, decided to move to a nearby city. There, a new job gave her promise of greater financial security. Her call to her mother with the news aroused the older woman's own anxiety about moving and the difficulties that would ensue. Instead of communicating her fears to Janet, she phoned her three other adult-children and conveyed her concern. Janet's older brother was selected to call Janet and share the "family's concerns." It's not surprising that big brother's well-intended questioning of Janet's judgment was not met with great appreciation.

Building with New Blocks

There are many more building blocks in the ideal parent–child relationship. You probably developed some that worked for you. What were some of your family rules? Take a minute to think about them. Before any changes can take place, it's important to take a good look at the starting point: your own workable and trusted rules.

The following anecdote was given to me recently by a parent searching for ways to have a more meaningful relationship with her adult-children and looking to her once useful tools for guidance.

> I always felt that the ideal family would have some specific time together each week. I don't know where I got this idea, but I do recall from my own childhood that family day was Sunday, and there was an expectation that all of us would take time out to be together, to put aside our own individual plans. It was usually a relaxed, comfortable time even for my parents. It was the one time during the week that allowed unhurried communication. I guess that's why I worked so hard to make that happen for my own family. It worked for a long time and seemed like an ideal way to make positive contact with each other. As the kids became adolescents, they pulled away more and more, and keeping Sunday for the family became more of a struggle than a pleasure. Now that the kids are adults, I still find myself trying to pull together Sunday family time. It's usually disap-

pointing because, when it's rejected, my feelings get hurt, and then my kids feel guilty.

Old rules die hard because they are so deeply entrenched. It's hard to know where our ideas come from or whether they still make sense in guiding our lives. It's easier to make changes in the way we see or do things when we have a good understanding of their origin. Let's see if your expectations of family behavior are still relevant.

Think about your own useful rules. Write them down. Think about their source. Here are some questions to consider:

1. Is this a way of being together that worked in your family of origin (the one you grew up in) or was it a family strategy that you *wish* had been used back then?
2. Did you learn about it from a friend or neighbor?
3. Were you influenced by books, magazine articles, or TV?

Now, evaluate how well your rules worked and for how long. Finally, determine whether you are still trying to use these rules in relating to your adult children. Here is a worksheet to help you organize your responses:

Family rule	Source	Evaluation	Still useful?

Did this activity help to clarify which rules are outmoded and which simply don't apply to this stage of family life? There may be a cluster of rules that you think may still be workable. If you discovered any that still work and are appropriate, you already have a good foundation for building even more satisfying ties with your adult-kids and their families.

If this exercise seemed really difficult, the reason may be that many of your family rules and models for communication were not systematically thought out, planned, and implemented. This "shoot-from-the-hip" style of family management is actually more common than any other. When a problem in communication arises, a solution is sought, but without a guiding principle. Rules, if they exist, may seem informal and implicit. If this pattern describes your style, you may have less to unlearn than parents who used a tighter structure. Remember, most strategies that worked for Phase 1 parenting simply won't be useful now. Giving up your notions of the ideal parenting style won't be easy, especially if you were successful!

Our families never did quite match up with the TV families characterized by "Ozzie and Harriet," "Leave it to Beaver," "The Brady Bunch," or, more recently, "The Cosby Show." It's easy to believe in the fantasy relationship designed and implemented by the media. It looks so real and it works so smoothly. When we try to imitate these clever parents, we tend not to get the same results. We set them up as a standard for a happy home life and invariably feel unsuccessful, not because of our shortcomings but because of an unrealistic requirement. The fact that you are reading this book proves that you did a sufficiently good job and that you still have some kind of relationship with your adult-children.

At this new stage the media offer you mere extensions of the old roles—once again working smoothly and effortlessly. We would probably all agree that this doesn't happen in real life. Still, it doesn't stop us from wishing that we could be as successful. It doesn't shield us from disappointment when we fail to re-create that perfect harmony, especially when we suspect others are achieving it.

Marking Time

Recently I met an old friend for lunch, and not surprisingly, we talked about our adult-children. This particular woman is in her late forties and has a daughter who is twenty-eight and a son who is twenty-five. I knew something about her life experience as a parent, which included a painful divorce when her kids where young. I also knew about the strain of being a single parent and later being a noncustodial parent when her daughter requested this arrangement as a teen. Donna was very candid about her feelings and experiences. Because she is also a therapist, it may be easier for her to talk openly about her sense of loss and grief when the struggles with her kids were most intense.

Our conversation focused on Donna's connection with her kids now that they are adults. Her words seemed paradoxical, but I have heard them again and again since that day:

> I'm really delighted with things the way they are now. Sometimes I'm amazed at how easily and comfortably we relate. I haven't forgotten how cautious and fearful I was when Brenda was a teen. I remember feeling so incompetent as a parent. It seemed as if whatever I did was the wrong thing back then. The contrast is so incredible. My daughter and I have something very special that I wouldn't have dreamed possible ten years ago. It's very perplexing, particularly since so many of my friends with adult-children seem to have a situation that is the reverse of mine. When I talk to them, I get the impression that they can't quite get into a mutually satisfying space with their adult-kids. Yet, these same parents had enviable relationships with their kids clear through adolescence, which everyone knows is remarkable!

I thought about this pattern when Donna presented it, but at the time I wasn't sure what to make of it. It almost appeared that relationships with kids might be time-bound in mutually exclusive ways. It suggested to me that, if your parenting skills were wonderful in Phase 1 (child parenting), somehow this might actually impede Phase 2 (adult parenting). On the other hand, did the absence of positive or clear parent–child interactions actually pave the way for the unbiased development of expert Phase 2 skills? While it didn't make sense entirely, it did give me something to think about and explore with others.

There's something about the need to shift gears that seems important in the transition from Phase 1 to Phase 2 parenting. Perhaps some sort of a historical life marker is necessary. Various cultures mark the passage of one phase of life and the beginning of a new era with a celebration. Marriage, birth, anniversary, graduation, bar or bat mitzvah, and other rites of passage, even including new job or career parties and housewarmings, are a few of the more familiar ones that symbolically or in reality set our expectations for a new way of being.

Such markers help to prepare all the players in life's production for a change that is necessary and to be welcomed, not fought or resisted. These events give people some time to shift gears in their hopes, wishes, expectations, and behavior. They mark an ending and a beginning that all can see and may signal some grief for a less-than-perfect outcome of the era passing.

Grief is a natural, but surprising, emotion often experienced when moving from one life stage to the next. It will pass if acknowledged with a few tears or some nostalgic review. Avoiding the grief associated with the passing of an era, for better or worse, results in the inability to move on to the next stage, free of the familiar tugs on our psyches to make things turn out perfectly. This view is summed up quite well by a newly freed parent:

> I looked forward to my daughter's emancipation, which is what I called her entry into her own life following college, and I anticipated relief in not having to be so responsible, financially and in other ways. Instead of feeling happy, I found myself depressed because I felt she would no longer need me for anything, and I could not see any other basis for

a relationship with her. The very thing I wanted, her emancipation, seemed to be backfiring on me because I felt distanced from her, and kind of useless.

This bitter-sweet account reflects many parents' ambivalence in letting go of an era that at least provided clear parameters for relationships.

Focusing on a related issue, Howard Halpern speaks to a young adult audience in his book *Cutting Loose* (1976):

Often our parents' inner child is not pleased by our being strong and independent. The child within them may be apprehensive and angry at the separateness and the loss of control over us implied by our own autonomy. It is in the nature of the young child that dwells in our parents (or us, or anyone) to want the sustained and dependable intimacy of those they are close to because their inner child depends on that involvement for their feelings of well-being, worth and adequacy. When we behave in ways that mark us as individuals separate from our parents, individuals with our own ideas, feelings and lives, the child within our parents feels an overwhelming threat of losing us and may react with disapproval, upset, hurt or anger. The child within us, seeking to avoid the disapproval or anger of the demanding child within our parents, may then enter into an unconscious collusion with the maneuvers of that child and develop specific ways of relating to our parents that keep us perpetually and placatingly reactive to their spoken or implied injunctions. (p. 17)

To paraphrase what Halpern wrote, whether we are parents or newly adult children, we often hook into the unconscious inner child of the other. When this happens, we no longer feel adult or rational, and this is both confusing and embarrassing. Rather than seeing this pattern for what it is, a remnant from the past, we become defensive and try to hide our reactions or explain them away. Since we are probably all "guilty" of this tendency from time to time, it might be best simply to acknowledge it when noticed and label it properly so that it can be seen more clearly the next time. There's really nothing more that needs to be done!

In her best-selling book *My Mother Myself* (1976), Nancy Friday describes her relationship with her mother, in which feelings are not acknowledged or accurately labeled. How painful that feels!

> In all the years we lived together, it is a shame we never talked honestly about our feelings. What neither of us knew then was that I could have stood honesty, no matter how frightening. Her angers, disillusionments, fears of failure, rage—emotions I seldom saw—I could have come to terms with them if she had been able to speak to me. I would have grown used to the idea that while mother loved me, at times other emotions impaired that love, and developed trust that in time her love for me would always return. Instead, I was left trying to believe in some perfect love she said she had for me, but in which I could not believe. (p. 45)

So much of what goes on in a love relationship does not take place on a rational or logical level. Learning to confront these murky feelings when we see them is critical if we are to avoid misunderstandings leading to hurt. This mutual process between parent and child doesn't usually come about until the transition to adulthood takes place and is acknowledged. The dialogue that Nancy Friday wishes could have taken place can, in fact, happen.

Challenging Old Rules

What makes the old tapes so indestructible? Partly it's the fault of the American work ethic and the illogical things we tell ourselves about how jobs *ought* to be done. It's an intolerable feeling for most of us to move away from a job that wasn't done perfectly. This is particularly true of the job of parenting.

Moving on to the next phase in parenting means closing off

the past—leaving the mistakes and unfinished business of the past still stirred up and pleading for completion or perfection. What makes this an even bigger problem is that some of the mistakes and unfinished business of the past stem from our own childhood, not from the childhood of our offspring, as we have just seen.

The old rules and the tapes on which they were recorded have had years to be reinforced, and while they aren't perfect, they are trusted and relied on. Zenith Gross, author of *And You Thought It Was All Over* (1985), sheds some light on the difficulty in establishing new patterns:

> Mothers and adult children have been in vehement, intense intimacy for twenty or thirty years, and their communications patterns are complex enough to include both love and hate, both affection and dislike, both acceptance and rejection. The pressures of the outside world have also infiltrated their responses to each other: The parents must face earning a livelihood as well as self-actualization and aging; the young people must endure growing pains, peer pressure, and the challenges of young adulthood. (p. 65)

It seems like an immense undertaking to negate the old patterns and start over. It would be, except that it's not necessary to go back to Square One. Much of what you already know is still useful. While technology and materials have changed dramatically, the cars of the 1990s still have as their primary function a role that is virtually the same as the Model T Ford. This metaphor applies equally well to the business of parenting.

Assuming that your desire to maintain contact with your adult-children is very strong, our next task is to identify the possibilities of a relationship, modified in form. It will be built on a foundation reinforced by years of history, tradition, and experience, altered by the passage of time. Our job is to shape and reshape a structure that already exists, and unlike in the equally creative art of sculpturing, mistakes are tolerable, and self-correction as you go along is rewarded.

It's important to remember that the change from parent to

"parent emeritus" is a process that takes place over time. First, there's a need for disconnection from the old ways or patterns, an unlearning of the rules that no longer apply. The next step involves coming to terms with disappointment. It's often hard to accept your adult-child's life when it looks so different from your own. The following chapter addresses the pain and the ways of coping with it.

Chapter 4

Acknowledging the Impasse

When the Seed Falls Far from the Tree

When I was young I remember hearing that I looked just like my mother. This was the ultimate compliment to be paid to her, and she smiled with pride and pleasure whenever someone made that observation. As parents we may not admit it, but it definitely feels good when our children are seen as being "like us": looking like us, behaving like us, and having aspirations and making lifestyle choices that are similar to our own.

Our children's "differences" are often not easily accepted. The child who grows into an adult and walks a different path is often not easily understood by his or her own family. Children choosing a course that seems alien causes discomfort, anger, and sometimes disappointment to well-meaning parents. Although most parents can acknowledge the values of equality and free choice, it is very uncomfortable when offspring act on these values and put their parents to the test. According to Roger Gould, psychiatrist and author of *Transformations* (1978), parents may intellectually "agree that we have a right to our own opinion, but emotionally they can't resist the temptation to exercise their waning power" (p. 58). He goes on to say that "The deep questioning of parental assumptions is more than adolescent play: it's a deadly serious business" (p. 60). The need to pull away from parents, emotionally, intellectually, and physically, is a developmentally appropriate behavior. Sometimes rebelliousness in behavior or values is a way of obtaining self-definition, so as to no longer "be defined by the family roles" (LaSorsa & Fodor, 1990, p. 604).

When your adult-child has an impediment, whether temporary or permanent, special accommodations are required for which few parents are psychologically prepared.

This chapter is about the feelings and reactions of parents who are trying to come to terms with the realization that their adult-children are different from them, have chosen an "unacceptable" lifestyle, or have limitations that they did not anticipate. It is about understanding the hopes and wishes that kindled the desire to have a family.

Roger Gould discusses the myth of family one-mindedness that is based on the destructive belief that "people must be identical in order for love to continue or hatred to be avoided" (p. 57). He notes the discomfort of acknowledging differences but the necessity of growth leading to acceptance.

In his book *The Middle Years* (1981), Donald Donohugh sets the stage for parents at midlife to understand some of the realities of parenting that were not pointed out by popular childhood experts such as Dr. Spock:

> We were told, too, that we could expect our children to use our values as a basis to form their own, rejecting some and modifying others. We were not told that they would reject all of them while living off the fruits of them. . . . Nor did we know that this total rejection would come at a time in our lives when we ourselves would begin to have doubts about our values and be in the process of rethinking them. (p. 271)

This chapter is also about the disappointment that grows out of the awareness that dreams and reality may be very far apart, that what you expected in the development of your child may never be realized. Acknowledging the disappointment is a necessary first step to understanding some of the tension between you and your adult-child.

Life is full of challenges. Who ever said that being a parent would be easy? We all were prepared for the "terrible twos," the "stormy adolescence," the breaking away of the young adult. We anticipated these stress points and saw them as signposts that measure movement along the path of normal child development. We could talk about the trials and tribulations of parenting publicly and with humor because everyone else who had a child could understand and identify with us. But what happens when the issues feel so far from "normal" that we find they aren't humorous or even speakable?

You may have had to come to terms with the special needs of your son or daughter before birth, at birth, or at any point along the way. Regardless of the specifics, there is a process that all parents of children who depart from the family norm must experience at some point in order to cope adequately with reality. The rest of this chapter focuses on the most representative problems that can interfere with parent–adult-child relationships.

Disabilities

Some parents know before birth that they will be bringing children with special needs into the world. Genetic defects, fetal accidents, and maternal illness can all cause trauma to the unborn child, and parents may be aware, from the very beginning of his or her life, that their child will be "different." But forewarned, in this case, is not forearmed, and parents of special children must struggle with their adjustment just as much as parents who learn about their children's "differences" much later in life.

Erma Bombeck discusses with humor and compassion the role of the "special mother" in her book *Motherhood: The Second Oldest Profession* (1984). She describes a dialogue between God and an angel in selecting a mother for a handicapped child. The angel asks, "But does she have patience?" God responds, "I don't want her to have too much patience, or she will drown in a sea of self-pity and despair. Once the shock and resentment wear off, she'll handle it. I watched her today. She has that sense of self and independence that are so rare and so necessary in a mother. You see, the child I'm going to give her has his own world. She has to make it live in her world and that's not going to be easy." Regarding selfishness, the angel asks, "Is that a virtue?" God responds, "If she can't separate herself from the child occasionally, she'll never survive. Yes, here is a woman whom I will bless with a child less than perfect. She doesn't realize it yet, but she is to be envied" (p. 11).

The short story is poignant. There is a predictable process that parents of children with disabilities must go through; it includes shock, coping, separation, and acceptance.

When a child is born with special needs or disabilities, he or she will be defined by the world as nontraditional, as different. Whether the disability will be permanent or is a temporary time-out that will improve over time, as a parent you will need to come to terms with unanswerable questions and strong feelings: "Why? What did I do wrong? How did I fail? It's not fair!"

Sometimes a child is born without severe physical or neurological problems but becomes disabled through disease or accident. Brain damage and mental retardation may follow an illness. An accident may result in spinal cord injury and paralysis. A psychological trauma, such as molestation or kidnapping, may cause severe emotional distress. Any number of circumstances can bring about a handicap that may be irreversible or not likely to improve much over time.

Spared the anguish described above, some parents encounter other types of difficulties associated with severe psychological problems or mental illness with an onset in childhood, adolescence, or young adulthood. For some youth, the transition from one life stage to another is quite traumatic. Parents, seldom prepared, usually have to respond to a crisis with very little understanding or experience. But whatever the cause or course of a child's difficulty, parents are likely to respond with disbelief and shock and to follow a predictable path in coming to terms with the reality.

Lifestyles

The problem you've experienced may not be a physical limitation, nor one that is cognitive or emotional. What about lifestyle choices that are repugnant and unacceptable to us? What about choices made by our young that separate us from them in terms of the very underpinnings of family life? How do we come to terms with these?

You may recall some discussion in the last chapter about family life and the ways in which hopes, wishes, and expectations are passed down from generation to generation. We learned the traditions of our family and the ways to behave that ensure our continued place in it. We learned to follow the cultural traditions and guidelines, to work in ways consistent with family values, to marry and have children. We also learned a role in the community and how to take our appropriate place in it. No script was written to accommodate the special needs, wishes, or limitations that life imposes.

Traditionally, women were supposed to marry by a certain time and build a family. Men were supposed to accept the responsibility of marrying and working to support the family that was created. Once a course was begun, it was supposed to be played out, without opportunity for detour. Marriage was forever. We worked until we were old and then relaxed with our grandchildren. End of story!

The story has changed significantly, but the expectations may have remained intact. In a more complex and diverse world, our young may not marry or may do so "too late" by our standards. They may marry someone from another social class or racial or religious group. They may *choose* not to have children. Work and the desire to "live the good life" may not motivate some of our offspring, who may not value the role of work in their lives.

Increasingly, gay and lesbian adults are not willing to live a double life, and they may wish for, or demand, acknowledgment by their parents and acceptance of their lifestyle. Can your values accommodate such a reality?

Alternate lifestyles may include living in a commune (less likely in 1990 than in 1970), living together out of wedlock, being an unmarried parent (either by accident or by choice), or rejecting work and living instead on public assistance. Certainly, there are others, but it's less necessary to identify each pattern than to understand the connection between them in terms of parents' reactions and coping abilities.

When a disability or an alternate lifestyle is identified, there is a tendency to believe that change is possible, that the situation or choice is reversible. This notion tends to get us, as parents, into a lot of trouble.

In some ways, it is easier to accept the limitations that God or nature or fate places on our children than to accept lifestyle choices that run counter to our beliefs. Somehow we can tolerate reality, however difficult, when the circumstances seem beyond our control. But where lifestyle is concerned there is a nagging hope that he or she will change, that given the right help, care, information, challenge, or reproach, these adult-children will rethink their "wrong" choices and assume their proper role in the family tree. Such thinking, on our part, indicates our disbelief, disappointment, and reluctance to accept the current reality. It also makes conflict inevitable. Sometimes we don't forgive their choices and create an impossible barrier.

Blaming*

When your child's life has not unfolded as you imagined it would, there is a gap between your expectations (dreams) and what has been realized (reality). This void becomes filled with

*Adapted from Chapter 3, "Who's to Blame?" in Toder (1987).

facts, rationalizations, judgments, assumptions, and other means of explaining this event. Unfortunately, we tend to review the past and examine our own past behavior for clues. It is not at all unusual, during this backward glance, to distort reality.

Memories are not particularly accurate. It may be especially easy to accept responsibility for what has happened to your adult-child by blaming yourself for things that you did or failed to do. You may have a strong urge to search the past for evidence of shortcomings in your character or behavior that led you to this point. Were you too afraid to discipline? Did your parents' early divorce deprive you of some basic parenting skills?

Finding some flaw shouldn't be too difficult since none of us is perfect. Looking back from a midlife perspective makes the shortfalls and mistakes more obvious: "The original scripts did not prepare adults for these real-life improvisations that they were called on to cope with" (Weick, 1989, p. 235).

"If I had only . . ." is a typical approach in reconstructing the past in such a way that the problem you are struggling with might have been avoided. This line of reasoning assumes that you failed, at some level, and that your failure was predictable and avoidable. It follows that you ought to be punished for your mistakes, and you may beat yourself with the negative qualities that you may believe are responsible for your pain. Some of these negative attributes include negligence, stupidity, and selfishness. How could you have anticipated this outcome? Would you have lived your life differently had you anticipated it?

The list of ways that you may have behaved differently is endless. If you were now able to redo the past and reconstruct it so that you could view yourself as the perfect parent and therefore as not at fault for the misfortune that has taken place, what might you consider? Here are some options:

If I had only
    taken better care of myself, him, her.
    paid more attention.
    set my priorities differently.

thought ahead.
been stronger.
been less selfish.
really heard what they were saying.
been home more often.
taken him or her more seriously.
done more.
anticipated this outcome.
not divorced.

Any parent who has gone through the experience of having a "different" child has probably considered some of the possibilities listed above. It is understandable to want to make changes in the past. It isn't really possible to see what went wrong and correct it. Still, the urge is very powerful.

If, as a parent, I'm to blame, then can't I fix it? The wish to change life events is not sufficient, no matter how strong the will. Even if the limitations are based on lifestyle choices and not physical limitation, you don't have the power or authority to bring about a change.

Whose Problem Is It?

There is a pervasive belief that if a child turns out to be an adult who is "different," someone has failed, usually the mother. For mothers "children are a piece of work—something they have invested a great deal of time and energy in shaping and guiding. Thus, they experience their daughter's failure as their own failure as a mother" (LaSorsa & Fodor, 1990, p. 604). This view seems to have taken hold when psychiatry set forth its theory that the first five years of life (particularly the first two) shape the psyche of the young child and that the mother plays a key role in this development and its outcome. Generations of guilt-ridden parents took responsibility and accepted blame for the difficulties of their offspring.

No matter what the problem, this blaming attitude made it difficult for parents to separate themselves from their children's afflictions. Whether your child was born with cerebral palsy, became deaf because of an illness, or had a substance abuse problem, there was a ready target to blame. It's easy to answer the question of "Why?" when there is a willing scapegoat. Accepting blame for sins, real or imagined, motivates parents, particularly mothers, to try to fix things.

The urge to "fix" things for our children can be very strong. It's hard to watch our kids (of any age) struggle, hurt, or fail. It's a natural inclination to want to step in and take over. Still, this action may backfire and communicate a lack of confidence, trust, and respect when the child is an adult and needs to be able to make changes on his or her own.

Though you may have difficulty tolerating the current situation, no really meaningful change can come about without the willing cooperation of your child. Children over eighteen are no longer minors, and you have very little say in their lives unless they are grossly incapacitated—and that requires a court order.

Whose problem is it? Do they really need or want your help, your well-intended advice, your decision-making skills? Chances are that, if your child is over eighteen (and you probably wouldn't be reading this book otherwise), he or she would resist your involvement.

If your adult-child is not resistant to your efforts, he or she may benefit from some help in developing a stronger drive toward his or her own autonomy. Fortunately, this need for autonomy peaks during adolescence and the early adult years.

When lifestyle choices are the issue, parents' views aren't appreciated. For whom are you becoming involved? Is the dissatisfaction *your* lack of acceptance of their lifestyle or is it their own dissatisfaction? The following example illustrates this point.

Your son Max is twenty-five and a college graduate. He has worked at a few jobs in the past three years, but for one reason or another he couldn't find satisfaction in his work. You have always been a very supportive parent and have communicated how important it is to have meaningful work. Max understood that.

Max is easygoing and comfortable with himself. He has some friendships that began in high school. Weekend soccer and softball occupy his weekends, while charcoal drawing and watercolor painting mark his days. Max does not see any of these activities as particularly marketable.

When the going got rough financially he moved back home easily, without defensiveness. He knew it would be OK with you. He seems perfectly at home and is mostly cooperative about his involvement in household chores and other family matters.

He makes few demands, but neither does he contribute to the family income. Still, his expenses are low, and family financial resources are not very much stretched at this point. This strong, healthy young man shows no signs of moving out on his own. When the subject is approached, he jokes about being the "oldest kid in the neighborhood." He appears to have little anxiety or self-criticism, but he is not easy to read. He doesn't share his inner thoughts or feelings. He seems to accept the current situation as is.

You, on the other hand, are becoming increasingly agitated and also annoyed at yourself for your feelings. After all, look how lucky you are to have a son who values his family and, unlike so many of his contemporaries, has chosen to remain close. Still, underneath your arguments, you have nagging worries and embarrassment. You may be thinking, "This is not normal. How can I explain this to my friends? What will people think? What have I done wrong? Why is Max so 'different' from his peers? Why is he doing this to us?"

What begins with your curiosity about Max's current lifestyle becomes almost an obsession as time goes by. Meanwhile, Max is undisturbed, keeps himself busy with interesting projects, and manages to meet his own needs for spending money by doing odd jobs.

Whose problem is it? It's sometimes difficult to ferret out who owns the problem. The possibilities are

the parent(s).
the child.
the parents and child together.

In this particular case it is abundantly clear that Max does not experience his situation as being a problem. That does not mean that beneath his calm exterior there aren't uncertainties and fears about being on his own. He may or may not be aware of these, but he certainly is not communicating insecurity in his behavior or language. He is clearly not willing to acknowledge the "problem" at this point. Nor does he see any need to change his work or living situation.

You see things much differently. You knew that Max needed a place to sort out his life, and you were only too glad to accommodate him. But you feel it has gone on too long to be "normal." You begin to question yourself. Who's to blame here? What did I (or we) do wrong to produce a young man with such complacency, unwilling or unable to negotiate the larger world?

When the self-searching ends, you wonder about his motives. Why is Max behaving this way? You consider two different hypotheses to explain his behavior:

1. *Revenge*. This explanation is based on "get-even" logic. Max is not moving on with his life in order to

challenge my (our) values.
punish me (us) for some past hurt.
get even for past competition waged and lost.
thwart parental satisfaction.

2. *Passivity*. This explanation depends on a constitutional deficit. Max cannot move on emotionally and psychologically. He is incapable of functioning on his own and is

weak in his character development.
easily influenced.
submissive and compliant.
a born follower with no initiative.

You entertain both of these hypotheses as interesting and useful ways of explaining why Max is stuck at home. You say to yourself, "Certainly he would not choose to live this way of his own free will." There is something wrong, and the urge to fix it becomes stronger and stronger.

Actually, there are additional ways to explain why Max may be stuck. Some possibilities are provided by Roger Gould (1978). He presents a number of false assumptions that, on the one hand, give young adults excuses for not accepting the reality of adulthood with full responsibility and, on the other hand, require parents to provide safety and security: "If we wait for someone to rescue us, we cannot build self-confidence or come to feel solidly independent. Those of us who choose this dependent response are miserably unhappy: we feel not only passive but chronically incompetent" (p. 74).

Depending on others—in this case, one's parents—to make things all right is also a false assumption that impedes growth. As this pattern plays itself out, feelings of passivity or hostility are likely to surface and to result in "a destructive conspiracy that prevents our developing a fuller, more independent adult consciousness" (p. 111).

As a parent, when you perceive that your adult-child has made a lifestyle choice that is not consistent with your views, values or hopes, it's easy to assume that the choice was not of his or her "free will" but was motivated by hostility or indecisiveness.

If the problem truly belongs to Max and he won't acknowledge it, then he won't be your partner in change. If he is content with his current life and you are not, then the problem is yours. If Max recognizes your discomfort and is willing to explore some of the issues with you, then the problem is shared, the solutions will be much easier to identify, and the likelihood of sabotage is diminished.

In the current example, without Max's acknowledgment of his role in the dilemma, the problem belongs to his parents. If they push for a solution, it will be without shared decision making and certainly without their son's blessing. This will not be easy. It's probably fair to say that when there is a lifestyle conflict between parent and adult-child, any potential change that takes place will probably need to involve a shift in the parents' attitude. This does not mean that the parent is to blame; rather, it means that the parent has more investment in bringing about a change.

The "Good-Enough" Parent

At the beginning of the chapter, we discussed the influence of psychiatry steeped in the Freudian tradition, which tends to hold parents responsible for the early psychological development of the child. That tradition explains the dysfunctions of the child in terms of parental (usually maternal) shortcomings. The theory gained its credence from the study of disturbed individuals and families. Unless you and your family are quite exceptional, it would be simple to place the finger of blame on you, as parent, for the difficulties of your offspring.

It is understandable that, if your child reaches adulthood and has significant problems in coping with life, you may want to explore your role or influence in shaping this situation. You may look for blame within yourself, and you will probably find some, since none of us is a perfect parent. Most of us, however, did the best we could.

In fact, we were probably "good enough"* though clearly less-than-perfect parents and somewhat disillusioned:

> So by middle age, we had hoped to see in our children the realization of all our hopes and dreams; some reward from late-at-night bottles, changing diapers, bandaging skinned knees, and comforting them when they cried; the results of all those investments in lessons, vitamins, braces and camps. And for the most part, we are doomed to disappointment" (Donohugh, 1981, p. 273)

*This phrase was coined by D. W. Winnicott (1989), a British pediatrician turned psychoanalyst, considered one of the most creative thinkers in contemporary psychoanalytic circles.

It is not enough to blame; blaming doesn't go far enough. Coping with painful realities is more productive. If I really am to blame for my thirty-year-old son's drinking, I'll probably go out of my way to

deny his problem.
rationalize my own parenting while searching for self-blame.
provide cover in public to protect him and avoid community awareness that would criticize him and therefore me.

However, if I was really a "good-enough" parent, then I can bypass much of this process and get down to really helping.

Before you get started, you need to believe that you and your adult-child are truly separate individuals, neither of you living your life for the other. You were separated at birth, if you are the mother, and now you must believe that your child needs to take a separate path and to walk it alone if she or he can. Even when there are severe limitations, so that physical or financial separation are not possible (as in the case of severe mental retardation or brain damage), emotional separation can still be achieved. You must believe, and be willing to accept, that you and your child have separate destinies. Your maternal or paternal instinct needs to give way to your own survival instincts, or your desire to "help" or "change" your child will cloud your own life. You may recall Erma Bombeck's comment in the first part of this chapter.

When you are able to understand the freedom of your child to live out his or her life, even when the choice is abhorrent to you, and to respect his or her individuality, then you will also be set free. Your adult-child has the right to make choices, and to fail. You have the right to be disappointed, but not responsible.

Accommodating to the circumstances of your adult-child's life requires a sensitive and accurate assessment of his or her limitations and needs. It also requires you to be able to tolerate what you can't change. However, it does not mean condoning behavior that is dangerous, hostile, or critical. Again, you may feel deeply saddened and disappointed, but you are not responsible for unacceptable behavior displayed by your adult offspring—toward you or anyone else.

I remember a consultation with the parents of a twenty-four-year-old man. He did not wish to see me himself because he sensed, correctly, that this was what his parents wanted. His anger at them was making their home life intolerable. But what had they done? It was not clear to anyone.

Benjamin had had his heart set on being an attorney. After college, which had not been particularly easy, he spent two years preparing for the Law School Admission Test and was unsuccessful in achieving a score high enough to be admitted to an accredited law school. He was agitated and became obsessed by this fact. Terribly annoyed and frustrated with himself, he lashed out at others, particularly his family. Fueling this fire was the fact that his parents were successful professionals—his mother a concert pianist and his father a pharmacist. Soon after his disappointment, Ben's younger sister was admitted to medical school.

There is no doubt that this young man's pain was being experienced by his parents, who had found a way to feel responsible for his troubles. Beyond that, his blaming, angry, and verbally abusive actions at home had exceeded the bounds of acceptable behavior.

While accepting his academic limitations, these parents were prepared to support Ben's efforts to find other career satisfactions. Their son, however, refused to move on in his thinking or planning, expressing energy only in the form of negative outbursts.

Limit setting is a difficult but necessary step in communicating what you will allow and what is definitely not tolerable. Most of us are better at setting limits on others' behavior when we are free of guilt or responsibility for that behavior. Making excuses and denying the seriousness of some behavior help a disillusioned parent look the other way to avoid some pain. At the same time, it takes a daughter or son off the hook. "She'll turn herself around," "It's only a phase," "This is a difficult time in his life"—

these may be ways of denying significant life problems or conflicts. It's important to differentiate between a stance that is emotionally supportive and nurturing and one that is overly tolerant because of guilt or self-blame.

Before you can come to terms with your adult-child, you need to see the problems, experience your disappointment and sadness, and go through a process that acknowledges your grief and loss. After all, the obstacle that got in the way of satisfying contact appeared over time and can be moved the same way. Whatever it is, acknowledging the nature of the impasse is a necessary first step toward healing and moving on.

Ben's parents needed to stop helping, to stop accepting blame for what they could not change, and to stop absorbing their son's disappointment. When these parents refocused their attention on themselves, they felt the helplessness that belonged to them and allowed their son to go through a similar process of loss and acceptance without their involvement.

Contemporary Lifestyle or Poor Judgment

Sometimes ignorance is bliss. Staying ignorant can be protective—as long as it works. If your daughter is thirty and single and her status is uncomfortable to you, it may be easier to avoid understanding what her lifestyle means. You can maintain your belief that the time for settling down has not arrived, and that you will need to wait a bit longer than you had hoped for grandchildren. But what if your daughter has no intention of having children? What if she is in a long-term, stable relationship but does not wish to marry or have children? Can you acknowledge her decisions, accept her as she is, and learn something about her values and choices that will increase your understanding? The alternative, of course, is to remain ignorant but no longer blissful.

When your values, beliefs, or desires come into conflict with your child's, there is a tendency to want to change her or his views and behavior. It's easy to cling to the idea that there's basically one "right" way to live. If your adult-child's choices are very different from yours, or from your family norm, it is easy to reject her or his way and label it "poor judgment."

As soon as you define your daughter's decision not to have children as deviant or unacceptable, you force both of you into opposing camps and into a win-lose battle that promises disappointment to everyone involved. Why define her way as wrong? If there is only one correct way, then any deviation must be incorrect and the road ahead is very narrow. What would enable you to maintain a relationship and meaningful contact with your daughter even though you don't agree with her choices?

If you go way back in your memory, you may recall an incident in which your child engaged in a behavior that was very unacceptable to you. Perhaps it was premarital sex, quitting college, or petty theft. At that time, you were probably anxious to separate your child from these actions so that you could still accept him or her as a person.

As parents, many of us have heard about what psychologists refer to as *unconditional positive regard*. This is the acceptance of people independent of their behavior. It requires the ability to appreciate and accept others as valuable and worthy of respect even if you don't agree with their behavior. You need to put yourself in their place and try to see the world as they do. It is necessary to become clear about your own views, then to place them on hold so that they don't interfere with your understanding of the other person. This is never really easy to do, as any psychotherapist can attest. For example, when I am consulted by someone who has values much different from my own, I know that to be effective I need to set my own values aside and not judge this person on my own terms. To be effective in helping them, I need to keep my own issues out of the process. Psychotherapists spend years learning how to do this. Even then, we're not always successful. There are some problems I just can't work with because I know I can't suspend my judgment: One such issue is child molestation.

Having a vested interest as a parent makes the process still more difficult. The next two chapters spell out how to accept without judging. Here are some guidelines to get you started.

Increase Your Sensitivity

Your perceptions of reality are not the same as your children's. Allow yourself to be open to learning as much as you can about their choices, decisions, and values. Honestly commit yourself to learning rather than preaching. Where can you learn more about their values and life choices? Certainly your own children are your best resource. They may also be able to direct you to books, support groups, and friends who can help you to learn what you need to learn in order to tolerate, if not condone, their choices.

Focus on Shared Values

Rather than focusing on conflicts, look for the similarities, the ways you share, your common ground. At the least, you have a shared history. Your joint memories of the past may provide a source of comfort and a neutral arena for communicating. You may discover other areas of mutual appreciation not contaminated by your differences: music, baseball, animals. Do what you can to keep the lines of communication between you open.

Look beyond Your Own Disappointment

After the guilt and self-blame come the disappointment and the anger over your children's choices and the unfairness of life or fate. Even as you try to remain open to learning about their decisions or limitations, you may feel cheated by their inability to actualize their potential, to become what they might have been. At this point, it may be useful to recognize that the struggle taking place has more to do with you than with your kids. Remember Ben's parents.

Challenge Your View of Yourself

This may be one of the final blocks to accepting your child. In the distant past of your own life, when you were a young child, you learned about the world from modeling others' behavior, and you developed your self-worth in part from the way in which others responded to you. You learned to feel good about yourself from your own internal experiences, but also from your achievements, successes, and other external sources of reassurance. You wished the outside world to mirror your feelings and behavior as a way of validating your worth. This is a normal part of child development.

In adults, there is still a desire to have the outside world, especially the people closest to us, mirror our attitudes, feelings, and behavior. When this happens, we feel reassured, comforted, and safe. It is a desirable but not necessary condition for maintaining our self-esteem. Still, when our self-esteem is very dependent on achievement, we may be particularly vulnerable if our children make choices different from our own.

The adult-child who does not mirror his or her parent in some significant ways makes waves in the family and threatens to capsize the family structure, along with long-held traditions. Parents may then see their child's behavior as "poor judgment" so that it doesn't diminish their own belief or value system.

The Struggles of Everyday Life

The struggles of everyday life are the nuts and bolts of intergenerational strife. These difficulties center on issues that are not necessarily serious or irreversible. Unlike the problems that grow out of lifestyle or disability, this category reflects common misunderstandings that, over time, erode a relationship. What starts out to be a "different view" escalates into a clash over basic worth. As this happens, polarities are formed and sides are taken that further intensify the misunderstandings.

In the struggles of everyday life, there are no culprits, just entrenched positions about how things "should" be. Letting go of a long-held idea or belief about how things should be may feel like defeat. But when both sides hold fast to incompatible views, an impasse will surely develop. Sadly, it represents a breach based more on stubbornness than on substance.

The struggles of everyday life have a characteristic tension about them. There is a feeling of being off-center that begs for correction. "If I can only make my point heard" and "If I hold out long enough, they will understand" are positions that demand capitulation or acceptance by the other side. Here the issues do not result in major value clashes but petty annoyances, which seem like relatively harmless differences but build to produce the "straw that broke the camel's back." Suddenly these petty grievances may be transformed into distrust, disappointment and hurt.

The typical struggles center on:
  value differences (career choice, money, education).
  family traditions (holidays, celebrations, visitation).
  rituals (weddings, rites of passage, religion).
  roles and expectations (grandchildren, stepchildren, adult-children and their spouses).

For example, the way religious beliefs or spirituality is expressed is often a source of hurt or misunderstanding between parents and adult-children. No matter how thoroughly you instilled your spiritual value system in your child, as adults they will inevitably question those ways and seek their own avenue to expressing their beliefs. If you provided them with a strong, traditional base, they are likely to alter it in ways that may seem significant to you. They may seek a less traditional approach, a different denomination, or a different religion entirely. They may find a partner whose views are more compatible with theirs and less with yours. They may choose to formally convert or to raise their children in a faith that is strange or abhorrent to you. None of these moves may have anything to do with you. Still, they may feel like a slap in the face or a rejection of your most basic values.

Sometimes the scenario may be reversed. Perhaps you didn't have close ties to the religion you were born into. Maybe religious belief doesn't have much of a role in your life at all. It is not unusual for the next generation to embrace religion with a zealousness that may leave you feeling very uncomfortable. Your adult-child may embrace practices that produce strong negative reactions in you.

In either of the above situations, family traditions will be affected. Your adult-child may not celebrate holidays or may celebrate different holidays. You may find yourself with grandchildren, stepchildren, or spouses of your children with whom you have little in common. Forming the bridge that leads to understanding and acceptance is a difficult but possible task. Experiencing the loss of your adult-children as you would have liked them to be leads to a grieving process that in turn allows healing and growth.

Stages of Coping

When you lose a person close to you, you go through a process that begins with denial and ultimately leads to acceptance. Sometimes the loss is real; more often, it is symbolic, as is the loss due to an impasse in a relationship—the subject of this book. What follows is a series of stages similar to the stages of coping with loss outlined in the classic *On Death and Dying* (1969), by Elizabeth Kübler-Ross.

1. *Disbelief*: Shock, anger, denial, and confusion. How could this happen? What have I done wrong? This is the stage that acknowledges the problem. Your adult-child may have been arrested for selling drugs; may have informed you of his or her marriage to someone of a different social, religious, or racial group; may have dropped out of medical school to pursue a

"lesser" calling; may have converted to another faith or joined a religious cult; may have come out of the closet with a homosexual lifestyle; may have had a child out of wedlock and by choice; may have had an accident which left him or her paralyzed or brain-damaged; or may have been hospitalized for severe depression or some other psychological disorder. If this list seems long enough, it isn't. In general, when your child's life radically departs from your own (or your dreams for that child) in ways that are unacceptable, this stage will present itself.

2. *Getting clear*: Realizing that your child is not the idealized person you created in your mind. Rather than being a mirror image of you or your family, your child is a real, complex, and separate person. This stage allows you to step back and take another look at the person who has jolted you into awareness. Who is this person? Have you missed noticing something along the way?

Nancy was a thirty-four-year-old woman relatively satisfied with her own life. Her mother described her as "strong and independent, always achieving and having little time for relationships with men, not ready to settle down because her career comes first, and lucky to have so many close women friends." Nancy tried to give her mother an honest picture of her life, sharing as much as she could about her wants, hopes, needs, and recreational activities. Her mother understood her through a selective filtering system that screened out upsetting information— unsettling because it suggested significant differences between them.

When her mother finally had to face the reality that her only daughter was a lesbian, she first responded with disbelief and then stepped back to get clear and see her daughter as she actually was rather than as she imagined her to be. This is a sobering step.

3. *Responding*: Learning to understand and accept. Use the help or consultation of others to comfort you and to clarify and change your own perceptions. If your adult-child is a willing partner, suggest the possibility of similar help and be supportive

in his or her search for solutions. This is the stage characterized by "doing." To this point, there is a focus on thinking, worrying, and searching. Now it is time to act. Action has its own rewards. Almost any action is better than waiting and watching. There is something therapeutic about wrestling with a problem head-on.

4. *Letting go*: Becoming less emotionally invested in the "right" outcome. This is a stage that evolves more-or-less on its own. It may represent the final acceptance of your adult-children's decisions and your understanding of his or her responsibility for guiding their own life. Or it may unfold when you are tired of the struggle, when you have exhausted all of the avenues for change and rehabilitation. You may have come to this point through soul searching, therapy, or endless talking with loved ones. You may finally be clear that the lives of your offspring and you are not inexorably intertwined. You and they are separate individuals. You are not responsible for their choices or their limitations, and these do not reflect on you. It may come as a surprise, but you can finally stand back and see the picture more clearly; you can see your role and define the limits of your involvement.

Whether your child is living with physical limitations or lifestyle choices that lead to a day-to-day existence different from yours, remember that it is her or his life. At this stage, you have reached a new equilibrium in which you can accept the current realities of your child's life while removing yourself (as much as possible) from a position of control. This stage is often experienced with a sense of relief.

I remember a young man with cerebral palsy. I knew him years ago when I was a county school psychologist. He had tremendous limitations in intelligence, speech, and body movements. The first time I met his mother, I was shocked by her ability to stand aside and watch him struggle. Watching their interactions certainly aroused my urge to take over and help this young man. I could barely tolerate the tremendous expenditure of energy required for him to carry out his limited responsibilities. Yet his mother stood by and did watch.

I later understood that the dignity and sense of accomplishment in this young man belonged to him and not to his mother. His growth was dependent on his feelings of self-worth and satisfaction in doing things for himself. His mother was effective because she did not see his limitations as a reflection of her poor mothering, her guilt at causing his handicaps, or her embarrassment in the community. She did not respond to him out of pity or disappointment, so she didn't have to interfere unnecessarily. He could achieve at a level that was appropriate for him. She could accept him as he was. Acceptance had not come naturally and without a struggle. Accommodating to the special circumstances of her adult-child's life was a process that required coming to terms with her own disappointment and self-blame. She could finally tolerate her inability to change the course of her son's life.

5. *Self-development*: Self-development happens when you no longer view your child's life as a problem to be solved. The energy that you formerly invested in your child is now more available for your own use. This is a stage characterized by a new interest in yourself and a desire to grow and develop in ways not possible before. You have reached the limits of your parental role.

The acceptance and relief of letting go opens up a new realm of possibilities that are within your control. Here you can develop your own autonomy, your own definition of yourself, and your own future. You may now be ready to expand more into life beyond parenting—the title and focus of Chapter 8 in this book.

Learning about Jack

Jack's parents, Betty and Mike, finally came to terms with their son's way of life. As they explained the process, it was clear that their experience was neither "totally out of control" nor finally "a perfect coming together."

As I listened, I became aware that the road they had all traveled together closely paralleled the stages of coping discussed in the previous section of this chapter. In a natural and informal way, they themselves had come upon most of the principles that work toward bridging big chasms caused by "differences that are unacceptable." While the names and details have been changed to protect the family's identity, the issues and feelings are real. This case illustrates a typical process, although the circumstances will vary in each family.

Jack's early years had been filled with the activities that are so typical of American families. He played Little League baseball and soccer. He was a good student who took his studies seriously. In fact, his parents later described him as "serious about most things." Perhaps as the youngest of three and the second boy, he had carved out a niche that was different from those of his outgoing sister and his easygoing brother. Jack's intensity about everything provided him a unique place in the family. Sometimes he was teased about this quality, but mostly he was appreciated and valued.

At twenty-nine, Jack was single, well educated, and attractive. He lived with a male roommate and enjoyed the quality of life that being a young professional provided. He participated in family events to the extent that adult-children involve themselves, but being single and childless, he was becoming less like his cousins and friends. More than anything, the fact that Jack seemed different from his age-peers served as a clue to his parents that there might be a problem.

But if a problem did exist, whose problem was it? There was nothing about Jack's life that called out in pain or for help. Still, his parents were becoming increasingly agitated about his "single" status and what that might mean. Finally, they approached Jack directly because the more subtle jokes and hints had not been acknowledged. They sought reassurance and an end to their nagging fears. Instead, they received an honest and clear but, as they saw it, devastating response.

Jack was gay and, according to his own recollection, had always had a homosexual orientation. When he was old enough to understand his sexual preferences, he had not yet been ready to make a public statement. He had had dates as a teenager, what had been as much a function of his own curiosity as of "looking OK." He had gone through a difficult transition as a college student but had kept his struggle mostly to himself. He had not felt capable of talking to his family at that time because "they would not understand, and I didn't want to hurt them."

Of course, Jack's instincts had been correct. His admission wasn't understood by his parents and resulted in considerable upset. Their reaction included hurt, anger, disappointment, and fear of the unknown. They experienced disbelief and decided that Jack was "going through a stage." The imagined loss of potential grandchildren was distressing. The life they had simply assumed would mirror their own was not to happen. Scrutinizing the past for hints of "problems" they might have missed caused them to blame themselves whenever possible for this "breach" of life rules. This was an agonizing time, and it lasted for about six months. Jack stayed away to sort out his own feelings.

During this time of emotional upheaval, Jack's siblings became involved. The parents, who had hoped to "bring Jack to his senses" before his lifestyle became public to the family, felt defeated. Ironically, the very siblings whom Betty and Mike had wished to shield provided the initial help. Their insights into and acceptance of Jack, the way he was, provided a calming effect that allowed Stage 2 coping to develop.

Betty and Mike were quite surprised when their two older children demonstrated a level of tolerance that they themselves could not muster. They tried to justify their reaction by dismissing the older siblings' attitude as naive. Still, the older siblings were able to maintain contact with their brother, while their parents' stance deprived them of a relationship they had always valued and cherished.

Probably because they felt their loss so intensely, a willingness to confront their own feelings surfaced. They readily agreed that they couldn't be objective about Jack. If he were someone else's son, they could understand and accept. Certainly they were open-minded! So they began to understand that their hurt, disappointment, and anger were connected with them as parents: guilt, shame, what had they done wrong? They were still focusing on themselves and not getting any closer to understanding Jack.

Getting clear means getting to know your child as he or she really is, in ways that you could not or would not see before. J. Brans and M. Smith are the authors of *Mother, I Have Something to Tell You* (1987), a book about adult-children who live nontraditional lifestyles. According to Brans and Smith:

> The mother of an untraditional child must listen, look and learn. She spends as much time as she can simply paying attention to her child, letting him talk, not judging but listening. What is it like, she asks herself, taxing her empathic imagination, to be this person, her child? And she tries to see her child, not as she wants him to be, not as she has assumed him to be, but as he really is. (p. 83)

Stepping out of your own shoes and into another's requires that you separate and temporarily store your own feelings and attitudes. Seeing others as they really are, not as you need them to be, means looking beyond the mirror that projects your own image, not theirs. Also, seeing them as they really are does not negate your own identity or threaten you in any way. It is a necessary but scary step.

Betty's and Mike's own instincts, coupled with the older siblings' encouragement, led them naturally to this point. Remember, talking things out is the hallmark of a healthy family. It's true that the issues were very highly charged, but talking, as well as listening, is a skill that most parents already have. "Tell me about yourself" is a very familiar line.and the starting point here.

Jack was tentative but anxious to share himself if his parents would not interrupt, judge, offer help, or criticize. He established the ground rules, and they accepted. He was clear that the problem was his parents' and not his own. He was not open to or interested in "rehabilitation."

The talking and listening that followed took place over many occasions and months. There were informative but formal meetings, not exactly pleasant and comfortable but definitely necessary according to Jack and his parents. Eventually, the talking began to shift to other subjects, and it seemed as if that shift was a clue to the participants' saturation level. Jack felt immeasurably more comfortable and less guarded than he had been in a long while. His parents now had information and understanding where a void had once been. Still, they needed something more to help them accept Jack's homosexuality. Talking and listening to Jack was not enough.

Jack's gay friends could have been a wonderful source of information at this point. Unfortunately, this was not the next step for parents who felt critical and confused. Quite naturally, they sought the help of others like themselves, who could share their feelings. They talked to their minister and found that there was a local support group for the parents of gay and lesbian adults. This was a self-help group that provided an important outlet for their feelings and worries. They had never shared so openly with others and were surprised by their great comfort and relief.

Increased awareness had its downside, too. As they became more open in their attitudes, they discovered that society at large was quite the opposite. Prejudice and intolerance were clearly visible and distressing. Their identification with Jack had indeed shifted their perspective.

Once they had gone full circle, it was now time for Betty and Mike to leave the circle that represented Jack's life. As parents, they had remained on the periphery, which is appropriate, until their awareness of Jack's "secret." Then they had been thrust into the circle, where they had struggled with their feelings, ideas, attitudes, and perceptions until the process wound down on its own. It was inevitable that all of this searching would lead to growth. The openness, increased awareness, and information helped bridge the gap between parents and son. The work felt finished even though it would still take time for additional healing to come about.

This stage is the "letting-go" stage. From intensely inter-meshed lives, the movement is again toward separation. It is a time for the parents to pull away and concentrate their energy on new interests of their own. The magnifying glass that had been focused on Jack's life needed to find a new target. The limits of parenting had been met in this family. The learning that had resulted was both cognitive and emotional, facts and feelings. All the players had developed depth as well as internal resources not available before. With a new way of experiencing the world, internal and external, these parents could move into the future with an appreciation of life not possible before.

Jack and his family had worked incredibly hard to reach a new equilibrium. All families don't have such a remarkable out-come. Still, the process of coping follows the very stages explored above and everyone with a "different" child comes to terms with that child through a similar process. Your family can adapt this model to suit your specific circumstances. Use the stages of cop-ing as a guide, and seek whatever additional help you require (Chapter 10).

Having read this chapter, you have already begun the pro-cess. The next section will detail specific problems and strategies for skill building.

Part II

RELATING, NEGOTIATING, AND ACCEPTING

Changing is never easy. Most of us avoid voluntary self-development and wait until our behavior or feelings are painful or unacceptable before committing ourselves to change. Even then, we tend to externalize the source of unhappiness and try to change situations or others' behavior first, before we work on ourselves. Usually, when all else fails, we take a look in the mirror.

Changing requires the ability to see a problem, feel the effects of it, and then put energy into resolving it. Part II of this book will help you to see things differently, do things differently, and build a new working relationship with your adult-child. It does require additional effort to tackle the difficulties head-on rather than to think, worry, and wonder about them. Still, the satisfaction that results from even small changes makes the effort worthwhile.

Part I of this book provided a picture of how past experiences, beliefs, and stereotypes feed current conflicts and misunderstandings. Now the job is to rebuild, repair, and renegotiate the old structure without tearing it down. This is not an easy undertaking because, initially, a great deal of the hard work will have to be done by you alone. Cooperation will probably come later, when some of your efforts to listen differently, attend differently, and see the conflict through a new filtering system begin to pay off. When your adult-children notice your serious attempt, they may respond with renewed interest.

In my work with parents who feel stuck in communicating with their grown kids, I hear again and again that trying something different alters the circular pattern that is so frustrating. The next three chapters will arm you with listening skills, communication skills, and negotiating skills to help you break out of the stuck pattern. Throughout the chapters, there are examples and exercises to guide you through the process.

There is something very powerful and hopeful about doing things differently. Perhaps it's a way of giving yourself another chance, a new beginning, and a vital opportunity to make things really better.

Chapter 5

Seeing Things Differently

Can We Talk?

"You haven't heard a thing I said. Why is it that the moment I start talking, you stop listening?" These are the words of a frustrated father who can see the problem in communicating with his adult son but feels at a loss to resolve it.

What is it that makes the communication process so full of conflict? What could be more basic than listening? Our capacity to hear is fully developed at birth, yet throughout the life cycle we frequently miss the things that are said to us.

Hearing is not the issue. Rather, the problems are in listening, a phenomenon that has little to do with the physiology of the ears. One way to conceptualize this idea is to imagine a radio that is receiving electrical power and emitting signals in the form of static. Although the radio is working satisfactorily, the message is distorted and not understandable. Hearing the sounds but missing the meaning creates annoyance, an emotional reaction. Likewise, listening is more an emotional experience than an intellectual one, particularly when the communicators have a relationship of some sort.

When you hear the words but don't get the message, you experience frustration and communicate it. The sender of the message may not understand your reaction or may misread your frustration as disapproval. At this point, the meaning of the words is lost, and the feelings take on a life of their own.

John, the frustrated father whose words began this chapter, has felt the same feelings many times before in similar circumstances. What's more, the feelings don't seem to be related to the subject of the conversation. No matter what the subject is, at some point in communicating with his son, Ray, this father feels as if he is talking to himself.

At this particular moment, the conversation focused on a seemingly neutral subject, whether to buy or lease a car. John couldn't remember who had brought up the subject, but it took a nose dive as soon as he interjected his opinion. He did not remember stating his opinion as fact, although he could see that it might have been interpreted in that way. Certainly, in the past, he may have expressed his opinions more forcefully.

In addition to feeling unheard, he also feels unappreciated. He recalls his disappointment: "After all, my words are well intended and designed to be helpful. I care about my son's struggles and only want to be supportive." He knows that all of his years of living and experiencing have given him knowledge that he wishes simply to transfer to his son. He has such a pure and straightforward goal, right? Wrong!

The communication process is anything but pure and straightforward. It is a complex transaction that is influenced by dozens of factors. Here are some of them:

History

Over time, communication patterns are developed and scenarios are played out over and over again, so that the patterns become fixed and reinforced. The process becomes very automatic, and attempts to change the process may not even be noticed by others. Often our expectation of how the conversation will end determines the way it actually happens. The history of conversations between John and Ray spans twenty-four years. As early as either can remember, there has been a style of communicating that follows the question-and-answer format of the expert and the novice.

A recent phone conversation makes the point. Ray called to let his dad know that he had some good ideas about investing a few dollars in a project a friend had told him about: "I'm excited but also a little cautious. I thought I'd let you know in case you have some interest as well." John responded, as he had many times before, by offering his suggestions and expertise: "I wish you had told me before you committed yourself to this project. These things are risky, and I'd hate for you to get hurt. Years ago, I had a similar experience, and fortunately, I did enough research to see the problems before I parted with my money."

At this point in the conversation, there was a lull, followed by a retreat from the topic. Both participants had become tangled in hurt feelings, and Ray's belief had once again been reinforced: "Nothing ever changes!"

Expectations

Ray was hoping against hope that his dad would understand his adult need to be responsible with money. He was attempting to share what he felt were his good judgment skills and gain his father's respect. John, on the other hand, saw Ray's venture as poorly thought out. John expected adolescent behavior from Ray, and he seemed to be stuck in this perception. He felt, "Ray never thinks things through. I don't know how he'll ever learn to manage his money."

Sometimes, parents have good reason to distrust the decision-making ability of their adult-children. When negative past experiences feed perceptions, there is cause for concern. On the other hand, the past does not always foretell the future. Offer reassurance for the person, not for the proposed project.

Roles

Can father and son roles ever shift enough to allow for changes in the behavior, needs, and goals of either person? This question does not mean to imply that the parent–child relationship will cease to exist. What it suggests is that the tight structure with clear rules that guided their behavior toward each other in the past is just too rigid now. John is guided by his long-useful role as mentor, teacher, and ultimate problem solver. Ray's role as learner and obedient recipient of knowledge was once useful but is now stifling.

Most of the time, adult-children outgrow their former role before their parents have recognized their own need to change. When the eventual shift begins to take place, it is viewed by the adult-child as a sign of growth and by the parent as confusing and uncomfortable: "Something's wrong here. That boy is not listening to me and respecting my advice. Let's see how far he gets without my help!"

Listening

Often, listening is semiautomatic. Saying nothing sometimes passes for listening. Since you can't see the content of a person's thoughts, you may not be able to tell whether she or he is paying attention or putting together a mental grocery list. The quiet that accompanies one person's verbalizations may not necessarily mean that the other is listening.

When Ray volunteered his ideas for investment, was his father listening to them? More than likely John was rehearsing his response but being polite enough to give Ray a chance to finish talking—and even this is a courtesy that isn't always given!

True listening is an acquired skill that is learned with much effort and is anything but automatic. It requires that you go beyond the words and understand the meaning and intent of the communicator. When Ray called his dad to talk about an investment idea, he was not seeking advice; he was showing off his new adult behavior and interest. John got caught up in the words and in his own assumptions about what that interaction meant. If John could have experienced this conversation through Ray's eyes, it might have taken a different course.

How does a parent know whether to respond to the overt message (investments) or the covert message ("Look, Dad, I'm taking care of my future")? The first message relays information, and the second pertains to the relationship. Since there's no exact way to know which is intended, a response that acknowledges both is a safe bet.

Empathy

Empathy is the ability to put yourself in the other's place and to experience the world through that person's eyes. This is hardly a simple task. Mental health professionals spend years in training and practice to accomplish it. This is one reason that people tend to consult psychologists and counselors, valued for their ability to listen and be empathic. Fortunately, these are skills that can be learned, and the purpose of this chapter is to provide you with some of the necessary tools.

Facts versus Feelings

In the case of John and Ray, you may already see that, while the son was communicating self-pride, his father was communicating information. It is not surprising that they were like ships passing in the night, both being misunderstood and becoming hurt and disappointed. Further along in this chapter, opportunities will be given for practice in matching feelings with feelings, facts with facts.

Listening Skills

Attending to someone's words is an active process. What does it take to truly listen? First, you might want to determine whether you already have the skills. Here is a way to find out how you rate. Consider taping the next phone conversation you have with your adult-child. In order to get an unbiased sample of your current interactions, don't tell your son or daughter that you are making a recording. Your purpose is to monitor your own behavior, and spontaneity may be lacking if both of you are aware of the taping.

After you have made your tape, find a time and place that will allow you to review it without distraction. You are going to listen with certain objectives. This is not the same as a replay of the conversation. It is more like the feedback session that a football team might have after its most recent game. The goal is to analyze the plays, correct mistakes, and develop strategies for improving future plays.

The first time you listen to your tape, notice the percentage of talking versus listening time for each of you. If your child called you to share an idea or some new information about her or his life, as Ray did, then your percentage of talking should be lower than 50 percent. Otherwise, you are lecturing, not listening.

In this first listening, you may also be able to pick up whether you are really listening to your child's words or rehearsing your own thoughts until the moment you can say them out loud. Write down what you found out. A worksheet is provided so that you can keep score. To simplify the score keeping, for each interaction rated during the phone conversation you should enter a plus sign for "acceptable" or a minus sign for "needs improvement."

The second assignment is to analyze the conversation according to the following guidelines:

- Percentage of talking and listening: This is an estimate.
- Mood conveyed: Did you experience sadness, pensiveness, tension, wit, impatience, elation?
- Closed versus open: Was there more advice giving and lecturing or curiosity and wonder?
- Competitive versus cooperative: Did the conversation move back and forth like a tennis match? Competitive dialogue has a gaming quality.

In your next listening, focus on your tone of voice. Without paying attention to what you are saying, try to stay tuned in to the way you are saying it. This is not a simple task. Pretend that you are hearing a foreign language so the words won't distract you from focusing on the feeling conveyed.

Is your style matter-of-fact, annoyed, tense, edgy, impatient, attentive? Even if you don't intend it, what you say is very much colored by your way of saying it. You may be surprised to find that you were sending information unknown even to *you*. Perhaps the annoyance that you felt but tried to cover over was conveyed just as clearly in your tone of voice. Now your adult-child is getting a very confusing message: Your words say one thing, and your nonverbal message is quite different.

An example of how this works also comes from Ray's dialogue with his dad. At one point in their conversation, Ray, looking for support and appreciation from his dad, said, "I'm really glad that I saw this business opportunity instead of just letting it pass by. I suppose I learned how to sniff out such deals from you." John, who was less than pleased by what he perceived as naïveté on Ray's part, responded quickly and without thinking: "I suppose things will work out OK in the long run." Although his intent was to be supportive, the sound of his words definitely conveyed the impression that John was skeptical and lacked faith in his son's judgment. To John's amazement, because he had really tried to be supportive, his son sounded more distant and detached, and the conversation moved to a level that was more comfortable but less meaningful. This conversation had really become quite confusing!

If you can tolerate another listening or two, here are some additional ways to explore your communication potential: Are you listening to *get* something or to *give* something? More specifically, are you interested in learning something new about your adult-child and the way his or her thinking is evolving? Are you curious about the person he or she is becoming? Are you truly interested in his or her life, as it unfolds, from his or her viewpoint? If so (and who can argue with these goals), then it means keeping your advice and opinions to yourself. This is definitely not easy to do because we all see the world within our own frame of reference, and shifting to the other's frame of reference requires a great deal of skill. This process is called *empathy building*, and some techniques for practice follow in the next section.

Listen to your tape one last time, and search for a power struggle. So much of the interaction between parents and children centers on who is right and who is wrong. As long as the adults are in the teacher mode, the offspring are the learners. Predictably, as children mature, they resist, and later they actively fight for equal power. As young adults, they are determined to demonstrate their independent thought, and most attempts by parents to "teach" an adult-child meet with resistance, at least. If your interactions even suggest, "I know best," "I told you so," "If you had listened to me," or "When I was your age," then the playing out of a power struggle is inevitable. Sadly, there are no winners.

What would it take for you to bypass the teaching–learning model and to assume that what you know as an adult is now matched by your child? It would probably take some time for you to adjust to this change. It would also take a willingness to catch yourself pulling rank and to stop yourself when you do so. While you may not know the same things, what each of you knows is valuable. Each of you may be able to learn from the other. The development of an assumed equality of ideas is a challenge that, when met, will make the communication process much more positive and maybe more interesting.

By now, you have listened to your tape at least four times and probably know the conversation by heart. Although you might benefit from additional listenings, I'm sure that you are getting tired of what may feel like beating a dead horse.

Though sometimes tedious, the listening and relistening to taped interviews can be very illuminating. It is a significant part of the training of mental health professionals and can help you as well. For most of us, including the professionals, listening skills are learned rather than intuitive, inborn qualities.

Are You Paying Attention?

The easiest way to develop and refine the listening process is to imagine yourself in a new relationship. The advantage of examining a *new* relationship is that the old, dangerous patterns and sources of misunderstanding that characterize ongoing relationships are erased. You start with a blank slate. The only fixed dimensions are your own personality and your own expectations.

How would you proceed to build a relationship with a potential friend, colleague, or peer? What do you believe are the important building or stumbling blocks? What would you definitely do and what would you avoid doing at all costs? Give yourself a moment to clarify your ideas before going on. You very likely know more than you think you do; it's just that spelling these ideas out is a new activity.

In communicating with a new potential friend, you are going to proceed somewhat cautiously. This is not done out of fear but out of increased consciousness. The following example shows how useful an asset increased consciousness is.

Imagine that you live in a climate in which snow falls in winter. Picture the first snow of the season. Pretend that the next morning you leave the house and go to your car as you do each morning. Usually, the process of leaving your house and walking to your car is automatic. You may be thinking about the work you need to do or unfinished tasks or phone calls you need to make. It is only when you notice the snow on the ground that your attention shifts to the new weather condition. At that point, you put your other thoughts aside and watch your footing, to avoid slipping. You try to size up the need for tire chains and assess whether the driveway needs to be shoveled.

When these issues are resolved and you finally get behind the wheel, you drive more cautiously than usual, paying attention to the details of stopping and turning that generally go unnoticed. Your awareness of these normally unconscious activities remains heightened until they, too, become automatic or until the weather condition changes. Your increased consciousness has enabled you to think of the best course of action. This is an active process that depends on your observation of the environment, your interaction with the environment, and the feedback you get, which allows you to self-correct (e.g., if you begin to skid, you turn the wheel into the skid rather than brake).

Developing a new relationship is similar to driving a car in snow. You need to be very observant and to proceed cautiously. In the beginning you pay attention to the subtle factors of the interaction that usually go unnoticed. What you say and how you say it are monitored on your end, and careful attention is also given to the feedback you get from the other person—verbally and nonverbally.

You proceed carefully not to offend the other person, and you watch her or his reaction for a need to explain, self-correct, or clarify a remark. You are likely to think before you talk rather than respond automatically. There is a certain level of cautiousness that helps to keep you conscious of your actions. Even while you are fully engaged in the process, there may be a part of you standing back to observe or analyze the transaction.

The other person is less apt to use trigger words that hook you into responding unconsciously or defensively. She or he simply doesn't know you well enough to identify or say the things that bother or upset you. Even if the other person inadvertently says something that feels unpleasant, you may take a moment to reflect on it before commenting. That extra moment of thinking time enables you to make a choice rather than react with knee-jerk quickness.

This level of patience and consideration will probably be higher than the level you tend to show in established relationships. After all, this new person needs time to understand, reflect, and respond. You watch for these responses to see whether the person truly understands your meaning, and if she or he doesn't, you try to explain the same thing in another way. Again, you look for a glimmer of understanding before going on. You're less likely to make assumptions about what the other person knows or "should" know. You don't show your annoyance when she or he is slow to follow. In this budding relationship, you are fully involved, but at the same time, you are watching for cues that will aid you in shaping your communication approach.

Clearly, this is an ideal and somewhat unrealistic picture. Most of us put far less thought into the way we think and behave. As in much of daily life, we tend to take many things for granted. It would really be impossible to give every event in each day our full attention and to examine the subtle nuances and novelties of each interaction. Taking things for granted is an expedient way to get through the day, but it is like flying on automatic pilot and sacrifices some personal thoughtfulness.

Increasing your awareness of your own thoughts and behavior can significantly affect how a new relationship will unfold. The chances of being understood and appreciated are expanded. Honesty and trust are enhanced because there is a level of respect for the other's feelings maintained by vigilance and consciousness. It is a delicate dance in which each dancer is paying close attention to the other's needs. Over time, of course, some of this attentiveness subsides, and some of the behavior becomes automatic. Assumptions take the place of observation, and misunderstandings begin to develop. Happily, at any point, either person can stop the process and start listening and watching more carefully again.

That takes us back full circle to communication with your adult-children. Somewhere along the way, you or your child may have stopped listening, watching, and understanding. The one factor that hasn't changed is that you both still care about each other, and this is the central reason why improvement in your relationship is possible. Now is the time to start observing your own behavior.

Actively Paying Attention

Notice the feelings as well as the facts. In a conversation, most of us are more attuned to the words that are spoken than we are to the underlying meaning or feeling. Mental health professionals are trained to look beyond the words, which are just the vehicle. The message is greater than the sum of the individual words. You can learn how to do this, too.

The following conversation was told to me by Joan, who was distressed about how she and her daughter Becky were relating to one another. Though they kept reaching out for each other and caring enough to maintain their ties, their patterns showed disrespect and impatience. Joan reported the following dialogue. Try to pay attention to what Joan and Becky were saying as well as to the feelings they were communicating:

> My daughter dropped in to see me unexpectedly. Of course, I'm always glad to see her, but I could see that she had a bag full of dirty clothes. I couldn't help feeling that she had come mainly to wash her clothes. She put down her bag and we had a chat.
>
> "I knew you'd be home tonight, so I thought I'd stop by," said Becky. "What have you been up to this week, Mom? I've been so busy with working and going to school at night that I haven't had a minute to myself. Do you know what it's like to fall asleep while you're eating dinner or forget your own phone number? I've been cutting it close everywhere. Last night I was at a meeting with a client, whose project I'm supervising. It ran so late that I missed the first hour of my class—and I got a speeding ticket on the way there."
>
> I replied, "I guess you have been pretty busy. I never seem to see you anymore. I've had a busy week myself, and I'm pretty tired this evening. It's getting kind of late."
>
> Becky said, "Let me get the wash into the machine, and then we can talk. I really am running around like a chicken with my head cut off, and it's really getting to me!"
>
> "You've always been pretty disorganized, and now it's catching up with you," I advised. "Why don't you take some time and make yourself a schedule."
>
> "A schedule," Becky roared. "Haven't I just finished telling you how crammed my life is now? Where would I get the time to work on a schedule? Besides, I came here to talk to you, and instead of hearing me, you give me this cheap advice."

I responded immediately. "You didn't come here to talk. You came to do your wash. If you wanted to talk, you would have picked a decent hour to come. I only see you when it suits you or when you want something."

Joan's tone of voice was *biting*. Her annoyance had leaked through unintentionally. Her body posture, the way she sat rigidly with her arms and legs crossed, also communicated her negative feeling. Becky, of course, having had years of experience in growing up with mother, knew (assumed) this nonverbalized message perfectly, and it made her feel like a naughty child.

The conversation continued, but it didn't improve. In fact, because it was already on a downhill course, it's not surprising that it deteriorated further, until mother and daughter retreated into silence, and the only sound heard was the washing machine.

This situation is not uncommon, nor does it imply the unraveling of a relationship. It could stay like this forever, it could worsen, or it could improve. If Joan and Becky do nothing, time will return them to their tenuous status quo. They will forget the interaction or dismiss it as trivial, only to have a predictable repeat performance sometime in the future. To improve their communication, they first need to understand what happened between them. Analyzing their interaction provides a good structure for looking at your own—and it's less threatening.

What Are You Looking For?

In every conversation, there are at least two levels of communication. One has to do with the content (the words that provide information), and the second has to do with the process (the feeling tone, the unspoken dialogue, and the hidden agenda). Conversations almost never limit themselves to information, except perhaps in the classroom. In a complex parent–child relationship, the secondary level is an important determinant of what takes place. On the surface, the facts are simple: (1) a daughter paid a visit to her mother; (2) the mother was tired; (3) the hour was late; and (4) the daughter had brought a bag of dirty clothes.

At the second level, the issues are far less clear. At the very moment that Becky arrived, Joan had two separate feelings. She was *happy* to see her daughter. Simultaneously, she was *annoyed* because Becky's dirty clothes appeared (assumption) to be the reason for her daughter's visit (hidden agenda). Both messages were sure to be communicated to her daughter, but because Joan wasn't clear about her annoyance, it could not be discussed.

Becky, instead of learning that her mother was *insulted* by a visit dedicated to the wash, felt that Joan was *disgusted* by her difficulty in managing time. Becky felt like a failure in her mother's eyes, and a surge of *guilt* washed over her. She *resented* her mother's advice, especially since it felt like criticism. She hadn't asked for advice or help; she was simply sharing her feelings of *frustration* about herself.

Since Joan's annoyance hadn't been verbalized, none of these feelings could be discussed (taboo subject). Becky thought to herself that nothing would ever change, that there was no point in trying to talk to her mother about anything important because Joan didn't really care. She retreated to silence and waited for the laundry to be finished.

Becky's silence signaled to Joan that her perception was right. Becky had come simply to do the wash and did not really want to share her life with her mother. She felt *disappointed* and *hurt* and wondered why most of their interactions felt so *futile*.

The feelings generated in this interaction had very little to do with the facts. Go back and notice all of the italicized words. The conversation did not acknowledge these at all. It's essential to go beyond the facts in searching for solutions. Otherwise the same vignette (process) will play itself out over and over again, but with different details (facts).

In my work with Joan, this seemed to be true. No matter what the subject of their interactions, she and Becky both usually came away with negative feelings. This is not an unusual phenomenon because, in addition to the history between them (nearly thirty years), there are taboo issues (issues not open for discussion) and unequal roles (parent and child) to further obstruct communication. Where do they go from here?

Look for some guidelines:

• *Listen at two levels.* The facts (Level 1) are easy to spot, but the underlying process (Level 2) is hard to recognize and is our focus here. Look for emotionally laden words or feelings in yourself and in the other person. Notice again that the feeling words are italicized. Look also for nonverbal expressions of feelings such as body stance and gestures, facial expression, tone of voice, and silences.

• *Emotional elements (feelings) are more easily distorted than facts.* Often, everyone can agree on the facts, but feelings are not communicated as clearly or understood as well. Feelings are not concrete objects that can be seen or touched. They are not like words, which have a precise, agreed-upon definition that can be found in a dictionary. They do not necessarily conform to logic or rationality. Sometimes they don't make sense. Furthermore, our feeling vocabulary is much more limited than our verbal vocabulary so that we aren't always very accurate or exact. When you say you are sad, I may understand you to mean that you are unhappy, but you may mean something else. Also, how sad is sad? Feelings have intensities ranging from weak to strong, and these intensities modify their meaning.

Identifying your own feelings takes a great deal of practice. Labeling them is still harder, and telling the other person about them, in a way that is constructive, is a real challenge!

Again, the first step in the communication process is to become aware of your feelings so you can exercise some control or choice in conveying them to someone else. As an aid in identifying your feelings, a long list of feeling words is presented below:*

*Alpaugh and Haney (1978).

abandoned	dissatisfied	loving
accepted	distressed	miserable
affectionate	ecstatic	misunderstood
afraid	elated	needed
alarmed	embarrassed	negative
amazed	empty	neglected
angry	enthusiastic	nervous
annoyed	envious	numb
anxious	euphoric	passionate
appreciative	excited	pleased
apprehensive	exhilarated	pressured
approving	fearful	proud
ashamed	friendly	put down
balmy	frustrated	puzzled
belittled	furious	reborn
belligerent	futile	regretful
bitter	grateful	rejected
bored	guilty	rejecting
bottled up	happy	rejuvenated
calm	hateful	relaxed
capable	helpless	relieved
competent	hopeless	resentful
confident	humble	sad
conflicted	humiliated	satisfied
confused	hurt	sensual
contented	identification	serene
crushed	inadequate	shocked
defeated	incompetent	startled
depressed	inflamed	surprised
desolate	insecure	tearful
desperate	insignificant	tense
despondent	jealous	terrified
discouraged	joyful	threatened
disinterested	lonely	thrilled
disparate	longing	transcendent
dispassionate	loved	trusting

uncertain	unloved	wanted
uncooperative	upset	warmhearted
understood	uptight	worthless
uneasy	vengeful	worthy
unhappy	vindictive	yearning

- *Everyday facts are easy to listen to, while emotions have a passion and intensity that bias both the receiving and the sending of messages.* This makes it very important to see the red flag of feeling statements and to proceed with great care in both listening and talking. Proceeding cautiously in advance is definitely superior to undoing the hurt inflicted by impulsivity.

- *Look at things through the other person's eyes.* This is a process referred to earlier as *empathy.* It enables you to imagine the other person's frame of reference, to search for his or her meaning. It requires that you set aside your assumptions and your own position. Remember the example of Joan and Becky. If she had not made assumptions about Becky's motives in visiting, Joan might have heard that Becky needed to talk to someone she trusted about her problem of disorganization. The laundry became the focus because it was concrete and tangible. It was easier for Becky to visit with the laundry than with a problem, especially a problem that had plagued her in the past and had been a source of conflict with her mother during adolescence.

If Joan could have been aware and set aside her own feelings long enough, she might have heard Becky's pain. She would probably not have felt victimized and might have been able to be supportive. Being empathic requires the ability to give up being egocentric (believing that your way is the right way), and this requires some maturity. At your age and with your years of life experience, you are probably in a better position to do this than your adult-child.

- *Listen because you genuinely care.* Be attentive to learn and to understand the issues in your child's life better. If you are doing this because you must, to "show her" or to "win," then you are not being empathic. With empathy, you are putting aside your assumptions and your preexisting knowledge about your adult-child. Just because Becky was a disorganized teenager does not mean that she is incapable of changing or that she likes a chaotic life.

It was important for Joan to see her struggle and appreciate her frustration without judgment or criticism. While Joan may have been able to catch her acknowledging her problems and win the round, she would surely lose Becky's trust. Paying attention to your child's sharing is not always easy because some of what he or she may share is alien to you. Perhaps worse, it may be contrary to your own values and beliefs.

• *Learn to accept another's values or ethics.* This step goes beyond empathy since, in addition to seeing the world through your child's eyes, it requires acceptance of what you see. This does not mean that you need to change the way you live your life to conform with your child's style. It does mean a recognition that, while your way suits you, there are additional ways of seeing the world. Communicating acceptance of your child's values depends on a variety of ideas including the following:

1. Judgments are decisions based on your own values. Judging implies that your way is right (the egocentric point of view) and that you can apply this standard to another. For example, consider a purchase that your grown child has made that you feel is frivolous. What makes it frivolous? Does your feeling reflect your child's faulty decision making or your own sense of appropriate purchases? Your way may not be her way, but her way may not be wrong either.

2. Generation gaps do exist, but a generation gap may benefit you in the long run. If you can allow the possibility that new ways, while different, are not necessarily bad, then you can learn to appreciate the current trends, fads, and styles without being threatened by them. You can reduce the generation gap from a chasm to a crevice. You may even, in fact, adopt a new position that will enhance your own life.

This memory is from my own past. My father lived in an era

in which goods and services were purchased for cash. He believed that, if you didn't have money in your pocket or in the bank, then you had no business buying. This notion was commonly held forty years ago, and the average person adhered to it. The sole exception to this style was the mortgage loan, since very few people could ever save up enough money to purchase a house for cash. Given this way of seeing the world, it was consistent for him to be appalled by my interest in obtaining a student loan to pay for my college education. I remember long debates trying to convince him that such a loan was possible and appropriate, to no avail.

He never did understand my "new" ideas. He never did move from his own firmly held position, which could have provided him with a slightly more comfortable lifestyle. Clearly, I didn't get what I needed either. We finally gave up trying to bridge the gap that existed between us. Sadly, it narrowed what we could talk about.

3. A person is more than the sum of his or her behaviors. You can accept your child's values without necessarily condoning her or his behavior. A woman in her fifties found it difficult to discuss her daughter's social life with her. Whenever the young woman, in her midtwenties, talked about meeting a man, her mother became uncomfortable. After much misunderstanding and many hurt feelings, it finally became apparent that the crux of the problem was the daughter's "dating behavior."

The young woman, who had been raised with traditional values, tended to socialize in a way that seemed unacceptable to her mother. Rather than meeting men at work, at church, or through introductions by a third party, she and her friends went to clubs or "singles" bars. The style was easy, comfortable, and informal for the young woman. This mother saw her daughter's behavior as inappropriate. If she expected her daughter's behavior to change and waited for that to happen, a lost opportunity in communicating would surely happen first.

4. Armed with your own self-knowledge, you will make fewer judgments. When you have accepted your own prejudices, ste-

reotypes, and intolerance, you will be able to monitor them better. None of us is judgment-free, and to think otherwise is naive. Yet it is possible to keep these ideas in check so that they don't get you into trouble with your children.

The following example is a case in point. Artie had been successful in sales for thirty years, since his midtwenties. He was proud of his life and had taught his work ethic to his kids. The three siblings were competitive with each other, especially to gain recognition from their father. Dana, the middle child and only daughter, was twenty-four when she proudly announced that she had been selected to be a regional salesperson for a national book publisher. Like her father, she had always been attracted to sales. This position not only fit her career plans but was also a promotion. With great excitement, she brought this news to her parents after she had accepted the offer.

Neither parent received the news with enthusiasm. Her father was outspoken about his belief that women in sales should not be on the road. He filled the conversation with his stereotypical views of saleswomen. Her mother's response was also negative, but for different reasons. She was unable to identify with her daughter as a traveling salesperson and dismissed her daughter's behavior as impulsive and radical. She summarized her feelings: "After all, a twenty-four-year-old who makes such a move is making a statement to the world that she doesn't want to settle down and raise a family."

Dana's decision seemed intolerable and an affront to her mother's way of seeing the world. Needless to say, Dana pursued her career plans without the blessings that would have facilitated future communication about her work with her parents. Does any of this ring a bell for you?

Reducing Power Struggles: Equalizing the Roles

A common power struggle that characterizes the early years in family life centers on a discussion with a teen or preteen child and goes something like this: The child says, "All of the kids are going over to the shopping mall on Saturday night, and I wonder if you could drop me off there. Someone else can probably give me a ride home." You say, "Sure, hang around a mall at night! I think you're all looking for trouble. The shop owners may think you're part of a gang and call the police or worse." The child says, "That's not true! It's never happened before. It's a way of getting together, and everybody is really responsible. Everyone is going. Why can't you trust me to take care of myself?" You say, "You're not going, and that's that!" And the feelings escalate. "But why? Give me one good reason." "Because I said so, and if you ask again, you can go to your room and spend some time thinking about it. I'm not going to spend another minute discussing this."

There was probably a time in your family when discussions and decision making could very well end like this. There may have been times when the answer was "no" and you, as the parent, had the power to have the final say and enforce it. Of course, you no longer have this power. What then takes its place in communication with your grown kids? What do you say when you don't like what they are doing, or how they are doing it? How can you tell them that you don't approve of their actions without alienating them? How can you get them to change their behavior? Or can you?

Your adult-children would most likely still appreciate your approval and good wishes. They would very likely welcome an open discussion of their ideas and hopes. Unlike their role of a decade before, they no longer are bound by your rules or philosophy. Mazor and Enright (1988), child development researchers, discuss this point when they describe the individuation process that allows the young adult to separate from his or her parents. They suggest two components:

> (1) An increasing differentiation of an individual's behavior, feelings, judgment and thoughts from those of his/her parents; and (2) changes in the parent-child relationship towards a growing co-operation, equality and mutuality, as the child becomes an autonomous person within the family context. (p. 30)

If they truly function as adults, your offspring must be free agents who will listen as long as listening suits their needs. They will stop listening when they sense that you are going beyond your new, more narrowly defined role, which equalizes power. Unfortunately, what sometimes masquerades as discussion is really a lecture that falls on deaf ears.

What will motivate the adult child to listen to and possibly accept your advice?

• Advice offered by one adult to another is acceptable to the extent that it is experienced as two-way. In equalizing the roles between you and them, it is critical to realize that your adult-aged children will not always regard you as an expert or a wise sage. If they are willing to see you in that role, even rarely, consider yourself lucky. Rather, they will tolerate your advice to the extent that you tolerate theirs. If you believe that their advice could not possibly have much value to you, then you are still tied to a power model that has no place in an adult–adult relationship.

Examine, even reluctantly, the view that your adult-child has advice that would be beneficial to you. What does he or she know about that you don't? Surely there is some area in which he or she has expertise that you lack.

I am reminded of a wonderful anecdote told by Klass, a psychologist, in a book chapter called "In the Midst of the Years" (1989). He provides a very personal account of his own life and the inevitable transitions within a family. Discussing his relationship with his adult sons, he notes:

> I was first aware of the sense of equality with the kids when we got our computer. . . . When I got in trouble, I would call Ben, my youngest, and he would figure out what I did wrong, help me fix it. . . . So the new age has come, and what I struggle to learn, the younger generation seems to understand intuitively. (p. 39)

Genuinely seeking advice from your offspring is a powerful message that is also bound to be flattering. Ironically, you may find that their advice is given as ungraciously as yours sometimes has been. If this happens, use the opportunity to laugh about it and approach the taboo subject directly. How can both of you give and receive advice more comfortably?

• Help, in the form of advice, may not be desired. There is a higher probability that your advice will be considered if it has been invited in the first place. There is one sure way to determine whether your advice is being sought, and that is to ask. It is not unusual for peers to discuss their problems without the expectation of help from one another.

Sometimes just talking to someone who cares and will listen is quite enough. Maybe a head nod or a pair of expressive eyes is all that is needed. It may suffice to be the audience for someone rehearsing a new idea or strategy out loud. Is this what your adult-child wants and expects from you? Can you limit your role to being an involved listener and refrain from problem solving?

If a good solid foundation exists beneath your relationship, your child may have the courage to tell you simply to listen and not give advice. Many adult-kids still get a twinge of guilt when they "talk back" this way. You can increase their comfort by offering them the alternative of listening without giving advice.

• Bring out the adult in one another. Equalizing the roles means that neither of you needs to play out the part of domineering parent or helpless child. Thomas Harris, a psychiatrist and author, makes this point in his now-classic book *I'm O.K., You're O.K.* (1973). An adult–adult relationship is the only model that can stand the test of time because it depends on mutual respect and equality. When power is unequal, there is a tension that threatens the balance of the relationship. When you invoke the powerful parent role, you are bound to activate a powerless, helpless, or resistant child. The powerless or helpless adult-child will sabotage your best efforts. The resistant adult-child sums it up with the following stance: "I tune out when she starts talking," or "When she says yes, I say no." No real dialogue can follow.

• Move from the parent role to that of the good aunt, kind uncle, benevolent grandparent, or caring mentor. Imagine a role without the power usually associated with parent–child interactions. I remember once hearing that being a grandparent is much easier and more pleasurable than being a parent because the responsibility for guidance, decision making, and discipline is not included in the job.

Imagine a shift in your responsibility so that you are freed from these chores. Would there be anything left to talk about? What do you talk about with your own nieces, nephews, grandchildren, godchildren, or special young-adult friends? You might notice that, though you take a real interest in their lives, you do not tell them how to live them. You do not feel responsible for their decision making. You do not feel compelled to make things turn out right. You probably recognize that you and they are separate individuals and that their choices don't reflect on you or diminish you in any way. You may also notice an increased tolerance of their ideas, whereas you own child with the same ideas might make you bristle. Keep this distinction in mind as a way to monitor your own behavior as time goes by.

• Give your child permission to be your peer. Sometimes it helps to have a ritual or a party or a symbolic gesture to clarify that parent and child will hereafter behave in an adult fashion toward each other. Maybe it can take the form of passing a family treasure, heirloom, or token, received from your own parent, to the next adult generation. Is there a book, tool, or treasured object that will symbolize the recognition of your child's adulthood? If not, create one. Start a new tradition. Celebrate!

Afterward, both of you have the responsibility to notice and point out when your peer status is being violated. This doesn't have to be a heavy or solemn process. In fact, when humor is used, the process of catching yourself (or being caught) can be laughed at. As I write this, it brings to mind my own son's light chiding: "Here you go again, making me into a baby, telling me things I already know!" I appreciate his gentle reminder, and it does get me to pay attention. He, of course, is most glad of that!

Now that you know a few more ways to observe your communication pattern, it might be useful to remember the beginning of this chapter and the discussion of new relationships. As you think about the skills you already have, you can also think about the new ways of listening, watching, observing, and monitoring yourself that were presented in this chapter.

What are the qualities most appreciated in you by your friends? Take a minute to reflect on them, and if you aren't sure, consult your friends for specifics. How do your best interpersonal skills become activated in new relationships? Think about the last time you wanted to get to know someone better. Perhaps your eagerness or enthusiasm gave vitality to your words or actions. How do you put your best foot forward? You may measure your words, or their timing, more closely. Finally, how does this information measure up in your relationship with your adult-child? If you can see a difference, and it points in the direction of shortchanging your child, then some of the ideas outlined here may give you the tools necessary to bridge that legendary gap.

This is not an easy transition. Most of us have difficulty acknowledging how quickly our children have grown up. It may be hard to fathom that the adult face and body across the table belong to our child. That face and body belonged to us not so long ago. Yet a quick glance in the mirror reminds us that time has passed and we are all adults now, wanting pretty much the same things from one another.

Gail Sheehy talks about reciprocal passages in her book *Path-finders* (1981). She describes the development of important friendships between parents and their adult-children: "One of the most joyous expressions of kinship can take place at such junctures. The two can engage in a reciprocal passage, each helping the other to find a new path and taking strength from the interchange" (p. 176).

When you find that your very best efforts don't work, there may be additional problems interfering with the development of a reciprocal relationship. These are discussed in the next chapter.

Chapter 6

Doing Things Differently

Barriers to Communication

"I've done everything I can to patch things up between us, but it seems as if the harder I try the worse it gets. The more I explain what I feel is wrong, the more I am misinterpreted. We are sort of at a stalemate now. Our conversations are brief and tense, and there is an air of apprehension. I feel that at any time one or the other of us will explode and the whole cycle will begin again." These words sum up the exasperation that Myra feels whenever she has an interaction with her twenty-two-year-old son, Jonathan. The problems, she indicates, are not exactly new, but they are more exaggerated than ever before. Myra recalls that life was always more difficult with Jonathan. His two older brothers, two and three years his senior, were more easygoing.

This family had undergone its fair share of stress over the years. Dan, the father, had been injured in an industrial accident. During the long period of recovery that followed, he could not work in the construction trade. Anger at himself and others began to surface. Dan felt worthless as he watched, but could not keep up with, the energy and stamina in his three sons, who were approaching adolescence. Increased unhappiness because of his disability, his diminished ability to support his family, and the strain these created may have been the catalyst for what first seemed like heavy drinking.

Myra struggled to keep the family together, financially and psychologically, while Dan participated in an alcohol treatment program. Her family role had expanded, but in the process, she felt that she might be having to sacrifice some quality time with her sons. The oldest two seemed to sail through this trying period.

It was difficult for Myra to pinpoint a specific problem. Rather, it seemed that the very way in which she and Jonathan related to each other was toxic. Myra felt that she would give anything to see improvement between them because she constantly dwelt on this conflict. No matter how happy and successful she felt or how happy she observed her other offspring to be, the nagging pain of her impasse with Jonathan would interfere and diminish her comfort.

In our discussions, Myra indicated to me that she agreed philosophically with the ideas presented in the previous chapter. She tried to listen and not give advice, unless asked for. Even though he frequently sought her help, she tried not to interfere in Jonathan's life. He had decided to quit college so that he could have more life experience, and his odd job pattern seemed to have no future. Still, she respected his choice. Jonathan's drifting seemed such a sharp contrast to the older boys' stable work style, but she found this difference tolerable.

Jonathan's father didn't say much about this, and for all she knew, it wasn't a problem for him at all. Most of the father–son contact was around activities like golf, carpentry, or televised sports. She said, "They don't get into heavy stuff, which I suppose prevents conflict. But I see their relationship as superficial, and I want more than that with Jonathan." Myra recognized that to have peaceful encounters she would need to maintain a polite but shallow pattern. She saw that option as unsatisfactory, and she rejected it.

Since she was at a stalemate, and very motivated to change,

she was willing to look at some of the issues that might be fueling the fire between her and her son. While she recognized that he probably had half the blame, at least, for their struggles, she realized that he wasn't particularly motivated to change things. It seemed to her that he could tolerate this deadlock forever. She, however, desperately felt that time was running out and that the current situation reflected on her role as a mother. Moreover, the negative tension between them affected her very core: her self-esteem.

Jonathan, on the other hand, did not seem particularly bothered, according to Myra. In fact, her incessant efforts to clarify and resolve problems were seen by him as annoying. This misperception, she claimed, was now part of the problem. "He doesn't seem to care," she said incredulously. "His well-being, our well-being, will always be central in my life." Of course, this was true for Myra, but it may not have been true for Jonathan.

Roger Gould, psychiatrist and author of *Transformations* (1978), points out the discrepancy in perceptions of family conflict: "Our children can't appreciate that this is our last family; they will go on to form a new family. We can't appreciate that after our children grow up and out, there's another life for us to lead" (p. 225). Gould talks about the "slipping away of safety" when conflict threatens our notion of family. Certainly this idea helps to explain Myra's sense of urgency. It also helps to explain why, almost invariably, the parents I talk to are more worried about conflict with their children than the reverse. For example, the younger generation can more easily lay old family conflict aside as they build new connections elsewhere. On the other hand, midlife parents are less future-oriented and tend to put much energy into repairing broken bridges that connect with the past.

Something needed to change, and Myra had accepted the challenge on her own, since Jonathan wanted no part of it. Naturally, she wanted to involve him at some point. "What's the point of me doing all the changing? I thought that communication was a two-way street," she said to me in a frustrated tone that continued in spite of her subsequent efforts. She believed deep down that without Jonathan's involvement the whole process would come to nothing.

The Deteriorating Cycle

As Myra became more aware of the destructive pattern that existed between her and Jonathan, she couldn't help feeling terrible sadness and disappointment. Talking to her friends about their children's successes and well-being only made her feel worse. Observing their healthy interactions or hearing about mutually satisfying conversations further troubled her. It was hard to pay attention to their words, which felt like blows to her already vulnerable sense of herself. Others' good feelings intensified her belief that she had failed with Jonathan. Now, on top of an already tense relationship, she had imposed even more troublesome thoughts and feelings, based more on her fears than on real interactions with Jonathan. For example, she worried that she would be alienated from his future children.

Over time, she communicated these thoughts and feelings, indirectly, to Jonathan through sullenness, greater silence, or sarcasm. He also read a tenseness in her, which, when added to these other behaviors, he interpreted as rejection. As you can imagine, the dance played on and on, and the spiral that had begun in hurt now escalated to anger and alienation.

This deteriorating cycle was like an invisible force that was not seen by mother or son, yet was clearly felt. Even if this cycle had been more obvious, neither party would have dared to talk about something that could get worse. How far does a deteriorating cycle need to go before someone takes the risk to jump into the middle of it and yell, "Stop"? The answer is one that mental health professionals understand very well. Generally speaking, people make decisions to change when remaining the same becomes more intolerable than moving on.

There is a delicate balance between the benefits and risks of psychological change. Since changing the way we see the world or how we interact with others is such a monumental task, it is not embarked on lightly. In fact, it usually takes a major life catastrophe to catapult people into action.

People make a commitment to change when confronted with threatened loss or real loss, and when they are face to face with the intolerable belief that time is running out, or has run out, and the present pain will go on endlessly if something doesn't change. When death takes a loved one, we are forced to begin a change process: a reevaluation of our lifestyle, relationships, goals, and values. In Myra's life, the loss was threatened—not a loss of life, but the loss of love and of potential satisfaction. Though it was a symbolic rather than a real threatened loss, it was still profound.

There seems to be a magical threshold between wanting things to be different and actually immersing oneself in the change process. Psychotherapists can usually spot when the threshold has been crossed because a great deal of energy and determination becomes invested in self-scrutiny. A person committed to change is willing to look at himself or herself and the world without rose-colored glasses. Not that this is ever easy, but somehow, at this point, keeping life the way it is becomes even more unbearable.

At this juncture, Myra was willing to look at herself more objectively, not so much to change herself but to facilitate her relationship with Jonathan. She had thought about working on this process alone, but in this morass of feelings and thoughts, she didn't know where to begin. Her thinking had led in circles and had always returned to the same spot. She could see the rift and the feared outcome: She would be forever alienated and irrelevant to her son's life. She was stuck in a circle that went round and round but led nowhere.

This is a commonly experienced dilemma, and most individuals do benefit from the help of a third party—whether a good friend, a member of the clergy, or a therapist. Myra believed that her friends could be supportive, but she was embarrassed to talk with them about her son and was afraid that they would fail to appreciate the desperateness of the situation. She didn't feel particularly close to a clergy member and therefore turned to a professional helper—a therapist.

A therapist is like a wilderness guide. Even though you still must walk the trail, the guide is there to point out the scenery, explain the terrain, discuss the alternative paths, and stay with you through the process. Certainly you could walk the trail alone, but it is easier and safer with a guide!

Where relationships are tense or tenuous, back-and-forth checking of what people mean or are *really* saying does not exist. This was true for Myra and is probably true for any of you who are in a similar situation. Making assumptions can cause trouble.

Zenith Gross, a seasoned journalist and author of *And You Thought It Was All Over* (1985), interviewed the mothers of adult-children about their relationships. She talks about "voices as weathervanes," saying that "the sensitivity, though more sharply developed on the maternal side, is not unknown among young adults. . . . The exquisite 'tuning in' that mothers and adult kids do to each other's voices would do credit to a skilled musician or an expert acoustical engineer" (p. 55). She quotes a forty-six-year-old mother: "My son just says 'hello' and I know pretty much what's what and when I hear the first word, sometimes I think to myself, 'Uh-oh—what now?'" (p. 55). This conversation took place by telephone and lacked all but the most basic cues. Tone of voice could be assessed, but nothing more, and still this mother "knew." If she had had the variety of cues available in a face-to-face conversation, would she have "known" even more certainly?

The extraordinary sensitivity to your offspring's moods and feelings has had years to develop. Over time, you have come to know the subtle cues that define their nature. You can identify with them, whether because they are part of you and have traits that mirror your own, or because their style is different but complementary. Either way, you feel their joys and pains intensely, often too intensely, and assume that they experience themselves the same way. It's easy to trust this instinct if your track record has been good. But acting on it, as if it were true and valid, is another matter.

In a conversation with her son, the mother who knew from her son's tone of voice that there was a problem probably stored that information. In good relationships, a "sense" is likely to be stored until there are more data. Also, a parent who has a comfortable relationship with his or her adult-child will check out an impression before assuming it is correct. Beyond that, the same parent will cautiously interpret the meaning of this feeling, knowing that he or she could be wrong. Ultimately checking with the adult-child will usually clarify the matter.

Assumptions can be dangerous. Where parent and adult-child are estranged, the assumptions made are usually more a reflection of the person who is making them than of the other person. This is commonly known as *projecting*, that is, attributing a thought, feeling, or behavior to someone else when in reality it is your own invention, for example, "I can see from his eyes how hurt he is," or "When I heard the sigh in her voice, I knew she was exasperated with me," or "I sense how helpless he feels." Whose feelings are reflected here?

In Myra's life, when her son became impatient with her expression of "genuine concern," she assumed this to mean that he didn't trust her. Jonathan, however, saw her concern as evidence that she didn't trust his decision making. Both felt the lack of trust and the disappointment of the other that "must be there." Neither, of course, felt safe enough to check out these assumptions: "Better to let this ride; it could get worse." Another dangerous assumption!

What other kind of assumptions do people make that cause them unnecessary grief? Albert Ellis, a prominent psychologist and author of the book *Reason and Emotion in Psychotherapy* (1962), outlines a number of "irrational beliefs" that are similar to my concept of assumptions. While these are not specific to relationships between parents and kids, they are important to consider because, like assumptions, they go unvalidated. They are acted on as if they were true, and they interfere with life because they color perceptions in very negative ways.

Ellis presents a scheme for understanding irrational beliefs: Something happens (perhaps your son speaks with you infrequently, hastily, or irritably). This is point A. You respond by feeling hurt, sad, or dejected. This is point C. What is actually responsible for C (or how you feel) is caused, not by A, but actually by B, which is an irrational self-statement that is hidden from view, an internalized sentence that you are telling yourself ("I am responsible for his annoyance" or "I have failed to make him happy") and that makes you feel a certain way (C).

Ellis says, "It is impossible for you to be harmed by purely verbal or gestural attacks unless *you* specifically *let* yourself—be harmed. It is never the words or gestures of others that hurt you—but *your* attitudes toward, *your* reactions to these symbols" (p. 72). "Erroneously, then, you believe that A causes C. . . . Actually, however, A has very little to do with causing C. . . . B is what you tell yourself . . . the utter nonsense you tell yourself about A. . . . And by telling yourself these catastrophizing, utterly false sentences at point B, you bring about . . . your results at point C" (p. 176).

For example, Myra feels that Jonathan's antagonism toward her, his withdrawal, or even his confusion is the source of her unhappiness. Ellis would rework this conversation because he would not accept the idea that Jonathan's behavior (A) could lead to Myra's unhappiness (C). Rather, he would see (B), an irrational belief or assumption, helping to explain Myra's unhappiness. What might that be for Myra? Perhaps she holds one of the following irrational beliefs:

1. "If I had been a better mother Jonathan's behavior would be better."
2. "The youngest of my three children was neglected by me."
3. "I should be able to make things OK, and since I can't, somehow I have failed."

4. "Since Jonathan is so angry he must not love me, or I'm not lovable, and that is intolerable."

Other assumptions are possible as well. Notice that all of these statements are ways of connecting Jonathan's behavior and Myra's feelings. They are a way of explaining how A is related to C. The only problem is that the explanations may not be true and are often unconscious, so that they are hard to explore, acknowledge, or give up.

As you can see, Myra assumes that A leads to C, whereas Ellis would say that A leads to B leads to C. Point B is what you tell yourself about A. It includes all those self-statements about how catastrophic the situation is or how awful you are. These self-statements and illogical, irrational assumptions, which have no basis in reality, lead to Myra's unhappiness, C.

Ellis indicates that, in addition to the already available valid reasons for being unhappy, people make themselves even more miserable by the things they tell themselves that may not be true. He contrasts the fears of animals with the fears of humans: "Dogs, in other words, fear *real* noxious stimuli, while human beings fear *imagined* or *defined* as well as real unpleasant stimuli" (p. 17). "The very facility with language which enabled them to be essentially human—to talk to others and to talk to themselves—also enabled them to abuse this facility by talking utter nonsense to themselves: to *define* things as terrible when, at worst, these things were inconvenient and annoying" (p. 21). He goes on to point out the extent of this problem: "Without human talk and self-talk, *some* degree of anxiety and hostility might well exist; but never, I realized, the extreme and intense degrees of these feelings which constitute emotional disturbance" (p. 22).

Certainly the relationship between Jonathan and Myra is confused and confusing, but the assumptions made to explain this state of affairs muddies the water even more. Learning to become aware of the way in which your self-statements affect your feelings and behavior is the key to change. When you can accept the notion that you may be contributing to your own unhappiness by telling yourself statements about yourself and about situations that may not be true, then you can begin to learn coping skills that will offset the negative effect of the critical self-statements. That is one of the first goals that Myra and her therapist set when they began working together.

Double Messages and Mixed Messages

Nothing is ever as confusing as being on the receiving end of a double or mixed message. It makes you feel confused and filled with doubt about what is being communicated. Double messages give two conflicting sets of information, and it's anybody's guess what is intended or how to respond. The only clarity in such a transaction is that it is consistently confusing.

Richard Lewis, the comic actor, gave an example of his mother's way of talking to the dog that gives a graphic picture of a double message: "My mother will throw a bone and say, 'Look, there's a bone. Don't get it. See if I care!'" Fortunately for the dog, his understanding of language is not sufficient for him to be confused. Very likely, he will respond to the sight and smell of the bone and possibly to Mother's tone of voice and disregard the rest. As humans, we don't have this advantage.

A while back, I was caught offering a mixed message to my nearly twenty-year-old son. He was working at a summer job in another city, and I realized that little time would remain between the ending of that job and his return to college. I had not seen him since spring vacation, and I missed him. A straightforward approach would have communicated that I missed him and wanted to spend some time with him before school started. Instead, I told him that I understood how important it was for him to work up to the last minute. I said that I valued his seriousness and sense of responsibility. But then I added that his eight-year-old sister felt deprived by his absence and wondered if he really cared about her: after all, he could have worked in the city in which we live!

In spite of my awareness of the need to be clear, I sometimes display this pattern (giving mixed messages) when I want him to accept my otherwise unacceptable ideas. The guilt and discomfort that this created for him were communicated to me in no uncertain terms. While it made me embarrassed and a bit sheepish, I really did appreciate the risk he took in pointing out my "crazy-making" message. What was I trying to do? Most certainly, at least two ideas were valid. I did value his attempt to be a successful worker and make his own money. I also did want to see him for more than a few days during the entire summer vacation.

Rather than stick with the facts and feelings and possibly have him choose what was good for him, but not for me, I loaded the deck. Surely, he would not want his sister to feel unloved and uncared for. Surely if he didn't want to see much of me, he wouldn't deprive her of his company.

The fact was plain and not pretty. I was feeling selfish and needy but didn't want him to see me that way. Honestly, what I wanted was to spend time with him because that would make me feel good. His visit would also send a message to the world that I was loved and valued by my son, who chose to spend time with me above other options—a priority even higher than making money!

The ploy, though mostly unconscious, didn't work. I learned something from it and was glad to have the opportunity to examine other messages *before* I sent them. In reality, whenever you have a vested interest in how an event turns out, you will probably try to skew it in that direction. Yet, most of us don't want our self-serving motives to be so obvious. It is the disguise that we use to cover our motive that makes our statement so confusing. What would enable us to be more direct in communicating our needs and wants so that they're not so distorted? The answer is more simply given then carried out.

Removing Barriers to Communication

Clear communication between two people requires the sending and receiving of accurate messages. This is a process that depends on words but goes much beyond. The subtle cues of a head nod, an eye wink, and a shoulder shrug impart a meaning that reinforces or even contradicts what we say. More precisely, good communication is built on active listening and a back-and-forth clarification and agreement to make sure that understanding has taken place. This probably seems like a very formal arrangement for a way of talking to your own children. Yet, as you saw earlier, the likelihood of misunderstanding is very high in situations where feelings and emotions are deeply involved. The stronger these are, the greater is the chance that each person will evaluate the other's remarks from his or her own viewpoint. When parents and adult-children each make assumptions about what the other means, the potential for misunderstanding is at its highest. To offset these odds the following guidelines may be helpful:

1. Paraphrase what you hear to get feedback on its accuracy. This kind of intent listening is not easy, but it's worth the effort. It conveys to the speaker that you are really listening and that you care to hear what is being said rather than what you think is being said. Paraphrasing requires that assumptions be disregarded or checked out with the sender of the message.

Each time one of you speaks, the other must first paraphrase what was heard in a way that seems satisfactory to the speaker. It is valuable practice for you, as the listener, to restate the ideas, feelings, and words in your own way and from your own viewpoint. The speaker can evaluate how close you came to her or his meaning. Only then do you get your turn to speak.

The nice part of this process is that *your* comments are also responded to in a caring and understanding way. Usually, the speaker experiences less fear of being evaluated and less defensiveness. While this procedure does not guarantee that you will always know what the speaker intends, it will get you much closer to the truth. Unfortunately, this way of interacting is more easily described than carried out.

To get some safe experience and rehearsal, try out the type of listening described above with a good friend. Probably you and your friend already have a caring and supportive relationship. This exercise it will help you see how natural the process can be when conflict, misunderstanding, and hurt feelings don't come into play.

The rules for practice are:

a. Make a statement about yourself—the way you feel, an idea you have, or a comment about your relationship with the listener.

b. The listener responds with the introductory statement, "What I hear you saying is . . ." or "What I think you mean is . . ." The listener simply conveys the ideas and feelings heard but does not go beyond to judge or evaluate or infer.

c. The speaker then gets to decide if the listener has heard accurately. Back-and-forth clarification takes place until the speaker acknowledges, "That is exactly what I meant." This is then a completed transaction, and the speaker and listener can change positions.

After each of you has had a turn, stop and talk to your friend about how this process felt. What did it feel like to know that your words were seriously pondered for their real meaning? What did it feel like to negotiate back and forth until the meaning was crystal clear? How did you feel about yourself, and about the listener?

The process may seem awkward at first, but it can become more comfortable with repetition, like learning to ride a bike. Even a little practice can greatly improve your skills as a listener. You will begin to pay attention differently. Better yet, without formally teaching your adult-child, you can still facilitate your communication with her or him. Imagine your child's surprise and relief when you repeat back her or his words to help you better understand what she or he meant or was feeling. If done with sincerity, this active listening can be catching!

2. Make personal statements using the personal pronouns *I*, *me*, and *my*. It is not easy to say how you feel, what you want, or what you need. Some risk taking is required because self-statements may expose your vulnerability. If trust and safety are

present, it is easier to take this risk. When you perceive that you are alienated from your adult-child, saying how you feel will seem awkward, or even dangerous, at first. Still, the payoff is high if it reduces the strain that currently exists.

What are some examples of "I" statements? Here is a small sample to get you started:

a. "I feel happy, scared, worried, angry, nervous, when . . ."
b. "I wish I could run away, cry, start over, tolerate, hold my temper, when . . ."
c. "I love you, hate you, worry about you, when . . ."
d. "When you talk to me that way I tend to withdraw, get angry, want to get even, . . ."
e. "My stomach gets upset when I, we . . ."
f. "I feel rejected, ignored, unvalued when . . ."
g. "My feelings are hurt when . . ."
h. "I become agitated when . . ."

Notice that in all of these self-revealing statements there is nothing for the listener to argue with. If you avoid criticizing or evaluating and stay with your own feelings, there is nothing for the listener to challenge. There is a big difference between saying, "You always hurt my feelings" and "My feelings are hurt when you turn your back on me, interrupt me, or criticize me." While the first statement implies intent to hurt and is global, the second statement is specific and doesn't suggest that the listener meant to inflict pain. For this reason, the second statement can be more easily and less defensively accepted than the first one.

Try to practice these personal statements with a trusted family member, and as your skill increases, try it with your adult-child. This way of speaking may require some getting used to by everyone. In the fixed role of parents, we are often not seen, even by ourselves, as separate individuals with hopes, fears, wants, needs, and other powerful feelings. Others may not understand that we are trying to change our behavior and may see our new style as playing games or being manipulative. They may also feel suspicious or confused and even try to change us back to the way we were, for their own comfort.

Identifying Negative Feelings

Nothing is as difficult as the expression of negative feelings except perhaps acknowledging them in the first place. Think about all the colloquial expressions that are designed to stop you from being negative: "If you don't have anything good to say, then don't say anything"; "Think good thoughts"; "If you're mad, count to ten before you speak."

Why are negative feelings so uncomfortable and distasteful for so many of us? We are all subject to these feelings, whether we like it or not, because feelings are emotional reactions to internal or external conditions. We are all different in our capacity to experience and react to feelings: One person may respond to criticism with anger or hurt. Another may feel a tightness in her or his gut. A third person may avoid the one who criticizes and take time out for a cigarette, a candy bar, or a few extra beers after work.

Our culture places a very high premium on happiness and satisfaction. Models of appropriate and adaptive ways of managing negative sensations are sadly lacking. The media reinforce the myth of exclusively positive emotions. Goods and services are sold through advertising on TV and radio and in magazines and newspapers by the display of happy, contented individuals.

The picture that comes immediately to my mind is the Thanksgiving Day ad for turkey, pumpkin pie, or stuffing mix. It shows a happy, multigenerational gathering of grandparents, parents, and children, all interacting in perfect harmony. All smile warmly at one another; all show respect and caring. Whose family is this anyway? It isn't mine, and it probably isn't yours. This image distorts reality significantly and may influence us to respond to the notion of negative emotions with much anxiety.

There needs to be a way to acknowledge that Dad has had much too much to drink before dinner and that it makes you upset. As unpleasant as it is, you need to be able to see the tension between your mother and your mother's mother—now an old lady but still relentless in her criticism. Perhaps there is an empty spot at your family table, left by your aunt's death. The loss doesn't disappear just because discussion and grieving are avoided.

Fear, anger, and sadness are seen as ugly, too unpleasant to experience and display. Even hurt, guilt, and disappointment may be circumvented because they evoke discomfort. It's not surprising, then, that our communication is often just the tip of the iceberg. Beneath the surface there is another, larger level that is typically covered over, but not hidden, by our nice words.

Rather than an iceberg with dangerous feelings lurking beneath the surface, there is really a continuum of emotions. Healthy people move back and forth. The normal expression of feelings includes happiness, joy, anger, and sadness as well as the more neutral states that may not be felt as strongly. For psychological well-being, it is important to be able to (1) sense or experience your emotions; (2) trust and value what you're feeling as appropriate; and (3) allow yourself the expression of these emotions. Few families provide good modeling of these three steps. You may be able to see the problem but be fearful of labeling it. You may find yourself irritable and short-tempered but not know why. On the other hand, you may label and act on your anger correctly but feel guilty or bad about yourself for having the feeling.

The mid-range of emotions is comfortable for most of us; less intense feelings are generally easier to feel and express. Positive emotions can be demonstrated, at least to those considered special, loved, and trusted. Few of us, however, are comfortable with the continuum of negative feelings.

Anger is a powerful emotion. The socialization process that begins in early childhood leaves, after years and years of shaping, only remnants of this feeling. Children are punished for the expression of anger and then learn to feel guilty and self-punitive for even experiencing the internal cues that characterize anger. A very common example is conflict between siblings. If fighting is punished, it may cease. The irritation or annoyance that led to the fighting may be denied to fit the profile of a "nice" person: "Nice people don't stay angry." In some cases, the feeling itself is not tolerable and must be disguised, so that any discomfort felt is avoided through distraction (e.g., spacing out, drugs, compulsive eating, or alcohol). When these cues refuse to disappear, they are sometimes distorted or denied through unconscious defensive operations that serve a protective role and come into play automatically.

When it's not acceptable to experience anger, anger tends to be converted into a less intense and dramatic feeling. Often, sadness and/or depression is substituted. When this happens, it's more difficult to identify and work on the original feeling, which has become disguised. Fortunately, when anger is acknowledged, the acknowledgment can lead to direct expression and resolution.

Sam and Margaret lived in the Midwest, not far from their childhood homes. Both had been raised in large families and had valued the richness a large family provided; at the same time, they wanted to go beyond their own experiences. Sam wished to give his kids more attention than he had received from his own father. Margaret wanted to instill a sense of specialness and individuality in her children. They believed they had done everything they could for their children, now grown. Their family life, as they now looked back on it, had been typical. In trying to summarize the past thirty years, they looked for evidence of mistakes that could explain the current state of affairs: "We weren't trendsetters, and we didn't invent our way of family life. We were very much like everyone else around us in the way we lived and the way we disciplined our children. Even our goals and plans were very much like those of our friends and neighbors. At the time, that was reassuring. We couldn't all be wrong. Now I wonder."

Sam was mulling over the past in an attempt to better understand the struggle that he and Margaret were having with their twenty-eight-year-old daughter: "It's not that Betty is a bad person. She's struggling like a lot of young people do today. With two kids and a job, she's probably doing the best she can. Her husband works hard, too. They're always so frazzled, and everything seems so chaotic. How could we turn our backs on them?"

Margaret acknowledges her daughter's hectic life. She conveys her concern, and possibly her annoyance, but also a sense of helplessness: "Whenever I try to make suggestions to her about ways to reduce some of the turmoil, she gets mad at me and I back off. I really wouldn't care as much if it didn't affect us the way it does. She constantly complains about things, but whenever I offer her some suggestions, she tells me I'm interfering. I really don't know what she wants from me!" Good question, I thought, and then I asked Margaret if, in fact, she had ever posed that question to Betty. My query came as a surprise. It hadn't occurred to Margaret that she could ask such a thing quite that straightforwardly.

Clearly, there was a great deal of confusion about how to be helpful to their daughter. But more than that, these parents, who had never said "no" to the needs of their children, found themselves in a situation where learning to say "no" would be most useful: "Whenever Betty gets overwhelmed and starts complaining to me, I try to help and she gets mad. I don't know what else to do; as a mother, that's what I've always done. Not only aren't my efforts appreciated, but I get snapped at besides. When my feelings get hurt, I get quiet, and then I realize that I'm not being helpful. The next thing I know, I'm feeling guilty because my daughter obviously needs me, and here I am being selfish and only thinking about myself."

Margaret went on to talk about her willingness to take care of Betty's young children as a way of providing some relief to her harried daughter. Sometimes, she and Sam had offered to take the kids, but more recently, Betty had just been stopping by with the kids and assuming that her mother or father wouldn't mind for a few hours: "It's not just her bringing the kids that bothers me, but she doesn't seem to notice that I may be getting ready to leave or may be into a project of my own. Sometimes I just don't want to see her or the kids, but here they are anyway."

While this is a common enough scenario with which most of us can identify, it is also a distorted picture of parent–adult-child relationships. Margaret and, to a lesser extent, Sam seem to believe that setting some limits on their child's demands would be unloving or cold, that a parent's love and help have no bounds. Beliefs such as these were held by many parents influenced by the child-centered philosophy that emerged after World War II. Setting limits and saying "no" tended to create guilt. Perhaps they had acquiesced to their daughter's demands too often over the years. It was easy to justify their behavior since they themselves had received little attention as children.

Now they feel some resentment toward Betty, but that feeling seems inappropriate, and so they rationalize it and double their efforts to be helpful. Perhaps this is a way for them to neutralize that uncomfortable feeling.

Since Sam and Margaret can hardly tolerate their annoyance at Betty, they certainly can't acknowledge any stronger negative feelings. Therefore, the anger that is covered over by resentment and rationalized away continues to fester and is expressed in a disguised manner: "Lately Sam and I find ourselves away from home more than usual. I'm not sure why, but it seems to be better for us. I found myself getting headaches and upset stomachs a lot, and it seems as if I feel bad primarily when I'm at home."

Only after much thought did I dare to suggest the possibility that Margaret's symptoms were connected with her daughter's demanding behavior and not with staying at home. This was a useful comment to Margaret, but it predictably activated some guilt and self-criticism. Sam was the first to see the link, and because his acknowledgment of it didn't seem blaming or critical, Margaret was later able to consider it herself. As she was able to step back and view her relationship with Betty a bit more objectively, she began to get in touch with the more intense negative feelings that had previously gone unnoticed. She felt exploited and dumped on. She became angry at Betty for not taking charge of her own life and her own family. Thus began a long but significant process of growth.

Learning to acknowledge negative feelings and emotions, and to value them as a source of strength, is a new idea to many of us. Learning to trust negative feelings as valid sources of information reduces the need to distort and deny their impact. Keeping yourself aware of your negative feelings goes a long way toward increasing your insight, self-understanding, and level of consciousness. After all, the more you experience at a conscious level, the less will be assigned to the unconscious, the level that is beyond the everyday reach of most of us.

Expressing Negative Feelings

Once Margaret and Sam could see that they had played a role in their conflict with Betty and that the way they were "helping" was counterproductive, they felt it was time to do things differently. Margaret wanted to let Betty know how angry she was at the way she felt she was being treated. Still, getting angry at Betty, without converting the anger to sadness, headaches, or self-loathing, was a big task that required much practice.

How do you learn how to express your anger? Before you can actually try out your feelings, you must be as frustrated as Margaret. She was finally able to feel the anger and, even more important, her entitlement to this feeling. She learned to identify a seething, warm movement in her stomach and a tightening in her shoulders. She also noticed that her teeth were clenched and her jaw tense. When Margaret saw the connection between these sensations and Betty's behavior, she understood that her body was giving her some useful information. While she still felt some sadness and the occasional guilt of a not-perfect mother, she felt ready to act. This was a significant starting point.

Keep in mind that an important incentive for learning to express anger is that, even when suppressed, anger continues on its destructive course though the conscious associations disappear. A clenched jaw and a tight gut or chest may eventually lead to stress-related disorders such as ulcers, bruxism, or muscular-skeletal pain.

When you take the risk of expressing anger or other negative feelings, the importance of the relationship needs to be considered. If the relationship has either very little importance (minimal consequences) or, paradoxically, enormous importance (great consequences), there are definite benefits in learning how to express negative feelings.

Here's a situation in which the consequences are minimal:

Imagine that you are waiting for the next available bank teller on your lunch hour. Someone cuts in front of you, whether accidentally or purposely. You feel yourself becoming angry but try to explain the feeling away: "Maybe she didn't notice me; perhaps she is in a bigger rush than I am; it could be an emergency." This line of reasoning doesn't make you feel better. In fact, your impatience increases with each passing moment. You'll certainly be late with still another person ahead of you. A sense of warmth creeps around your neck and face. This is a definite signal of your agitation.

It makes sense to tell the person whose behavior was anger-producing that you are next and that you would appreciate it if she or he would wait her or his turn. You may not need to say more, since most people correct their behavior when they are given this kind of feedback. Most people don't want to be rude or to act inappropriately. Still, no matter how the other person reacts, you have had a chance to *do* something that will probably make you feel less angry. Even if the person doesn't respond appropriately or with appreciation, you have no vested interest in preserving this relationship at all costs. Never seeing this person again will not adversely affect your life. It's worth the risk.

Here's a situation in which the consequences are great:

In Margaret's relationship with her daughter, the consequences of failure are great. Confrontation will be uncomfortable, awkward, and frightening because of the fear of alienation if the new behavior doesn't work or, worse yet, backfires. Yet, there is a sufficiently strong bond between mother and daughter to ensure the continuity of their relationship over time. In most relationships between parents and their adult-children, the expression of negative feelings may create some initial distance, but in the long run, the honesty that marks such a confrontation will strengthen the bonds and allow a deepening of the relationship that was not possible before. In other words, constructive confrontation has a high risk but also a high payoff.

You are now ready to design your practice. You need to be sure that the following preconditions have been satisfied:

First, you must be aware of and feel entitled to your negative feelings.

Second, you must feel that the consequences (outcomes) are sufficiently unimportant or critical to allow you to take the risk that comes with verbal expression.

Clearly, the actual practice can't take place until you know what you want to say. Consider the following:

1. Think of an "I" statement that communicates your feeling.
2. Identify the behavior that upsets you.
3. Clarify the link between 1 and 2.
4. Be aware of what you would like to see as an outcome. How would you like the other person to change? What are you willing to change in yourself?

As you already know, communicating your negative feelings to your adult-child, the very person who needs to hear them, is unpleasant and frightening. It may cause you to feel bad about yourself or guilty about causing even more grief for your own flesh and blood. You may feel unnecessarily critical or cruel. A sense of betrayal or abandonment may be activated. In any case, you probably won't feel ready to talk to your child directly until you have had some practice with a more neutral person.

In addition to a more neutral person, you will need a third person to observe the two of you and to give you feedback about how accurately and clearly you said what you wanted to say. In this practice session, the one who is on the receiving end of this confrontation will try to respond honestly and in a way that seems realistic. In your first practice, give yourself no more than fifteen minutes to explain how and what you feel and what you want to see happen or change. During this time, the "receiver" can act the part of the adult-child by asking questions, expressing his or her feelings, and defending his or her behavior.

At the end of fifteen minutes, the observer should give you feedback about the effectiveness of your communication, especially pointing out what you did well, as well as what you still need to practice. The observer will have paid attention to:

1. Statements that you made about yourself and your feelings.
2. Statements that showed that you were listening to the other's words and feelings in an attempt to truly understand.
3. Clear statements of wants and expectations.

The "receiver" will also give you feedback about how your words felt. Were you straight and honest, but firm? Did you cave in the first time you were challenged? Did the "receiver" feel punished by your words or simply informed of your wants, hurts, and worries? Were you too soft or too abrasive in your approach? All of this and more can be gleaned from the "receiver's" experience in this practice.

You may find it useful to play this scene over and over with the same partners. On the other hand, this practice may remind you of other dialogues that need to take place and may give you the confidence to practice additional situations. If the first scene involved saying "no" to cosigning a loan for your daughter, then the second scene might entail saying "no" to caring for her dog when she is out of town. You may also find it helpful to rehearse the same scene with a different emphasis or approach. Instead of saying "no" to dog-sitting, you may want to offer a conditional "yes"—on your terms.

It may even be worthwhile to replay the same words but

change roles so that instead of "actor" you become "receiver" or "observer." In each role, you can learn something different about how your message is communicated. As in the theater, rehearsal gives you skill in remembering the lines and courage in delivering them. Of course, unlike in the theater, the goal of this performance is not entertainment but increased understanding and behavior change.

In the drama of life, the very performance may influence the subsequent dialogue and even the outcome. When you know what you want to say and believe in the importance of saying it, you increase the likelihood that your adult-child will take your message seriously. Surprisingly, the most feared outcome—the destruction of your relationship—may never materialize.

At some point, you will be prepared to have the real-life interaction with your adult-child. Readiness for this assignment, like all psychological change, depends on a shift in balance—when moving ahead (having the feared encounter) becomes more comfortable than the status quo. As in the theater, you need to expect the possibility of cold feet and some uncertainty. Push yourself a bit to get the words out. The observing part of your psyche will help you clarify the meaning of your fumbled thoughts. Because this is a dialogue, you will have the opportunity to say something again in another way or to give examples to make what you say more meaningful. You can also communicate warmth and caring so that your adult-child understands it's his or her "behavior" and not his or her "being" that you have difficulty accepting.

Be prepared to hear your child's negative feelings, too. Confrontation, like communication in general, is a two-way street. Your willingness to open this hidden arena to dialogue may give your adult-children permission to speak in ways that are new and very frank. After all, you were their role model in so many ways during their formative years. Now you are signaling that negative feelings are *not* taboo and can be discussed. Just remember that your adult children have their own grievances. Get ready to hear about their loss, hurt, frustration, anger, guilt, and pain. Be prepared to listen actively, to ask for clarification, to be tolerant and nondefensive, and to understand that these are the feelings of your children—valid simply because they are experienced. Be prepared to learn a whole lot in a very short period of time.

As in the aftermath of a severe storm, intense and raging emotions will eventually subside and give way to a calmness that comes from greater awareness. Each of you has finally given words and meaning to feelings that have been seen but not entirely understood. Now you have expanded the foundation on which your relationship was built.

Following up on our earlier excerpt from family life, Margaret finally got to the point of confronting Betty. Predictably, feelings ran high. Margaret stuck with her own feelings of anger at being used, and Betty cried and said that she felt betrayed. Margaret didn't get sidetracked and didn't rescue her hurt daughter, though she very much wanted to. Instead, she stayed with her *own* feelings as well as her wants. It wasn't easy, and it wasn't pleasant, but Margaret did say everything she wanted to say and managed to tolerate Betty's angry and hurt feelings—knowing that the feelings belonged to Betty and that they were Betty's responsibility.

Betty's defensive feelings eventually gave way to statements of annoyance that she could spell out in behavior. She could tell her mother how annoying it was to get a message that said, "It's fine to leave the kids. I don't see them enough, and I always have time for them," and at the same time to get a second, nonverbal message that said, "I'm not glad to see you or your kids. You're interfering with my plans. Go away and take care of your own problems." Betty had never known which message was real or accurate. Betty had never known which message required a response. Betty had picked up on her mother's anger but didn't know what it meant. Now the two of them could discuss what had and had not been said, and the cautiousness that had marked their interactions before their first confrontation disappeared.

The Less-Than-Perfect Parent

One predictable by-product of confrontation between parent and adult-child is the airing of mistakes made on both sides. Giving up the image of perfection is a symbolic gesture that allows your child to complete the rite of passage from adolescence to adulthood. Without this shift, you can't be seen as a real person, and your child can't talk to you as an equal. Without this shift, you can't take the risk of being vulnerable in front of your child. What are you actually giving up?

The shattered need to seem perfect to your child is a necessary loss. Giving up this idealized state (being seen as perfect) may feel damaging to your self-esteem. There is a certain glory to parenthood that is reinforced by the adoration, trust, and naïveté of our youngsters. When they are very young, they tend to see us as all-knowing and infallible. We are flattered but understand that the perfection projected on us is merely an illusion. On the other hand, it's reassuring to be seen in such a way, and it even gives us courage and confidence when the internal supply runs low.

By late childhood and certainly by adolescence, our image is tarnished by reality. When we don't follow through perfectly, when we disappoint, or when our judgment is incorrect, we are seen as withholding, mean, or intolerant enforcers of rules. Still we may not be seen as faulty or imperfect. There is more of a sense that we *won't* cooperate than that we *can't*. It is difficult for average adolescents or young adults to accept the fact that their parents can't solve all their problems, can't make them feel better, and can't take their struggles away. Since they are still dependent on us in many ways and don't trust their own perceptions entirely, they continue to see us as "all-knowing."

The process of breaking away allows them to see our limitations and flaws more accurately. At the same time, they may try to keep us infallible in an attempt to bolster their own comfort and offset their fear that we are no wiser than they. As this drama unfolds, we become aware that our image was always distorted in their eyes; we were never perfect, and we surely aren't the source of all their unhappiness either.

As a midlife parent, it is critical for you to present a realistic picture of who you are, with all the strengths and limitations that define you. It isn't easy to talk about the mistakes you've made, the personality traits you can't seem to change, or the bad habits that keep you from succeeding in certain ways. It isn't easy, but it is necessary. Only when you can be real, showing your vulnerable side, can you expect to have honesty and equality. As in every other surrender, there is an up side. The benefit of letting your adult-child see you as you see yourself is that her or his fresh observations may be surprisingly accurate and useful. For example, your stubborn and tenacious qualities may be finally appreciated, now that they no longer pose a threat to your adult-child. Given the opportunity to give you her or his perspective, she or he will take on a more adult role and become more involved in your life as a co-adult.

Recently, a phone conversation with my son made this business of equality abundantly clear. We were discussing an upcoming visit, and I was mildly protesting his decision to stay only a few days. (It's probably obvious that many of my conflicts and negotiations with my son are about visiting.)

He talked about why his decision was good for him, and I found myself upset nevertheless. I understood his reasoning, and I accepted it. At least I thought I did. Why was it so hard for me to just let go? While the answer didn't come to me directly, I did get some help from an unexpected source. My son, Matt, carefully and cautiously reminded me that I was making assumptions about our relationship based on my own relationship with *my* mother. He said that I was worried that less time together would translate for me into less closeness, less connection. He went on to say that the distance and pain between me and my mother had nothing to do with him and me.

Though I bristled at hearing such words of insubordination, I chuckled to myself that he really understood me. In fact, I knew he was right, and not only was this new information help-ful to me, but it gave me a new respect for his ability to see and understand the world. It also told me that his acceptance of my humanness didn't diminish me in his eyes. In fact, unless he goes overboard in his interpretations of my behavior (a parent-psychologist's nightmare), I will continue to be delighted by this expansion of our already-good relationship.

In the final analysis, building a relationship is not like build-ing a house. With a house, the storms of life and time are often ravaging. With a relationship, time, raging storms, and changing or interchanging parts have a positive effect. Peace and tran-quillity may preserve the appearance of a house, and even the appearance of a relationship, but the periodic expression of neg-ative feelings through constructive confrontation makes a rela-tionship flourish.

Building a relationship is more like excavating an archae-ological site. You don't realize the potential until a great deal of digging has been done. What you find may be incomplete and may require more digging or exploring. There may be false starts, much frustration, and a lot of dirt to sift through. The job re-quires perseverance and respect. In the end, satisfaction and increased understanding make the effort worthwhile.

Lillian Troll (1989), a psychologist affiliated with the Univer-sity of California at San Francisco, carried out research on the formation of intergenerational family relationships and sums up the experiences of those she studied. They "described transfor-mations of relationships with their grown children over time. First, they dropped their authority, then providing protection, and, last, counseling. Friendship was what remained" (p. 214). For the sake of friendship, take a good look in the mirror, roll up the rugs, look eye-to-eye at your adult-child, and tackle the impasse.

Chapter 7

Getting It Together

A Workable Model

In an ideal world, it would be possible to change the models for family structure and relationships as changes were needed. When our children were young and required parental supervision and guidance, we were there. Later, as they became emerging adults who wanted to try their independence and autonomy, we would know enough to back off—graciously. Still later, our parental role would cease to exist altogether, except by request from our adult-children in times of stress or crisis. The rest of the time we would have a role similar to that of a favorite aunt or uncle, the person who is credited with more life experience, and who is loving but less involved and less liable to interfere.

Again, this is an ideal picture. Adapting to changing life circumstances is not so easy. A shift in one dimension (our children's maturation) requires a countershift (in our expectations and behavior). Rebalancing leads to a more effective status quo.

In the world of science, balance is achieved by adaptation to changing information. On a balance scale, the removal of weight from one side requires an equal removal on the other side; otherwise, the balance will be off. When we talk about families out of balance, we are really talking about tense and stressed relationships in which the weights have been altered on one side but not on the other. Without some kind of planned intervention or adjustment, these relationships may deteriorate through frustration, anger, and withdrawal. The idea of shifting roles to maintain balance comes in very handy in understanding how to build a good adult-family model.

The following example comes from my psychological work with young adults at a university health center. It is typical of the rebalancing efforts that adult-kids tend to make. Since most of the examples in this book focus on parents' initiation of change, here is a scenario showing the same effort from the young adult's perspective.

I remember a young woman named Mary. She struggled with her conflicting feelings about whether to go to her parents' home for the Christmas holidays or to stay in her own environment. While she had continued to show her parents, over time, that her priorities were shifting and that she was more and more the center of her own world, her parents had failed to pick up the message. In a discussion with me about this issue, she said, "They've always supported my independence, and now that I'm trying to exercise it, they seem so hurt. I know that they were expecting me for the holidays, and I've reassured them that I'll come for a few days including Christmas. I felt that this was a compromise for me because, quite honestly, I had thought about going skiing with some of my friends. I knew that not going home at all would be intolerable to them, and it also made me feel a little guilty and irresponsible. So finally, after much thought and soul searching, I decided to spend some time with the family and the rest on my own. It seemed like the perfect solution."

Mary's dilemma is very common. Day in and day out, I hear college students wrestle with what they "owe" to their parents and what they "owe" to themselves. These young adults are expanding their own limits and are often surprised to find that their parents are resisting their efforts even though the parents had always been supportive in the abstract. It is easy to see this resistance as nonsupportive or rejecting. What these young adults fail to see is the internal struggle that parents face in backing off and letting go. This dilemma is articulated by Dennis Klass (1989) as he reminisces about his sons' transition to adulthood and how that affected him:

> But if we relate as peers when we are together, we are not separate but equal in my sense of self. When people ask me how it is going, I catch myself telling them about the kids. They are living in a very different world than I did, and yet I find that a part of my self-hood is living in the world with them. Their successes feel very much like my successes, and, fortunately, there have been few failures. Now that they are moving into their own lives, one of the tasks before me is to reestablish an identity separate from them yet including them. (p. 39)

Young adulthood is not a time for challenging the rules, as was true in adolescence. It also may not be a time for pursuing solid goals, which tends to come later. Mazor and Enright (1988), researching the stages of individuation from childhood to adulthood, point out that the contradictions in the way adolescents see themselves, in relationship to their parents, become clearer in early adulthood. They observe:

> At this level, individuals develop an appreciation for parental support and long-term influence as an important part of individual values. The greater equality in the relationship enables individuals to recognize parental needs, such as reliance on their children. (p. 44)

Compromise, acceptance, and integration characterize this level.

Gail Sheehy, in *Passages* (1976), her best-selling book about the stages of adult life, discusses the work of the twenties decade:

> The Trying Twenties is one of the longer and more stable periods, stable, that is, in comparison with the rockier passages that lead to and exit from it. Although each nail driven into our first external life structure is tentative, a tryout,

> once we have made our commitments we are convinced
> they are the right ones. (p.85)

In Mary's case, she was convinced that her solution was correct. Unlike at an earlier time, she was not interested in consulting her parents and then doing the opposite. In fact, at this point she didn't want to consult her parents at all! Parents, generally unprepared for this stage, often react with hurt or anger. Ironically, parents who have done an adequate job of preparing their offspring for adulthood are likely to find themselves out of a job.

Sheehy sheds some light on the desire to achieve self-determination that is characteristic of this period:

> People in their twenties commonly insist what they are doing is the one true course in life. Any suggestion that we are like our parents raises our hackles. Introspection is a dangerous thing. It doesn't disappear, of course, but it is not a signal characteristic of this period. Too much introspection would interfere with action. What if we were to find out the truth? That the parental figures, unknowingly internalized as our guardians, provide the very feelings of safety that allow us to dare all these great firsts of the twenties. They are also the inner dictators that hold us back. (p.89)

Mary had internalized her parents' message that she "must do what was right" for her. She was acting consistently with her parents' values. Still, the rest of the script was unraveling as her parents resisted the changes that were natural and inevitable. The old contract had been modified in subtle ways, over time, but without notice. A new contract needed to be created so that the business of living could go on more smoothly. At this point, Mary needed an exploration of a new working relationship with her parents and, ultimately, a new contract.

Negotiating a New Working Relationship

The idea of negotiating within a family probably seems a little strange because we usually think about this strategy in the world of work. The best strategies that businesses have to offer may very well fit into the context of family life. Businesses are, after all, designed to succeed and be profitable.

Interestingly, the role of the negotiator in business is very similar to the role of the family therapist. The family therapist facilitates a process, as does the negotiator hired to resolve a business or labor dispute. For this reason, the ideas that follow would be at home at the bargaining table or in the family therapist's office. I use the business analogy because it is probably more familiar to you than the realm of psychotherapy and takes away some of the discomfort or stigma that may be associated with the use of mental health services. I hope that the knowledge you gain about negotiating will give you a head start in problem solving or will at least clarify your starting point before family therapy begins.

Negotiators are not trained as therapists, which should offer encouragement to those of you who are not therapists. But negotiators are professionals in their own right. The Center for Dispute Resolution located in Santa Monica, California, is a company that provides consultation to all sorts of organizations including businesses, industries, and governmental agencies. Some of my ideas are based on this center's work. When I attended one of its seminars, I was struck by the similarity between its approach and goals and the work of the family therapist. Families in turmoil can use these negotiating methods quite well without professional help. This process is especially suitable for the family of "equals," made up of parents and adult-children, not usually the target group for family therapy. (More information about family therapists is provided in Chapter 10.)

What follows is an outline of topics that you will want to consider and perhaps include in your negotiation process:

1. *Search for mutual gain.* Developing a win-win strategy is an imperative step. Since this process is anything but easy, everyone involved needs reassurance that there is something in it for them. Young adults tend to feel that they have gone along with the family agenda for their whole lives and may not be willing to give up having things on their own terms. Conversely,

parents believe that they have sacrificed and given much more than they have received, and they are not interested in more of the same.

It is useful for the parties on both sides to try to communicate what they would like to happen for them or what they could live with as an outcome. What this really means is that neither will feel exploited and both will feel they've gained something valuable.

A young man lived about an hour's drive away from his parents. He understood his mother's desire to stay connected with him, and he felt guilty when he avoided contact with her. His subtle attempts to regulate the relationship did not succeed because he wasn't clear and specific about what he wanted: a way of protecting his mother's feelings. He felt desperate when he began the negotiation process with his parents: "I would be ecstatic if you could give me room to develop and not demand to be part of my everyday life. I feel you are stifling me, and that's why I stay away. I would be willing to have a phone conversation once a week. In fact, I would enjoy that, especially if I can let you know when you are probing too much." His mother's response, her own "win" scenario, went as follows: "You are a very important part of my life, and I really want to have more contact with you than you are willing to agree to. But I can live with weekly phone contacts as long as they aren't as superficial as the ones I have with the plumber. I'm afraid of that possibility, but I'll try to let you know if I am feeling that way."

Keep in mind that this little vignette is very specific and is stated in behavioral terms, that is, selecting the specific behavior changes needed by each to make the negotiation successful. If what each party wants is vague or nonspecific, it will be really difficult to measure success. "I want you to love me more" is a wish that is probably universal, but there are no guidelines for carrying it out or for knowing precisely when it happens.

2. *Take stock of common issues, shared beliefs, and values.* Establish a common ground. This provides reassurance that not everything is in need of change. Clearly, a variety of issues may be

bringing you into conflict, but there is also something keeping you from calling it quits and walking away.

It may be only shared history or shared genetic material that binds you together, but that's a starting point in negotiating. Since you want to put some effort into improving the relationship, you probably share much more (e.g., a sense of humor, a food preference, and a love of nature). While there's no best way to do this task, it should include all of the family members involved, assembled in one place.

In contemporary family life, the family may be limited to a divorced or widowed mother or father and an adult-child. It may also include a variety of other combinations, including both parents and any number of adult-children. While the goal of this task is serious, it need not be deadly. It can take on the quality of a game that involves everyone, since no special expertise is needed.

3. *Identify the "hot spots."* These are the areas so sensitive to one or both parties that negotiating would come to a halt if these were encountered early in the process. Remember that your goal is to come together, not in the old conflicted pattern, but in a more harmonious way. An old emotional hurt may need to be aired before healing occurs, but working on it before a solid base is laid may result in a fear of further deterioration and in withdrawal.

What are some potential hot spots? Usually these have to do with a young adult's departure from traditional values. Has an adult-child chosen an alternative or "unacceptable" lifestyle, sexual preference, partner, career, or political party? People have very strong emotional reactions to these kinds of choices. Identify the issues, but agree to table them for now.

4. *Develop a problem-solving process.* Remember that change in the way we do things or the way we think about things is slow. If it were easy, we would all readily adapt to each other's changing needs as we became aware of them. This simply doesn't happen. Instead, the process must take place over time, so that everyone has a chance to move ahead, make mistakes, self-correct, and get

back on track again. Time allows a tentative back-and-forth fine-tuning of the possibilities.

5. *Set objectives, establish priorities, plot a course of action, and work on a time line.* I know that this sounds like a plan for a year-end report or a project proposal, and you may be wondering what it has to do with family life. Again, planning is the first step in the change process in any aspect of daily functioning, and if this process is successful in business, it can be adapted for family use. The main drawback is that it takes some effort. It really is much easier to just let things happen or evolve over time. To get you started with your own planning, I have come up with a composite sample from my own work with young adults and their parents.

Sally and her husband, Mark, were very frustrated by their interactions with Annette, their twenty-eight-year-old daughter, a single parent who lived in another city. Because contact between them was sporadic and usually problem-oriented, there never seemed to be an occasion to work on building a more satisfying relationship. In fact, Annette was comfortable with the current arrangement. She felt that, with the precious little time available, she did not want to spend it locked in a struggle with her parents. The tense status quo seemed to meet her current needs. In this example, it was the midlife parents who were grossly dissatisfied and whose energy provided the necessary impetus for change.

Sally and Mark reluctantly talked with their daughter on her next visit. They were careful to set the stage for a cooperative, joint, win-win venture as outlined above. Annette was initially defensive. She couldn't see how any of this would benefit her, since she liked things the way they were. Her parents had a clear picture of what they wanted to happen, and so they took the lead in this process. They initiated a dialogue that will seem very familiar to many of you: "We feel that, when you come to town, you see our house as a full-service hotel. We care about seeing you and the kids, but you often leave the kids and take off to do your own thing. We feel used." The defensive daughter replied,

"Maybe you don't want to see us. I thought you enjoyed seeing the kids. You make me feel guilty and selfish, and right now I wish I hadn't come."

While this is a predictable reaction, it's important to push beyond it. These parents didn't get sucked into their daughter's negative feelings. Instead, they stated what they wanted to happen, what was most important, and a time frame for implementation: "We want to know in advance when you're coming, and to have you check with us to see if it's OK. We both work, and as much as we would like to see you and accommodate you, sometimes our separate plans won't work with yours. We also can't always be depended on to baby-sit. You need to ask, and we need to be free to say 'no.' Of course, we want to spend some time with you, not just the kids."

Annette initially reacted with hurt and anger because she had never seen her parents as separate people outside the parent role. Yet the adult part of her could accept their concern and their request for change. In fact, in some inexplicable way, this dialogue helped to foster her sense of equality with her parents— who were no longer there to anticipate and meet all of her needs. She agreed to try to meet their terms, and they all decided to take another look at how things were going in three months.

6. *Minimize potential misunderstanding.* Make the terms of the agreement definite enough. Harriet Lerner, author of *The Dance of Intimacy* (1989), focuses on taking a stand in working through conflict between parents and adult children. She points out that "the degree to which we can be clear with our first family about who we are, what we believe, and where we stand on important issues will strongly influence the level of independence or emotional maturity" (p. 189). Being clear by putting the specifics in writing may increase commitment and compliance. You may want to resist at this point because putting things in writing makes them sound so terribly formal. Certainly, you can bypass this step but be prepared to carry it out down the road if anyone says, "I didn't remember agreeing to that."

As an alternative to writing out your agreement, you may

want to tape-record your discussion and make copies as necessary. In my experience, people usually want to honor an agreement, especially one of which there is a permanent record! If I am being asked to alter my behavior and it takes some effort, I am likely to remember what is most convenient. Memory is often colored by wants and wishes. On the other hand, I'm sure you know how easy it is to remember those things that are truly important to you.

7. *Assume a cooperative stance; it tends to be mirrored.* Cooperation is experienced as psychological movement *toward* the other person. In contrast, an aggressive stance is felt as a move *against*. It makes sense that a withdrawal stance is felt as a move *away*. Because these are sometimes subtle signals, keep in mind how your approach will be interpreted, and try to assess what you are communicating even without words.

8. *Demonstrate your willingness to participate and adapt.* Make a good-faith or token gesture. This can be a hug or an immediate action. For example, Sarah had become increasingly annoyed during her visits with her parents. Her father had never been one to show his feelings. His style was on the stoic side, but deep down Sarah and her siblings knew he cared.

The annoyance she felt was not new, but now that Sarah saw her parents infrequently, she resented his behavior even more. Her father appeared bored with talk. According to her, "Dad's idea of being there was to be in the room but disappear into the sofa, and away from the family. He only seemed to show interest in the newspaper or TV." Previously, her discomfort had been vague; she had felt upset with her dad but wasn't sure why. Now she was clear that his behavior made her feel insignificant and angry at the same time. On the day that she finally communicated her dissatisfaction, she really didn't expect anything to happen. She was amazed with delight when her father remained in the room, interested and attentive, following the family chat. He stayed for the duration which was his way of saying he cared. According to him, he hadn't known that his behavior was such a problem to Sarah. Of course, this awareness marked a beginning, not an ending. Still, how simple, but powerful, a token gesture can be!

Being Clear

In the best of all possible worlds, what is said by one person is perfectly understood by the other. In reality, our communications fall very far short of this ideal. Being misunderstood is an all-too-common phenomenon. Add to this the difficulty of being clear with someone who doesn't understand or care about your point of view, and the challenge is apparent!

When the communication process has been disrupted by bad feelings between people, it is likely that all the verbal exchanges will take place at more than one level. Hidden messages and innuendos are sent in addition to what is actually said. A simple statement made by a hurt parent to his or her indifferent adult-child will probably communicate much more than was intended. Also, the response will seem distorted or defensive to the parent receiving it. Unchecked, the dialogue takes on a life of its own, and both parties feel misunderstood, hurt, defensive, and/or angry. Whatever follows this interchange will be a wasted effort or, worse, a confirmation that no communication is really possible!

Here is a typical telephone miscommunication: "I'm calling because I haven't heard from you in a while. You must be busy, and I thought you might be under a lot of stress on your new job."

Angela meant well in her opening statement, but she triggered some discomfort in her son, Fred, when she referred to the "stress" of his "new job." This feeling, combined with his mother's worried voice and her tendency to probe for his problems, led him to snap back at her: "Can't you ever start a conversation by simply saying, 'How are you'? I don't know why you look for ways to make me feel bad. I haven't called for a while because I've been busy, but there's nothing really wrong. I have a lot of things on my mind—its normal!"

Fred defended himself angrily. Remembering back over the years of conflict around privacy, he realized that he was still sensitive to his mother's probing. When his grandparents were alive, she had directed some of this "caretaking" to them. He reflected that these annoying ways of showing she cared had probably been learned from her own parents. Simply understanding did not fix the problem. He still felt attacked, and his voice conveyed impatience and irritation. He thought to himself, "Same old thing; here she goes again."

The strong reaction was not so much to what his mother said as it was to her tone of voice (nonverbal cues), her history of probing for problems (assumptions), and her offering of unsolicited emotional support. These combined to make Fred feel less than adequate.

Even in the brief exchange that took place between this mother and son, they managed to sidetrack the conversation. They steered it away from any current topic back to the old, tired, but familiar war zone where they continued to battle. Neither side heard either the words or the intended meanings. Both acted out an ancient script, generations old, in which Angela wanted something and Fred felt intruded on and held back.

Analyzing this scenario points out some rules for clarifying communication that lead to a more positive outcome:

1. *Pay attention to the tone of your own voice.* Does it sound whiny, demanding, irritated, upset? Be aware that your feelings will be communicated even if your words say something else. You may want to postpone your phone call until you feel better, so that your feelings and what you say have a better opportunity to match. Otherwise, the "receiver" will have to choose between your verbal and your nonverbal messages and may not choose what you intended. (Remember the double messages and mixed messages in Chapter 6.)

2. *Be certain that your message has been received correctly.*

The receiver, because of a history of misunderstanding and misinterpretation, needs to provide feedback on what she or he heard. This provision of feedback should be agreed upon in advance to prevent a mutual nit-picking session in which the total picture is lost.

A simple procedure to follow is to restate what was heard. For example, "I heard you say that I don't call you often enough." Sam reflects what he thought he heard but missed the mark. Because he said what he thought he heard, his mother now has the opportunity to clarify both what she said and what she meant. She might now say, "I didn't mean to tell you that you don't call often enough, only that it has been a while. I recognize that you are busy, so instead of waiting I picked up the phone myself. There is no blame attached." The replay allows another chance to avoid unpleasant feelings leading to an impasse.

3. *Avoid sidetracking.* Stay with the current dialogue, and don't bring into the conversation old agendas that are activated by your bad feelings. If your son hasn't called you for a while, it is probably not important to remind him. Rather, you are calling to make contact and to share some information. Stick to your goal. Talk about what you have been doing and other family information, and ask him plainly what he has been doing. If his response is defensive, don't be sidetracked. Get back to your reason for calling.

Poor timing is another way of sidetracking the communication process. Try to assess whether the timing is right before launching into a sensitive subject. Timing is off, for example, when either party has had a bad day. If your goal, however, is to evade sensitive subjects or to avoid dealing with your concerns, then poor timing is a useful tactic!

4. *Maintain a focus on the present.* Try to stay away from past mistakes or future fears and fantasies. The phone conversation is about you and him, now, at this moment in time. This is an opportunity for the two of you to connect, separate and apart from the pain of the past and the uncertainty of the future.

Statements that include such key judgmental phrases as

"you always" or "you never" or value-loaded words such as *right,
wrong, good, bad, better,* or *worse* should be avoided. Rather,
focus on the common issues that are currently relevant. Rehearse
ahead of time, if necessary, so that your statements, questions,
and observations will be presented as clearly as possible.

5. *Offer help only when asked.* Adult-children are very sensitive and ambivalent about help or support from their parents.
Even when they desperately need it, and perhaps especially
when their need is the greatest, they are inclined to become
angry rather than grateful. For this reason, it is best to respond to
their need when they initiate it. Otherwise, you are responding to
their need before they are aware of it or before they are comfortable sharing it with you, and you may activate a child–parent
interaction that is intolerable to them and will become punitive
to you. The acceptance of support needs to be clear and explic-
itly agreed to.

6. *Reframe the issues when necessary.* Clarity is enhanced by
saying things differently. "Let me say this another way . . ." is a
good way to start. Perhaps a new context will move the discussion to a less emotionally charged arena, where hurt and anger
won't interfere as much with what you are really saying.

Here is an example of reframing that Angela could try when
it appears that Fred has misunderstood: "Let me say this again a
different way. I called you because I wanted to, with no strings
attached. I called you because I miss the contact with you. I am
doing what makes me feel good. I am not calling you to make
you feel bad." Saying things a bit differently may allow the words
to pass through the defensive receiver's invisible screening-out
device.

An alternate statement might be "Let me start over. You know
how you call friends you haven't heard from lately? You are glad
to hear their voice and to find out how things are going with
them. You don't have any other motive. Well, neither do I." This
way of phrasing things places the conversation in a context that
is pleasant and comfortable and outside the war zone where the
meaning of things becomes so distorted.

Maintaining Flexibility

At the beginning of this chapter, Mary's holiday dilemma was discussed. She had offered her parents the perfect compromise, or so she thought. Much to her disappointment, her parents seemed unbending, which led to an impasse. The need for greater flexibility was clear, but in this apparent power struggle, neither side wished to capitulate.

For some inexplicable reason, the idea of "backing down" met with tremendous resistance. If this notion could be reframed so that compromise had a more positive feel, then some progress might be made toward a new balance in the relationship. Remember that Mary had already shifted the balance by deciding to visit her parents differently from before. No amount of talk or coercion would make her want to change her mind. In fact, precisely because she was now an adult, she would cling to her stance and exert the equal power that she expected to share with her parents.

The wise parents, at this point, might be looking toward accommodation and see this as an opportunity for growth rather than as a sign of loss. This is more easily said than done. Unfortunately, loss is often experienced first, and it may get in the way of compromise. The losses are real, of course, and as presented earlier in this book, they spell an end to the parent–child family model and to the old methods of communicating and problem solving.

If our children are now adults, are we, as parents, obsolete? If we let go of things the way they are, will our relationship erode even further? These are significant and fearful issues. With the passage of time and the dwindling of future time, we may feel an urgency to build new bridges to our adult-children's lives.

This may be a good time to consider the value of bending, which is not necessarily the same as "giving in." The earlier concept of balance comes from the field of physics. The notion of bending comes from the field of physics also. Bending is a process that discourages breaking. In a strong wind, flexible trees bend. Rigid ones break. Likewise, buildings that meet earthquake standards have a built-in flexibility that reduces the possibility of collapse. Even a steel structure can be made flexible!

Flexibility is a critical tool in reworking relationships between parents and adult-children. It helps to have some guidelines for making flexibility a palatable as well as a workable idea. Consider the following:

1. *Change takes place over time.* Flexibility is also increased over time. Gradually, like pulling gently on a piece of taffy, the tension gives way to stretching and a new equilibrium. When changes are suggested, try to keep them as gradual as possible. Stretching too far too fast is likely to be resisted, by people and by taffy!

Mary's holiday visit plan, presented at the beginning of the chapter, was a departure from the past but not a drastic change. Certainly, it could have been more gradual or still more extreme. A more extreme position would have been the decision not to visit at all or to invite her parents to visit her for the holidays on her own turf. These positions would make accommodation very unlikely. Most parents would not be able to assimilate so much change at once.

2. *Don't look for a single solution.* There is no right answer, and no bells will ring if you arrive at a good resolution. Instead, this guideline suggests an open attitude that allows searching for new ways rather than the *one* way. If you think that bending in a certain direction is the only possibility, then think again. I have seen numerous impasses come about even when both sides think they are flexible and agree to consider an alternative, if they rigidly adhere to the new position when it's not acceptable to the other person. For example, Fred's mother, in her haste to relieve the tension between them, volunteered to give up calling her son. This was a sacrifice that was· intended to show her flexibility. Fred, however, felt that this arrangement put the whole responsibility of communication on his shoulders. Your idea of flexible may not be what the other person had in mind. Give that person an opportunity to help you self-correct.

Mary was disappointed by her parents' unwillingness to accept her decision to vary her vacation plans. She could maintain her stand and try to convince her parents that her way was best. An alternative plan would be to hold firm and not try to convince her parents—but this would lead to an impasse. A more flexible approach would create other options. It would require her to think about her priorities to achieve major goals while letting go of only minor points.

Her more flexible statement might look like this: "I very much want to have my Christmas plans the way I arranged them, but I can see that you feel hurt by that. I really do want time for myself, and ten days away from my own place feels much too long. I would be willing to stay an extra day or would welcome a visit from you the following weekend." Here Mary has provided two alternatives and has made it easier for her parents to accept her changing needs. They also get to have a choice.

3. *Be aware of blocks to new ideas.* "Yes but . . ." is the monkey wrench that stops the wheel from turning. New ideas are always tentative, and their consideration doesn't require their implementation. Besides, creativity must be nurtured, and this won't happen if there are too many stumbling blocks in the way.

Blocking new ideas is rarely a planned strategy for sabotage, even if it seems that way. Rather, it is a defensive maneuver based on fear of change. Prematurely closing off new ideas serves to reduce anxiety. Acknowledging the discomfort of trying new ways may be all that is necessary to get on with the process. Considering new ways to behave and interact is never easy for anyone—this is definitely something on which you both can agree. Give plenty of time for "What if . . ."

Envisioning the Future

1. *Imagine the possibilities.* No matter how much information is available, it's hard to break out of the old circular track. Sometimes it helps to imagine the possibilities, the "what if"

prospects, in bridging the distance between your life and your child's life.

• How do I want things to be between us? There are no standard dimensions for relationships. They can come in all sizes and shapes. Clearly, it takes two people in agreement to make something happen. But if you are imagining the possibilities, none of the limitations need to be considered at this point. What is necessary is an unclouded picture of what *you* want, what *you* can tolerate given the reality of your differences. Here is a case in point.

The mother of a twenty-year-old woman who was mentally retarded had never stopped to think about what she wanted in a relationship with her daughter. It had never occurred to her that she could think about such a thing. Since Andrea had been a baby, the focus had always been on helping the family adapt to the needs of a special child. As a parent, Marjorie had committed herself to making sure that her daughter received respect and dignity at school and in the community: "It hasn't been an easy life when I look back over the past two decades. I always had to pay such close attention to everything that others take for granted, and it certainly put a strain on the family, which may have contributed to my divorce. But my relationship with Andrea is strong and loving, and I feel blessed to have her in my life."

When asked what she wanted for the future, Marjorie replied with surprise, "I never thought about what I wanted. I've always just responded. I just do what needs to be done, take each day and problem as it comes. I'm a little shocked and excited that I can go beyond that—but I also don't trust that I really can."

There is something very freeing about imagining the possibilities. It is a way of shaking loose the shackles that bind you to currently limiting circumstances. This mother took the task very seriously. Although she was worried that such thinking would lead to disappointment, there was a certain excitement about the task that gave her energy. She liked the feeling: "I want to see a time ahead in which Andrea and I can have a more normal relationship. She really is capable of living independently in a sheltered community. She has the potential to work. But here I am thinking about what's good for her and not what *I* want to see happen. It's so easy to get sidetracked. As for myself, I want to spend time with Andrea but less time than now. I would like to see her develop her own life, to the extent that she can. I would also like to make some changes in my own, perhaps toward my own independence. I would look forward to our phone conversations and getting together once a week or even once a month later on."

It was very difficult for this mother to stay clear of current realities and let herself dream. Still, it didn't take long for this process to lead her to the first steps of change. When she began to take her dreams more seriously, change began to take place, and the resulting sense of satisfaction led to more change. Looking back, it seems that some of her hopes did indeed become realized.

• What are the current realities? What changes can I make now? Tony's son had joined a religious community with beliefs that seemed alien and rituals that made this father very uncomfortable. For the time being, he was satisfied with weekly phone contact. Actually, he was relieved because in-person get-togethers seemed too tense and irritating. He needed time to understand his son's lifestyle and sort out the reasons behind George's decision to join a "cult." In some vague way, he felt that he must have let George down. The guilt that gnawed at him served as a reminder that he must be responsible for George's situation.

Tony wasn't really sure what he wanted in the long run. His relationship with his son had been stalemated for months. He needed time to think, to understand, but the longer the time that passed without contact, the more overwhelming any potential contact felt. Phone conversations limited to safe subjects were a possibility and eased this father's pain.

• "What if I . . . ?" This step gives your imagination wings. It allows you to try out new ideas, thoughts, and wishes. You may produce totally unworkable and unrealistic notions, but production of *new* information is the goal. Seldom do we let imagination prevail without being critical and judgmental. We tend to shoot down our dreams almost as fast as we come up with them. Here the goal is to write them down, however silly and trivial. Sure, you will discard a great many items, but if you identify even one workable new idea, you may be giving yourself the key to unlocking the circle that entraps you.

A father was estranged from his twenty-five-year-old daughter, Doris. It was not a sudden rift but a process of growing apart that had taken place over many years. During her early years, she had lived with her mother, his former wife. When he finally had a chance to get to know her as an adult, he found that her values were very far from his fundamentalist religious beliefs. Anger and intolerance severed their somewhat tenuous ties. While this father grieved and felt the pain of his loss, he felt unable and unwilling to "give in."

He wished for a solution, and one came to mind. The idea was to send Doris a postcard each week just to say, "Hi." It could be newsy or it could pertain to family matters. It really didn't matter. Of course, his first tendency was to discard this idea when his rational side responded.

Still, it really didn't matter that Doris might not respond because Dad was acting on his own behalf. He was trying to keep some form of contact alive until he could come up with another solution.

2. *Learn to brainstorm the possibilities.* Brainstorming is a process that depends on the rapid-fire presentation of new ideas and associations without interruption. It allows you to be creative, without the constraints that reason usually dictates. Everyone involved contributes as much as he or she can about a certain topic in the form of words or phrases, and these are written on a large sheet of paper for everyone to see. The participants are allowed to offer no negative comments. The idea is quantity, not quality, and strange ideas may generate useful ones in time. An idea can be useful even if it doesn't work. Remember, the success of the brainstorming process depends on a lively flow of ideas.

No judging or criticizing of offerings is permitted because that makes people self-conscious and reduces creative thinking.

The process looks chaotic because it purposely lacks order to maximize the creative flow of ideas. Usually, a time limit is set, after which the ideas are looked at, sorted, and clarified. The remaining piece of paper contains many ideas, some of which are impossible or improbable. Nevertheless, it becomes a jumping-off point for creating new options and is also a symbol of your openness to change.

Brainstorming is also a natural tool for envisioning the future. It gives you a chance to look at the future without the constraints that a logical, reality-based approach depends on. You can use your creativity to think beyond the obvious possibilities for building a satisfying relationship between the generations in your family.

Most people are so involved in the daily problem solving of life that the idea of working on future possibilities seems beyond reach. Yet I am often amazed to find that people can plan work and financial goals for years ahead. They can outline and track their career paths for a decade. Even recreational activities are thought out well in advance. People commit themselves to buying a "place for retirement" or a recreational vehicle that will require monthly payments for a long time. Vacations are sometimes budgeted for years before the actual trip takes place. The media aid us in this process by providing magazine articles, news stories, and commercials that pique our interest in work and recreational outlooks. In contrast to retirement planning, working on relationship goals for five or ten years in advance is seldom considered.

We behave as if the stability of our relationships is the one aspect of life that is unchanging. Understandably, it is hard to see daily changes in the way we look at or the way we see and feel things. It is still harder to recognize and acknowledge the changes in others close to us. We are jolted into noticing that our children are no longer babies, children, or adolescents: "Where has the time gone?" "Why haven't I noticed that she or he was changing?" We mark the passage of time with surprise and sadness at losing what was so precious. We tend to want to capture the moment or the past moments and generally try to slow down the passage of time. Again, acknowledgment of our kids' changing activates the dreaded feelings associated with our own aging. Yet in avoiding that potential pain, we are painting a future that is built on a past that no longer exists.

One way to minimize the impact of eroding time is to build a future that is equally exciting and meaningful, even if it is different. Look ahead and anticipate the needs of your family members at various points of time in the future. Contemplate the ways you will need to adapt to changes that have yet to happen. In most relationships, we tend to wear blinders as we move forward into a future that seems strange and unsettling. But that can be changed!

Although you can't predict the future with any accuracy, you can look at the current lifestyles of young adults ages twenty-five to forty to better understand the typical struggles or issues. Talk to young people five or ten years older than your own children, and learn about their interests, conflicts, and relationships with their own parents. These may give you some ideas about ways to grow, adapt, and prepare for the needs of the future.

What would you like the next year, the next five years, even the next ten years to look like? If you have newly established adult-children now, what will they need from you when they are twenty-five or thirty-five? What sort of relationship would you like to have with them? What can you do right now to enhance the chances of succeeding?

Envisioning the future offers a starting point for planning with your adult-children. It requires some research because you will probably be starting with long-held or stereotyped ideas about what the future can be, and so will your children. You need to probe beyond these fixed ideas. Discuss the idea of planning in advance with your adult-children so that they have the opportunity to think about and explore what they see in their future.

Allow ample time for research by collecting information from as many sources as possible. You might want to read the observations of some of the leading futurists, who forecast change. Here are some authors and titles to get you started: J. Gerber, *Life Trends: Your Future for the Next 30 Years* (1991); J. Naisbitt, *Megatrends: Ten New Directions Transforming Our Lives* (1982); and A. Toffler, *Future Shock* (1970) and *Previews and Premises* (1983).

A more practical approach to research might include looking at other families or individuals who seem like good role models. Allow time for talking to people you admire who are at different life stages. Perhaps a retired family member can offer a retrospective glance and philosophy that will give you some new ideas.

To aid your research, take another look at Chapter 1 of this book. It is based on a lengthy questionnaire and interview process. The results were grouped and summarized into statements by adults of every age group, describing the kind of relationship they would value (or would have valued) with their parents. You are likely to find a few ideas there. Remember, all the individuals surveyed were giving a retrospective picture based on their experiences as well as their wishes. Some of these ideas will seem implausible and some fantastic, but your goal at this point is idea collection. Those that don't fit or work can be discarded later.

When the time has come for the actual brainstorming, you can follow the rules discussed above. Your prior information gathering will allow new ideas to get an airing, even if they are later rejected.

Here is a sample brainstorm that will give you a tangible picture of what you can expect to see. Notice that the items are not arranged in any order, just listed as they were dreamed up. Later they could be grouped, clarified, or tossed out:

get-togethers
equality

doing activities together
respect
mutual respect
freedom versus obligation
friendship
new roles
I don't want to baby-sit (Mother)
I do want to baby-sit in five years (Father)
value me as a person
trust me
go fishing (shopping) together
open talking without rank-pulling
politeness; don't take me for granted
short visits
interdependence
no guilt
no strings attached
comfort
enjoy watching me live my life
be honest no matter what
I don't need you
relationship based on appreciation
no demands
I want to be included
share
mutual sharing
no one's in charge

This activity took only fifteen minutes once it got started. It was a first attempt that did not focus on specific time frames in the future. Again, this is a creative process, and when you become involved on your own, you will do it in the way that best suits you. The greatest benefit of this exercise is that the process of looking forward becomes associated with positive anticipation rather than fear. It is a tool that can be used over and over again, and it provides a structure that is safe. Best of all, no one loses!

Letting Go

Letting go is both an attitude and a behavior, perhaps the most difficult step in "getting it together." It acknowledges that whatever you have accomplished so far, and whatever your wishes and hopes for the future, the final version of your relationship will fall short of your expectations. It is a disappointing fact of reality that nothing will match your dreams of harmony or absolute goodness. Understanding this reality in advance allows you to appreciate any changes that are positive instead of concentrating on the conflicts that won't budge. You and your adult-children will never see eye to eye totally. There will always be some unfinished business from the past that interferes with your longed-for scenario. Being happy depends on accepting what *is* rather than demanding what *could be*. This is like looking at the garden you toiled to cultivate and noticing how fine it is, notwithstanding the few weeds or the crabgrass.

Taking this step requires an awareness and acceptance of the limitations of another person in successfully meeting and fulfilling your needs. It means giving up some childhood fantasies about how parents and children are *supposed* to be. It means living with the ultimate disappointment that you will never be loved and understood perfectly.

Before you protest that these ideas had never even occurred to you, it's important to know that these are basic human wants that everyone has. These struggles are primarily unconscious. Rather than beating yourself for having these needs for perfect harmony and sensitivity, just understand that the needs exist. Then you can learn how to minimize the psychological pain that accompanies your awareness.

This was Arlene's experience. At twenty-four, she had just undergone surgery following an auto accident, and she was frightened and in pain. Her husband had been supportive and comforting. Her dad and her sister had shown their concern, and Arlene felt that she was lucky and should have appreciated the caring that had been shown to her. Instead there was something missing that made her very sad and depressed. She sought some professional help at this point because, although she continued to improve physically, she felt more sad and empty than ever. It still seemed as if something was missing from her life that, when found, would allow her to feel happy again. It appeared that she was putting her life on hold while she looked for the missing puzzle piece.

It didn't take long to find out that her mother was the missing piece. Arlene had built a very successful life for herself and had achieved all that she had set out to do. She felt good about her accomplishments and had previously been so busy that she had managed to avoid the sadness connected with her mother. Fortunately (although it didn't seem fortunate at the time), her recuperation had given her plenty of free time, with no pressing jobs to distract her. She realized that her estranged relationship with her mother was causing her much grief. At her request, no one had notified her mother of her accident. At the same time, she was angry that, once again, her mother was not going to be there to care for her. This awareness bothered her because she had told herself for years that her mother was a "lost cause" and could not be depended on. It angered her to think that, in spite of all the caring she had received from her family, what she had really wanted was her mother's attention.

Arlene's mother had been an alcoholic through much of Arlene's childhood and adolescence. As a survival measure, Arlene had successfully repressed her angry feelings so that life would be more bearable. All of the milestones in Arlene's life had been contaminated by her mother's undependable behavior. Her mother had been drunk at the time of her senior prom. Her mother had missed her high school and college graduations. Arlene had learned not to rely on her mother at all. But now, at this crisis point, the annoying wish to be cared for had intruded into Arlene's consciousness.

This very basic wish, to be loved and perfectly understood by a good and nurturing mother, made her furious, as well as sad.

She had rejected that wishful feeling and tried to stuff it away in her mind. But still she couldn't get herself to move ahead with her life. She was definitely stuck, and until she could truly "let go" of her disappointment, she would be unable to move on.

Arlene finally did move on, but not before she took a good look at the roadblocks in her path. In thinking about her struggle and the similar efforts of others with whom I have worked, the following ideas seem to be relevant tracks that need to be covered in the process of "letting go":

1. *Let go of what you can't change.* Arlene's mother had grave limitations associated with her alcoholism. She was still drinking and would continue to be undependable. It wasn't Arlene's fault that this was the case, and as much as she would have liked to, she couldn't make her mother behave differently. Similarly, if you are the parent of an adult-child who is a substance abuser, or who has a lifestyle that is unacceptable to you, be prepared to give up the fantasy that, with enough love and caring, he or she will change.

This "letting go" is incredibly hard because it means coming to grips with the fact that your parent or child will never be the same as you, never be a perfect mirror of your needs, values, and hopes. It means that you will never be perfectly understood, cared for, or reassured. No one will be able to read your mind, see what you want, and give you what you need—without asking. Nothing in life is more difficult to admit, and nothing is harder to accept. Yet, for most of us, the awareness of this disappointment, although painful, is not intolerable. The first step is adequate grieving for this profound loss.

2. *Recognize and stay clear of the areas that can't be resolved.* Whatever relationship *is* possible depends on your ability to work around the impasse. It's important to see that some kind of contact is possible, allowing some mutual sharing of lives, without focusing on the area of impasse. Arlene felt that she was not ready to reject her mother totally or permanently but knew that depending on her, in any way, would only activate old hurt feel-

ings. She realized that, in most of her interactions with her mother, she looked for opportunities to remind this woman of how her drinking spoiled everything. Not surprisingly, on these occasions, her mother would become defensive or hostile, and the circular scenario would play itself out in very predictable ways. Both sides would lose sight of the purpose of the contact, and it would always end in hurt and disappointment.

But the unresolvable conflict between you and your adult-child can be avoided. Making this happen depends on your willingness to let go of what you can't change and to find something mutually satisfying on which to build a new foundation. Arlene decided that limiting contact to just family events and holidays would be possible. She tended to be less critical of her mother with others around. Also, even limited and superficial contact made her feel more "normal." Excluding her mother caused her to feel defensive and guilty. Clearly, this was not an ideal relationship, but it did leave the door open for future possibilities.

3. *Accept each interaction in good faith.* The hurt and the pain of the past will never disappear, but it can be left in the past. Assuming that you and your family truly wish to find healthy ways to connect, you need to be willing to suspend your suspiciousness and critical eye.

When Arlene's mother sent her a birthday present, rather than appreciating her mother's effort, Arlene became enraged by this "superficial gesture." She immediately launched into a tirade about her mother's past track record of forgetting all sorts of important events. Her anger from past hurts blurred her ability to see the present display of caring. True, this gift would never make up for past mistakes, but Arlene's mother really didn't have an ulterior motive in sending it. What would it take for Arlene to accept the good wishes in good faith?

It took some work for Arlene to see that the gift was not intended as a peace offering for the past. That would never happen, nor would Arlene ever accept it. Still, the gesture was real and meaningful and needed to be seen in the context of the here and now. This gift would not repair the past, but it could be acknowledged and remembered as one good experience with the Mother, perhaps the first of many. If you are the hurt parent, can you also find the ability to accept current tokens of caring without tieing them to past injury?

4. *Proceed slowly.* Once you've decided to work toward a more positive relationship, it's easy to get carried away with anticipation. Old hopes, wishes, and fantasies are rekindled. Instead of working toward mutual respect, acceptance, and tolerance of differences, there is a tendency to aim for perfect harmony and perfect understanding—today!

Looking at interactions one at a time allows you to grow separately and together. If you can accept each positive interaction as a sign of caring and effort, then it will also be easier to tolerate the occasional bombs. When an interaction is unsatisfactory, it's crucial to see it as one interaction and not as a repeat of past history or a preview of pain to come.

Doris is a woman in her mid-forties. Her son, Frank, is a college senior, living about five hundred miles away. Over the years, there has been a great deal of tension between them. Frank's parents divorced when Frank was eight or nine. Often there was competition for Frank's time and attention. His choice to live with his father was painful to Doris because she lost the day-to-day contact with her son.

Judith Wallerstein is an expert on family life following divorce. Since the early 1970s, she has studied the consequences of divorce for parents and children. Her landmark book, *Second Chances: Men, Women and Children a Decade after Divorce* (1989), written with S. Blakeslee, describes the life experiences of several families. These authors find that, even ten years later, there are lingering feelings of hurt, anger, and rejection that need to be acknowledged and then resolved:

> Loyalty conflicts, sometimes flipping from one parent to the other and back again, are a common experience. . . . Even when children are encouraged not to take sides, they often feel that they must. However, when they do take sides to feel

> more protected, they also feel despair because they are be-
> traying one parent over the other. (p. 13)

These issues are exaggerated for the noncustodial parent.

> The visiting parent is a new kind of parent, and there are no
> proven guidelines for how to maintain this relationship suc-
> cessfully. Few visiting parents and children do not have
> some question as they part, about the forthcoming visit.
> (p. 17)

Misunderstandings persist for years and feed a sense of rejection
and failure. Tension often remains high until a healing process is
begun.

Doris hoped for a turning point in her relationship with
Frank: "When Frank left for college, I was relieved. I believed the
tension would subside. But he continued to live with his father
when he was not at school. That hurt me, and I couldn't seem to
hide my feelings. Frank was defensive and often angry at me
whenever the subject was even close to being raised. It made for
very tense phone calls and increasingly rare visits. We were prac-
tically at a standoff in communications when I finally decided to
do something about it."

Doris painstakingly went through the process detailed in
this chapter. Thinking about things differently and trying out
new ways of talking, listening, and negotiating had a positive
effect. A challenge still remained. Placing so much importance on
a single interaction could forecast "happily ever after" or "doom"
in the way she viewed their relationship.

She discussed her latest phone call. She had tried to stay
grounded in the present time rather than recalling old pain or
wishful thinking about the future: "It was not easy to hear him
say that he would not be visiting during his summer vacation. We
didn't discuss this as we would have in the past. Instead we
focused on what each of us would be doing. He was more talka-
tive than usual, and I found myself very excited and happy to be
having such an upbeat conversation. Then I understood that
letting go of old baggage and expectations made a lot of differ-

ence. It may not always feel so good to talk with Frank, but I won't forget how good it felt *this* time."

As the saying goes, "This is the first day of the rest of your life." Keep in mind that each successful effort you make increases the likelihood that more will follow. Today truly does have an effect on all the tomorrows s'.ll to come.

Part III

BUILDING YOUR
OWN TOMORROW

Midlife! A dead end, a turning point, a time for reevaluation and retuning, an opportunity for shifting gears? It can be all or none of these things. However you look at it, this is a time in the life cycle that never existed at all until the twentieth century. Five decades ago, midlife was viewed as the end of the line, where the formal jobs and assigned roles of life ran out, and a passive wait began.

Taking a very broad perspective of the life span in history, Donald Donohugh, author of *The Middle Years* (1981), underscores the recency of the midlife concept:

> Fossil remains of prehistoric eras show that the average age at death then was about 18. In Greek and Roman times it was still in the twenties. Throughout the next millenium and more it hovered around 30. At the start of this century, it was still just thirty-seven. . .∴. People who are now 45 have already lived as long as the average person born in 1900 could expect to live. (p. 5)

Thanks, in part, to the increase in the life span, midlife has become more than an idea. Also contributing to this development is a social phenomenon that has allowed more flexible roles for men and women. No longer is it necessary or even tolerable to play out the life scenario as it was traditionally defined by society, family, and maybe you.

There are a number of changes that take place at midlife. The body, for example, shows signs of aging that are no longer subtle. Hair may become noticeably thinner or show a dramatic loss of color. Previously good near vision may seem to deteriorate overnight. Work, once interesting, may have lost its luster. Family challenges shift as a generation passes. We use these cues to clock ourselves, to mark the passage of time. These milestones also indicate a turning point in life's direction. Momentum builds and leads us to try fresh ways of experiencing life.

Now that your children are grown, the demands of day-to-day parenting are behind you. The skill building necessary to tighten or repair relationships with your adult-children has begun. The struggles of everyday life have changed. The focus of life has shifted. New ways are sought to give life meaning.

The awareness of death is also a strong motivating life force at this stage. The generation of parents, aunts, and uncles is passing in front of us. More of our contemporaries succumb to illnesses and die "before their time." These are sobering thoughts, and we start to pay a new kind of attention to our own lives. The sense that time is running out is an impetus to get on with life, to win the race by *making* things happen rather than hoping, wishing, or waiting for desired changes to take place. Midlife signals us to act and, in some cases, makes action possible.

Myths and Old Wives' Tales

Bernice Neugarten is a sociologist and one of the first researchers to study adaptations in midlife. She was surprised by her findings about how women cope with the "empty nest." This is a period when the children have grown and left their family. The parents are alone (as a couple or as single individuals) once again, or perhaps for the first time. Is this a time of great stress and sadness?

According to the myths and old wives' tales, this is a particularly hard time in the life of a woman. Not so, says Dr. Neugarten (1976):

> Rather than being a stressful period for women, the empty nest or postparental stage in the life cycle was associated with a somewhat *higher* level of satisfaction than is found among other women. Evidently for women in this sample, coping with children at home was more taxing and stressful than having their children married and launched into adult society. (p. 19)

This time frame may need to be seen as one of liberation rather than crisis—for both men and women! The ties that bind individuals to work and family begin to loosen, and many experience a sense of relief. It's not that the pace of life slows down or the stresses diminish; rather, the challenges are new and therefore more interesting if not more exciting.

There is a myth that says that men at or close to retirement experience a loss of meaning and a sense of purposelessness. The findings for men in Neugarten's study don't support this view. In fact, some researchers were "unprepared for their discovery of no significant losses in life satisfaction and no increased rates of depression following retirement" (p. 19).

It's clear that midlife, as a concept, has got a bad name. Midlife simply is not a time for crisis, except where the timing is off. The facts call for a new definition. Ironically, though individuals actually experience midlife as positive, there is still a fearful anticipation of this stage—because of the myths and tales that are just not true, at least not at the end of the twentieth century.

The Issues of Men and Women

There is no shortage of theories about the separate effect of midlife transitions on men and women. The business of living life is certainly carried out in as many ways as there are people. Until midlife, men and women are likely to have different influences pressing on them and yet the basic struggles are not so different. According to Lillian Rubin's research on midlife women (1981), "All spoke to a fundamental theme in women's identity—the distinction they experience between *being* and *doing*. *Being* is internal, *doing* external; *doing* is work, *being* identity" (p. 57).

During the first half of life, so much energy is expended on *doing* the job, whatever it is, however it is defined. Certainly, the jobs of women and men are experienced as different during these earlier times, and an identity is formed around the job: "Unlike men, whose core identity rests with their work, women have an alternative identity—wife and mother—that is central to definitions of self" (Rubin, 1981, p. 176). Interestingly, both men and women are *doing* their job, based partly on their own internal choices and partly on environmental and cultural influences.

Now, at midlife, there is a shift that is natural and inevitable in both men and women. There is a convergence that results in stock taking and then movement toward the development of the weaker part. According to Schlossberg and Troll (1978), psychologists studying older adults, "Men and women seek to develop the unfulfilled aspects of their personalities. This idea connects with the crossover in sex roles . . . as men become more affiliative and women more assertive" (p. 97).

At midlife, men and women begin to feel the need to develop the side of themselves that has remained underdeveloped. For men, it is the more "nurturing" side, and for women, it is the more "aggressive" side. It is as if the whole person cannot really exist until all aspects are tried on and fit.

Mitchell and Helson (1990) studied the factors that define the "prime of life" for women. They suggest that the fifties are the decade in which balance is achieved: "The prime of life for women is a time when various forces converge to support them—the formerly subordinate and adapting sex—in a sense of entitlement and self-efficacy in the real world. It is an opportunity for autonomy, androgyny, and generativity" (p. 168).

George Vaillant (1977) studied ninety-five healthy men over a forty-year period. His work culminated in an insightful and beautifully written book, *Adaptation to Life*. In describing men in their forties, he suggests that if they are depressed it is

> because they are more honestly able to acknowledge their
> own pain. . . . If they are no longer satisfied with their ca-
> reers, it may be because they wish to be of more service to
> those around them. If their marriages are sometimes in dis-
> array and their groping toward love seems adolescent, it
> may be because they are less inhibited than they were in
> their thirties. (p. 222)

Men who have experienced success in the world of work are likely to experience the need to have more meaningful contact with family and friends. They may feel the need to nourish the development of younger people and to take a more active role in society, in the community, or in causes. These needs are natural and timely. After all, only at midlife, when the earlier demands to achieve are no longer primary, can this gentler side be expressed. It may seem obvious to you that men's midlife position is the flip side of women's. Women typically spend the first part of their lives nurturing others and only at midlife have the freedom to choose another path.

Daniel Levinson, a psychologist who pioneered the work on men's adult development, wrote about the five stages in men's life development in his book *The Seasons of a Man's Life* (1978). The fifth stage is the midlife transition. It starts, not surprisingly, in the early forties, and it is reminiscent of the difficult time frame that marks the transition between the teen years and early adulthood, a time of turmoil, as a young man becomes aware of the discrepancy between who he is and who he wants to be.

It means giving up a way of being that is secure and dependable—but no longer valuable. Dissatisfaction with work, marriage, or recreation no longer gets pushed aside and ignored. This is a time to see and then act. It is marked by strong feeling because change is often uncomfortable and distressing. Some men think about working for themselves, tired of building another's business. Other men recognize that their sedentary life has taken a toll on their bodies, which are no longer strong or full of energy. Still others sense a dullness in relationships and may think about fleeing.

Change also means loss, which brings grief—inevitable, unavoidable, and necessary for growth. This can be a time of great uncertainty in a man's life and is sometimes recognized as the "midlife crisis." But the part that makes this stage tolerable is the opportunity for growth and self-development barely beyond reach. The lure of self-development is so characteristically human! When the instinctive, biological demands of life have been met, the search for meaning and personal fulfillment can begin.

No matter where you look, in whatever social class or ethnic group, men at midlife and beyond broaden their view of life to include ways of being that were stifled in the earlier crunch of demands to be productive. Because men live long enough in the 1990s for this stage to happen, it's important to see this as a natural part of the life cycle.

Contemporary psychologists and sociologists readily acknowledge the expanded picture of life after forty, but this is a relatively new phenomenon.

In 1989, J. Oldham, a psychologist contributing to the book *The Middle Years*, discussed a process called the *third individuation*, which, like the second individuation (adolescence), is an important developmental stage. He writes, "Although the third individuation is stressful, it is also a process of growth and maturation, leading to a new equilibrium which can be quite rewarding" (p. 95). This new equilibrium is an important stage in its own right.

When Erik Erikson wrote the classic book *Childhood and Society* in 1950, he described the eight stages of man. When the book was published, there had been very little prior focus on the last stages because adult development was not seen as a separate phase characterized by growth and development. Adulthood had been seen as the vague and amorphous "end of the line," to be mentioned only as a way of marking the end of life. Not so, said Erikson. Although it took another twenty-five years to describe and define these stages adequately, at least he acknowledged them.*

It was Erikson's belief that the last two stages were critical in rounding out a person's life. According to him, the midlife crisis is resolved during the stage of generativity, which he contrasted with stagnation: "Generativity is primarily the interest in establishing and guiding the next generation . . . a parental kind of responsibility" (p. 231).

This is a time for taking stock of who you are and what you know and to begin to share it with the next generation. But as you do so, the unfinished business of self-development is uncovered, and the unrealized hopes and wishes become apparent. Painful stuff! Time is running out, time to take risks and develop what is necessary for fulfillment. Pull out the oil paints, become a tutor, join a bicycling club, go back to school.

Erikson talked only briefly about stage eight: "ego integrity versus despair." Still it's an important stage in providing a sense of closure and satisfaction with life. This is the culminating stage and the one that allows you to see, in retrospect, that you met your goals, satisfied your basic needs, and achieved your humanness. If the midlife issues are successfully resolved, which this book hopes to facilitate, then the backward glance of stage eight will be very satisfying.

Erikson's words say it best:

> Only he who in some way has taken care of things and people and has adapted himself to the trumps and disappointments adherent to being, by necessity the originator of others and the generator of things and ideas—only he may gradually grow the fruit of these seven stages . . . ego integrity. (p. 231)

This is a time for acceptance of your own life as meaningful, worthwhile, and righteous.

---

*In 1950 the reference to "stages of man" presumably included women, although research on life development was generally done on samples of men.

Midlife is a pivotal point and a time of convergence when men and women cross over into the unexplored and unchartered paths of their lives. Schlossberg and Troll (1978) echo this idea:

> In the middle years . . . both sexes may reach a turning point: Many women find that the pivots of their existence are gone. Their children have grown up and no longer need them; they may be widowed or divorced or simply isolated from their husbands by the years of leading separate existences. For their part, men may find that the world of work no longer holds the challenge or the promise that it once did: they have reached the peak of their careers (or have failed to do so and feel that they cannot go any further). It is not surprising, then, that at this point there can be a crossing over of paths and an apparent reshuffling of roles. Looking back on their lives, both sexes may feel that they have missed out on something and thus may redirect their attention to the neglected areas: in the case of men, to human relationships, their own inner selves, the meaning of life; in the case of women, to achievement in the external world. (p. 33)

Robert Bly is a poet and facilitator of men's self-exploration. He talks about men's need to connect by communicating with each other at a level not previously acceptable for men. Until now, that role has been reserved only for women. Connecting, a self-development task appropriate for men, is particularly relevant at midlife.

Curiously, women's midlife task is to learn to "unconnect":

> For most midlife women, becoming mother meant that they aborted their own hopes and dreams and invested them instead in their children. . . . There exists another powerful set of needs and emotions that helps to neutralize the pain—the longing for freedom, the wish to find and claim a well defined and differentiated self, and the relief that, finally, this may be possible. (Rubin, 1981, pp. 21–23)

"Connect" and "unconnect" are so apparently different goals!

Yet the means of achieving these developmental tasks are not so different. Whether you are a midlife woman or man, the road from here to there already exists within you. Trust yourself.

The following chapters emphasize your own development. After all, your kids are grown. "Moving on with them" has been the focus until this point. "Moving on without them" comes next.

Chapter 8

Life beyond Parenting

Until recently, midlife seemed little more than a way station between youth and old age, not worthy of much thought or discussion. . . . Middlehood as a stage in the family life cycle—a period when the tasks and responsibilities of earlier phases of adulthood are done—is a relatively recent part of human experience, the product of the closely intertwined biological and cultural changes of our century.

LILLIAN RUBIN

What Midlife Means to You

Midlife as a point in time is very elusive. You can't pin it on a specific chronological age. A midlife person may be thirty-five or forty-five. You can't tie it to a particular change in your life, like the departure of your adult children or your partner. It may or may not accompany retiring from or joining the work force.

Midlife isn't a point in time, or a step toward old age to be dreaded. To further confuse the definition, if you selected two people of the same sex, age, and life circumstances, they might have very different ways of defining and experiencing midlife. Midlife is a developmental stage, much like adolescence or young adulthood, in which new opportunities are presented and the achievements of the past stages are reviewed and stored in memory. In his book *Midlife Myths and Realities* (1985), W. Van Hoose says that middle age is

> the first time we can begin to comprehend the life cycle. It is the first time that we have the facts and the experience to understand all the options and possibilities for leading a full, satisfying life. For the first time, middle-aged men and women have the freedom and the independence to make personal decisions and to plan for the future. (p. 110)

While it sounds like an idyllic time, not everyone welcomes and embraces this idea.

There's something very taboo about midlife, which is thought to happen around the age of forty. Unlike "sweet sixteen" or "twenty-one, the legal age to party," this stage in life is loaded down and camouflaged with negative attitudes and feelings. Just go to your favorite greeting-card store and see the "over-the-hill" section designed to usher in humorously the dreaded decade when "everything stops working." Of course it's intended to be funny, but humor is a common way of coping with an experience that produces anxiety or fear.

I have my own prejudices. Among the many vivid memories of my grandmother, one relatively minor image comes to mind as it has numerous times before. I can picture her sewing. I see the outline of her soft gray hair and the warmth of her face as she concentrated on threading the needle. Unless the daylight was strong, or she was sitting near the window, the process could be pretty frustrating. Sometimes I would help her find the needle's eye with the good vision of a child. Grandmother always seemed old to me, but if I were to calculate her chronological age at the time of this recollection, she was middle-aged.

As a child, I had hundreds of mental snapshots of my grandmother stored away. There was no particular meaning or power then. But now I understand! One time while sewing, in the year that I turned forty, I found myself moving the needle back and forth to focus on it well enough to get the thread through the eye of the needle. To my surprise and horror, I realized that I was just like grandma. It was a painful realization that I was also an old woman (i.e., middle-aged).

Although the *event* was trivial, the *feeling* of "being like grandma" was a shock. In all the ways I could have identified with her, what I chose was her age-related visual problem, far-sightedness. That incident became a marker of the beginning of my own midlife. There was a change taking place in me that I didn't want and couldn't control, and it was hard to keep myself from coloring all of my experiences with this feeling.

You have your own symbolic markers, and these experiences are bound to color how you see yourself at midlife. What comes to mind about this time of life? Did you have a grandmother who spent her days in a rocking chair after her children were grown and gone? Can you remember your middle-aged dad complaining about aches and pains for days after a morning of shoveling snow? On the other hand, was there a wise mentor in your past whom you hoped to emulate when you were "old"?

Before going any further with the facts of midlife, you have an opportunity to examine your own personal values, stereotypes, and judgments. The way you perceive yourself and your experiences has a great deal to do with how you begin the journey through midlife. The self-evaluation that follows will tell you something about your hopes and wishes. It will also suggest your energy level for pursuing the future and changing unsatisfying behavior.

Here is a short survey focusing on how you see yourself at this point in time:

My age is _____. I see the rewards of being _____ as _____.

I see the drawbacks of being this age as _____.

One thing I specifically like about being _____ is _____.

When I look in the mirror I see _____.

It makes me feel _____.

When I think about my life to this point I am aware that
_____. This makes me feel _____.

If you remained candid in your responses you may find that you feel one of the following ways:

1. You are on good terms with what goes on inside you and your age does not scare you.
2. You have age-related stereotypes but, when challenged, they evaporate.
3. You are surprised by your age-related stereotypes and realize that you take them seriously and that this affects your self-perception in negative ways.

Again, keep in mind that this is a beginning point, and your awareness, however painful now, will serve you well as time goes on.

A Time for Reflection

If life is a journey, then midlife is a stopover, a place where you change planes or board a new train or take some time out to think about your direction. It may be the first time in your life that such a deliberate and conscious view was possible. For many people, it's the only time that the forward movement of life has slowed down enough for them to take a good look or notice that something is missing.

When your children are grown, and the press of their daily needs subsides, there may be a sense of quiet that has not existed before. It tends to bring the focus of life back to yourself—a time to explore the achievements and the needs still unmet. What is experienced as missing varies greatly between people, but the sense of having worked very hard for others and not having had much time for oneself is a common thread. This is a widely held feeling throughout adulthood, but it is intensified at midlife when the first wave of "quiet" settles. The phenomenon is not specific to either sex or to a particular social class. It seems to be an American trait left over from an early Puritan influence.

We have become accustomed to getting all of the work done before we allow time for leisure, play, or other "nonproductive" activities. We value ourselves when we have been constructive and useful, when we have taken care of everything that needs to be done—usually for others. The problem is that the cycle is never-ending and therefore not rewarding.

A mid-forties father carries home a briefcase of work every weekend but doesn't get to it. Instead he plays catch-up at home, fixes things, and drives his kids around. He reflects on his situation: "When will my time come, when the grind of everyday life stops and I can get to do what I want?" He doesn't get an answer, nor is there such a time. Time is not the issue.

D. Donohugh (1981), an internist who has a philosophical style, writes:

> Awareness and acceptance are the keys to success in this period, success in becoming the person you never became, the person you *can* become. . . . In your favor is knowing that most of the answers you arrive at now will be your last. You have the experience of a lifetime, which you did not have when you first charted your course. You can now recognize externally imposed values for what they are. . . . You have the satisfaction that the changes you make through the rest of your life will be based upon the truth as you see it, not upon the perception of others. (p. 211)

Fueling this process of self-discovery is the growing awareness that when the journey starts up again, it will move faster than ever toward its final destination. And the "final destination" now takes on even more meaning as the sense of mortality becomes increasingly real:

> We somehow stop believing that our stay here on earth is infinite and realize for the first time that it is not. . . . From then on we are changed, subtly but significantly. Whether or not we understand life any better than we ever have, or

whether we ever will, we at least begin to try from then on.
(Donohugh, 1981, p. 3)

This is the first place in life that people report time as mea-
sured in *how much remains ahead* rather than in *time passed
since birth*. There is a growing realization that time is running
out and that wishes, dreams, hopes, and vague plans need to be
clarified and acted on before too long or they won't be realized at
all. Suddenly, tomorrow is today. What a sobering thought!

While a time urgency is felt, it doesn't necessarily feel like
panic. In fact, because it's experienced at midlife, rather than
adolescence or young adulthood, there is a maturity and wisdom
that comes from having lived for forty-plus years that leads to a
powerful and natural partnership. This is truly the ideal time in
life to search for personal meaning and relevancy. The combina-
tion of maturity and motivation for change, sparked by the
awareness of one's own mortality, heralds in an exciting phase of
development.

Darlene was forty-five and alone for the first time in her life.
Her children were grown, and a divorce eight years before had
ended her only marriage. She had friends who were special, both
male and female. She had a job that paid her bills and gave her
some satisfaction, yet she felt a sense of stagnation and disappointment.

At first, she identified the feeling as boredom, but it had
grown into uneasiness and then spread to a general discomfort
that could not be ignored. Though she tried to make sense of it,
the feeling that "something was wrong" persisted. Increasingly,
her life seemed less and less interesting, but she tended to see
this as a weakness in herself, a self-centeredness that had long
ago been defined as "selfish" and driven away by her parents.

There was no way to deny that her feelings were real. Since
she couldn't successfully intimidate herself or evoke enough
guilt to get herself back on track, she finally decided to consult a
psychologist. That is how I met Darlene, and what I've described
to you is how she presented herself to me.

She talked about her life experiences, which were in many ways typical of women raised traditionally and born between 1940 and 1950. While she was troubled by her current state of unrest and her building dissatisfaction with life as it currently seemed, she was not someone who could be described as emotionally disturbed. In fact, she had accomplished much of what she had expected of herself. As she looked for keys to her unhappiness, she looked backward toward her past and considered the major influences on her development: "My parents did the best they could. They were loving and supportive. But then, I knew how to please them. I never went too far to the right or left of their values, so I didn't take too many risks. I always thought I had chosen my own direction, my own path, but now, as I look back, I can see how many forces were weighing on me, shaping me."

As she spoke, I could feel her sadness. Her body seemed heavy under the weight of her awareness. Darlene was being very hard on herself. I asked, "Are you feeling sorry about your choices or feeling somehow that they were not, in fact, your choices?" After some time in apparently painful soul searching, she responded, "I don't regret the way I've lived. Caring for my husband and the three kids made me feel good and important. Working enabled me to have those things that it takes two incomes to buy. It was just something I did to help us maintain a higher standard of living."

While focusing on Darlene's life beyond family and work, it seemed more clear that other aspects of her daily living were also oriented toward the help and support of others. While she gave unselfishly to her parents, her church, the PTA, and the Scouts, we could see a pattern of responding to others' needs, others' requests, others' demands. What did Darlene want for herself? What did Darlene need? She recalled, "I never had time to look inside. Maybe I didn't know how to do that or felt it was selfish. Maybe I didn't know that I had an inside to consider. Probably it's just as well that I wasn't aware of an inner life. What a conflict it would have created!"

What Darlene was realizing was that precisely this dilemma, unwittingly sidestepped in the past, had now surfaced at a time when she could finally address it without a great deal of conflict. Her current situation was actually an opportunity for self-discovery at a point in her life that would support the changes she needed to make. For the first time in her life, the pulls and pressures from outside had ceased to be the primary focus of Darlene's attention. Her children were mostly self-sufficient; that is, they didn't have the same daily need of attention and care that they had needed in their childhood and adolescence. (Clearly, a parent will always have a small place in his or her head and heart reserved and on alert for his or her children of any age.) Her husband was gone. Her parents' expectations had generally been met, and many of her volunteer commitments had been taken on by the next generation of women. Finally, Darlene could look within herself for stimulation, for satisfaction, and for direction. This opportunity, however, presented new struggles.

Darlene continued, "I feel like a small child learning to walk. I keep looking around for someone to hold my hand so I don't fall. At the same time, I want to walk by myself. So I don't dare do anything but stand still and wait—wait for something to happen. It feels as if that's where I am in my life right now—waiting. I'm afraid to move ahead on my own, and I'm waiting for something to happen because I'm afraid to take that step by myself. But at the same time, I'm looking for external guidelines. Won't someone please tell me what to do? Won't someone, something, rescue me from having to decide what's good for me?"

It's this process of self-discovery that characterizes midlife. Darlene was grappling with a profoundly important idea labeled by the psychological theorists as *locus of control*. When someone asks, "Who's in charge of my ·decision making?" he or she is talking about internal versus external control of choices. Darlene believed that she had decided on the big things in her life: whom to marry, whether or not to work, child-rearing practices, how to spend disposable income, and so forth. And of course she *had* made these decisions, but not without considerable reliance on the world around her, outside her.

It's likely that she had unknowingly based her decisions on the expectations of other people and institutions. Although probably not consciously, she had checked her plans with the outside world and had shaped them accordingly: "Will father approve? Will people think I'm different, unfeminine, irresponsible, acting inappropriately, incapable? Will I displease my husband, disappoint him? If I take this promotion at work, will I anger, hurt, abandon my friends on the old job?"

Of course, the process is subtle, so subtle that unless there is a major conflict between what you want and the feedback you get from others, you will simply not notice the forces at play. These battles get fought in an unremarkable way, and yet they are very powerful in determining one's life direction. Because most of us prefer to avoid struggles and battles, we tend to take the path of least resistance, which often means avoiding our internally derived wants, needs, hopes, and wishes. We tend to sacrifice at this level to maintain a status quo that prevents conflict with the outside world.

This dilemma is really no different for men and women. While the specific issues affecting men and women at midlife have particular focuses that set them apart, the "locus-of-control" debate burdens both sexes equally. For example, the pressures on men to "settle down," "be responsible," "get a good job," and "be dependable" often successfully drown out the internal tentative wishes that are simply not practical by external standards. In the process of "shaping up," the dreams seem less and less realistic, while the press to take care of others financially silences the internal, but weak, voice. "Doing the right thing" is rewarded and is ultimately rewarding—until midlife!

Stan didn't know he was sacrificing, nor would he want to look back at the last twenty years in this way. Still, one day it became very clear that, while he had everything that was considered a sign of achievement and accomplishment, he really was not sure he had anything that was particularly satisfying. He kept conjuring up an image of his own eulogy, which described him as "hardworking, a good father, a dependable person." He shuddered to think about how blandly it portrayed him and how ordinary it seemed. Not that he was always so morbid, but within the past year, his father had died, and Stan could no longer avoid his own mortality. To this point, he had been able to live much as before, day-to-day, event-to-event, season-to-season. He had never seen himself as particularly philosophical, and it kind of annoyed him that this life-versus-death debate was taking place within him.

Like others for whom the internal dialogue begins to play too loud, Stan consulted me when troubled by his apparent inability to stop his own disturbing thoughts. He was increasingly distracted by self-criticism and thoughts of disappointment in himself and his achievements. In his own eyes, he "had not amounted to much." At the time he did not understand, but the feelings that were pushing into his consciousness made sense in light of his father's recent death. His loss had caused him to pause and look at his own life much more closely.

Ann Weick (1989), dean of the School of Social Welfare at the University of Kansas, studied the process of change in adult life. She writes, "By the time most people reach midlife, they are beginning to make an important discovery: life has not been what they were led to expect. The scripts society has written have become blurred because the things that were expected to happen did not and many things that did occur were not expected" (p. 244). Stan's backward glance at his internal life made him uncomfortable about the future.

On the outside, nothing had changed; even the wear and tear of forty-nine years, now more apparent in thinning hair and expanding middle, were not especially upsetting. Yet inside, worry about his unrealized potential and long-lost dreams was a serious distraction that was beginning to affect Stan's daily life. While his condition would not be considered a serious emotional problem, he sought professional help when the usual ways of talking himself out of his feelings did not work. As with Darlene, the awareness of a long-denied inner calling was both unsettling and exciting at the same time. Self-discovery, they both found, was a double-edged sword.

Shifting Gears

Middle adulthood is anything but static. No longer is it necessary for a person to *adapt* and *adjust* to be normal. No longer is it necessary to put aside oneself to accomplish the jobs taken on long ago without much thought or choice. This is a dynamic time, perhaps unsettling, as is anything that involves movement, but definitely offering opportunities for self-growth not possible before and not likely later. It is a transitional time, involving movement and producing change, but it need not lead to crisis.

By midlife, many adults have become stuck. Like a once-powerful and sharp tool that could effortlessly perform, the midlife adult, through years of wear, begins to feel dull and to grind to a halt. Even once-satisfying and meaningful jobs lose their appeal. How long does it take to get tired of an activity? Even an activity that is central to your life, such as child rearing or a career, may not remain a challenge and may become boring, tiring, or grim. Is it normal to have such feelings? Rather, is it normal to *not* have such feelings?

Judith Bardwick (1990), a professor of psychiatry at the University of California, echoes this concept in her study of adults reaching midlife at the end of the twentieth century:

> For the majority, work will be mastered, promotions will end, and the responsibilities of child rearing will be over. Thus the commitments made in the past no longer provide satisfaction in the present or guidelines for the future. People ask themselves what they give and what they gain from work, spouse, children, friends. The future is shortening. One may have spent twenty years in an occupation and may face spending the next twenty doing the same thing. Likewise, twenty-year-old marriages are often comfortable but

> rarely exhilarating, yet ending one means losing roots and injuring a spouse whose only sin may have been being around too long. (p. 202)

If the feelings described above are normal, then what is the midlife crisis we hear so much about? For a midlife crisis to take place, it is necessary to have both a *rapid* and a *major change* in personality or life circumstance, by definition, one that was not anticipated and planned for. While a midlife crisis does take some of us by surprise and proves to be disturbing or destructive, most of us can see the issues and struggles unfolding. The unsettling feelings that result also become the catalysts for healthy change.

Any of the turning points in life can be stressful, whether it's graduating from college, getting married, having a child, changing jobs, or moving away from one's family. But stress in manageable doses, and in the appropriate time frame, need not be negative. It can be exciting and exhilarating, leading to a sense of aliveness and energy.

Neugarten (1976) talks about the normal turning points in life as

> markers or the punctuation marks along the life cycle. They call forth changes in self-concept and in sense of identity, they mark the incorporation of new social roles, and accordingly, they are the precipitants of new adaptations. But in themselves they are not, for the vast groups of normal persons, traumatic events or crises that trigger mental illness or destroy the continuity of the self. (p. 18)

This time is for looking, evaluating, and reworking life goals. Now it is possible to consider letting go of functions or positions adequately performed but no longer appropriate or meaningful. The moment may be right to dust off old dreams and fantasies and see if they still fit. It may also be an opportunity to reassess old values in light of new or emerging beliefs about yourself, about life, and about the world.

Rubin (1981), in a discussion of women's early-life role development, points out that women "learned to suppress elements of self this world doesn't want to see, doesn't want to know about" (p. 42). Men's issues, while different in specific ways, also include a suppression of self-determination in favor of correct life roles.

Taking Control

Learning to assume control of your life is definitely a midlife issue. This may also be the first time that such an idea could be considered. But when your life history requires choices made for the benefit of others (e.g., parents, children, spouse, or religious group), you develop great skill in making decisions for others and learn little about your own needs. This is true of both men and women.

In the mid-sixties, a psychologist named Julian Rotter (1966) coined the phrase *locus of control*. He believed that the locus of control affects how people shape their lives. An external locus of control is associated with a sense of powerlessness in managing forces outside of the self, such as societal limitations, the influence of others, and fate. A person with an external locus of control believes that the ability to make things happen or change is not under his or her control. These beliefs, in good times, tend to make men and women more passive and responsive than they need to be. When times are bad, a sense of hopelessness may prevail. Individuals with an internal locus of control feel a sense of power over their own lives and believe in their ability to shape their lives.

During the early adult years, the roles of man, woman, mother, father, and worker are fairly clear and demanding. At midlife, the ability to feel in control of life separates people into two groups. One group believe they can plan and act on their plans, and the other group believe that their decision making will have little impact on what happens to them, so why bother trying?

These are two distinct ways of viewing personal power. Both greatly affect the experience of the midlife transition. "Externalizers" have a rougher course to sail because they are so accustomed to searching for markers and guides outside themselves. If we use a sailing analogy, it's like navigating by compass, buoy, map, and stars. "Internalizers" tend to have more self-confidence, like dolphins using built-in sensing devices. The internalizers trust their hopes, wishes, and decisions and take them seriously, believing they can happen.

Feeling helpless and out of control is never a normal or tolerable state. It leads to a host of psychological problems related to depression and anxiety. Stress and distress may be increased to a level where health may be jeopardized. When the future is relatively unstructured, it may seem terribly frightening. The bad news is that, if your style allows changes only when the feedback from the world is supportive, midlife may be a struggle. The good news, however, is that control over your own life can be *learned*. Some first steps might include:

1. Taking chances before all the "outside evidence" is in.
2. Taking a small risk, knowing that it's OK to make a mistake.
3. Purposely avoiding asking anyone for advice on a particular decision, just for practice!

In the previous vignettes, both Darlene and Stan were afraid to act on their own, fearful of taking a step into the unknown without being sure or being reassured by others. For each of them, tuning in to an internal, but weak, voice for direction was necessary. This resulted in blocking the very strong voices that were usually sought from outside.

Over time, Darlene and Stan learned to depend on their internal guides and voices to move ahead and plan their futures. The changes were not dramatic, but neither were they fearful. Instead, changes that were subtle were also comfortable and eventually welcomed.

Chapter 9

Designing the Future

The conditions required for leading a full life are more available after forty than during young adulthood. Middle-aged people have more control over their lives, more experience in coping, and more awareness of their own capacities than younger people.

WILLIAM H. VAN HOOSE

Reconsidering Choices and Values

Even for the slow starter or slow developer, midlife is a time when most of us feel it's unnecessary to ask permission. Perhaps it's the fact that we've done everything that was expected of us, and now it's up to us. Clearly, the idea of picking our own life course is a bit scary. But clinging to safety limits the opportunity to change. Roger Gould makes this point in *Transformations* (1978). He notes that, in the forties, "whatever we must do must be done now. We must let go of our childish desire for absolute safety or we lose the opportunity for fundamental repair" (p. 218).

Fortunately, at midlife there is a degree of safety provided for individuals whose children and spouses are generally independent. This is the decade with the fewest external de-mands and the greatest opportunity for self-exploration and self-development. In his book about midlife myths, W. Van Hoose (1985) underscores this idea: "By 40 to 50 we are more free to examine the ideals that guide our conduct, more willing to follow our own conscience, and less likely to conform to the views of others" (p. 113).

Knowing what you do about midlife choices, let's play with the idea that you *do* have control over your life and can *choose* your own ways of living. Take a few minutes to consider which activities are "musts" and which are "choices" in your own life. Make two lists of five items each:*

I have to:	I choose to:
1.	1.
2.	2.
3.	3.
4.	4.
5.	5.

The items that you placed in the "I have to" category are ones that probably seem fixed, given, outside your decision making, or not freely chosen.

Place an asterisk next to the "have to" items that you would also choose. These items are ones that you are obliged to do but at the same time would continue on your own, if you were free to choose.

Place a cross next to the "have to" items that *once* fit you but now seem irrelevant to your life or that interfere with your life. Place a zero next to the "have to" items that you have incorporated into your life but that were defined or imposed by someone else (e.g., your parents, spouse, or church).

Now go back to your lists and see if you can move any "have to's" out of that category by:

1. Realizing that they are choices (you want to do them anyway).
2. Retiring the no-longer-necessary items.

*Adapted from "Have to" vs. "Choose to" in Schlossberg and Troll (1978), p. 120.

3. Examining the consequences of saying "no" to a particular "have to."

Take some time to summarize what you have found out about yourself. You may be surprised by your responses. You may still feel stuck, but you may be aware that change is a possibility. If nothing else, you will probably sense that initiating change requires only your permission.

Know yourself! Not everyone jumps into a new life course with both feet. In fact, some people make no real changes until they've sorted through all of their thoughts and plans a thousand times. It really doesn't matter what your style is; even daydreaming is a step forward.

Sometimes a new approach is useful. The following exercise provides a view of life from a seldom-used perspective. It gives you a chance to see your life from one end to the other. Just as when you use a wide-angle camera lens, you can see a much broader view of things:

Draw a life line with birth as the beginning and death as the end. Place yourself on the life line at a point that represents you currently. There's no need to be precise because this point is not exact, nor can it determine how much life remains or how you choose to fill it. But it does provide a marker of your current status and a starting place for your self-evaluation.

Choose a symbol for yourself to place on the life line. If you don't feel very creative, start out with a check mark, an X, or some other simple character. If you are feeling more creative, design a symbol for yourself. It needs to have meaning only to you. Here are a few ideas to get you started (draw one of the following: heart, star, sun, or tree), but you'll probably do better on your own. Place your symbol on the life line below:

Give yourself a few minutes to appreciate your efforts. Did this feel like a significant and meaningful gesture or a requirement by the author that was carried out minimally?

Now that you've located yourself on the life line, what other symbols belong there with you at this point in your life? Again, this is an assessment of what currently *is* your life, not what *could have been, was, should be,* or *might be* in the future. The symbols reflect actual people or routines that are part of your daily life. If your children live apart from you, do not place their symbols on your line unless you have daily contact with them.

Here are some items to consider. Pick any that are relevant (also create your own) and develop symbols for them: spouse, children, parents, work, hobbies, friends, unpaid work (volunteer), others _____.

Below is a cross section of the "present time" marker on your life line. The circle represents the sphere of influence in your life and can contain all of the symbols of your current life. Arrange them within the circle and around the center point (yourself) in terms of how close or distant you feel they are from you in terms of *importance* to your present life.

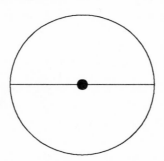

Take some time to design your symbols and to place them around yourself. Rearrange them as seems necessary. Stay aware of your feelings while you are doing this activity. Take some time at the end to see how you feel about the way you have represented your current life. Did you include or leave out a certain symbol that now surprises you?

Next comes a lifestyle function survey, which is designed to give you information about your current daily "work." It is the kind of checkup that is best done annually just the way you would take an annual physical exam, and it may be used similarly, as an appraisal of your current health. You use it to note changes, to measure changes, and then to evaluate whether the changes are "good" or "bad." Like a physical exam, this survey will lead to a plan of action or "treatment" meant to make improvements. The following "work" checkup gives you additional information:

Work Satisfaction Survey

Select the *one primary* activity—paid or unpaid work, job, career, homemaking, volunteer work—that is the focus of your daily life. Do not select the one you feel is most important or meaningful, but the one that actually absorbs the major portion of your daily time and energy. This is an exercise about how your time is *actually spent*. The following questions do not necessarily lead to yes or no answers. You don't need to write your responses in detail. It is really a *thinking* assignment, and when it has been completed, there will probably be much to think about. Again, the goal is to assess how much satisfaction you actually derive from the activity in which you spend the majority of your daily time.

When you have completed this exercise, you may feel pleased with yourself and satisfied that the time you spend is meaningful and fulfilling. If not, the remainder of this chapter will get you turned in the direction of positive change.

Please respond to the items below:

My primary job is _____.

Am I satisfied? (yes, no, explain) _____.

Have my goals changed over recent years? (yes, no, explain) ___

_____.

Is my current "job" meeting my expectations? _____.

Are my strengths being utilized or acknowledged? _____.

How can I achieve greater satisfaction in *this* job? _____

_____.

What else can I do? _____.
Would this require a major or a minor adjustment? _____.

Now that you have completed a number of exercises designed to clarify your goals and values, you probably have uncovered some new ways of seeing yourself. You may now have an expanded picture of who you are, where you are, and perhaps where you are headed.

Exploring the Self

What do I want to do when I grow up? *How* do I want to be when I grow up? *When* will I grow up? These are the challenges of midlife just as they were during adolescence. The questions may be the same, but the capacity to answer them is greatly improved. You surely know so much more about yourself and the world than you did then. Yet, asking the same questions now may seem like an admission of failure. You may reason that, once answered, these questions need never be raised again. Wrong!

Midlife is tumultuous because no turning points can ever be motionless. As I write these lines, I approach my fiftieth birthday—and do so with mixed feelings. In many ways, as a psychologist, I am forced to stay in touch with my self-feelings and self-appraisals. I am keenly aware of changes in my body, memory, endurance—none of these in the directions I would choose! Some of the personality traits that were troublesome to me in my youth are still nagging reminders of my imperfections: I am still stubborn and pushy and tend to blow up when angry. These are behaviors that still get in my way, notwithstanding my efforts to change. But on the plus side, I have (and you also have) the benefit of years of life experience. Learning that is rich and varied is part of the legacy of middle age.

One of the beauties of midlife is that, while you make the changes in your life and self-correct your course, you have the benefit of knowing yourself better than at any other stage in life. Self-knowledge is cumulative. You continue to gather information about yourself throughout life. Even when the traits and styles that you identify are problems (like my stubbornness or perhaps your competitiveness), the shortcomings can be minimized as you learn to work around them. For example, If you tend to be most comfortable when you are well organized and orderly, then you can count on this characteristic to continue in the future—for better (e.g., reordering your priorities) or for worse (e.g., controlling others' behaviors). However, as in modernizing a house, there is comfort in knowing that the foundation is solid, even though some rooms need updating.

Costa and McCrae (1989), who have researched the permanence of personality traits across adult life, support the idea that "who we are" continues to influence "who we become." They report, "The personality dispositions that form an essential part of our unique identity endure across adulthood as formative influences on the life course" (p. 71). The advantage of the midlife perspective is that a foundation is already in place and the once-powerful social roles and environmental pulls simply don't exert so much influence over our lives.

"Who am I?" no longer depends on hopes and wishes that are untried and untested. This is a time for taking stock of what already exists: abilities, shortcomings, and accomplishments. Begin to make lists of your talents, skills, and gifts. Also note your faults and weaknesses, but be certain to avoid getting sidetracked by them. They are a part of you, but rather than focusing on their elimination, put your energy into developing your assets. The work ahead of you is internal; it is self-searching, so it doesn't have to depend on what others think. Neither will the process necessarily be visible to anyone but you.

You may ask yourself why you must bother with all of this introspection at this point in life. Why not just talk yourself out of any annoying doubts? The answer, simply put, is that time is running out! This is a most acutely urgent feeling. It provides an impetus to resolve the pressing issues.

Basically, I like myself. I feel I have done pretty well with my life, but if I died tomorrow there would still be unfinished business. I have a certain amount of wisdom that comes with age, and I can be a mentor to others who are younger, because I've traveled so much of life's path. Probably this is true of you, too.

Self-growth is the task ahead, requiring a focus on the positive and a sorting of things to gain clarity about ourselves. That process, in fact, is what gives us personal power. As we discover more and more of the qualities that make us unique and then take the risks to express them, we affirm an interior power that does not require others' approval. To make this idea more concrete, here is an analogy. Think about your garden or your favorite place in the outdoors. What may have begun as a well-planned and orderly garden with fine plants, shrubs, and trees may now look crowded, unkempt, or disorderly. The greenery grows closer and closer and may eventually interfere with growth. At the same time, there are some volunteers, plants that grow from seeds scattered by the wind or animals. Some of these may be very pleasant and others unwanted, but until weeded, they continue to grow at the same rate or speed.

Over time, the basic shape of the garden or woods may have changed, but without plan or purpose. If it's your garden, you can weed and rearrange things based on your personal preferences. You know, after all, what you like and what you don't like. If the green space does not belong to you, and changing it is not possible, you can still imagine how you would like it to be, based on your desires.

It's very hard to take charge of your "self" in the same way you would a garden. But it's not impossible. Again, from the enormous number of possibilities, you want to select those that will optimally enhance your internal garden. You will also want to start new growth that is consistent with your present likes and dislikes. Reworking your internal garden is a potent way to empower yourself.

Developing Internal Power

Who am I? Asking this question doesn't negate the past but builds on it. It assumes that the building blocks are in place but may need some repair, polishing, and a general sprucing up. You may also want to remove a few pieces and replace them with a new shape, design, or texture. Your goal is to improve on the structure that is already there, not to tear it down and start over. This is meant to be reassuring, since a move toward midlife growth and change must be seen as safe and worth the risk or it's not likely to be ventured.

The risks involve looking at your present life—objectively, in the full light of day—and making choices based on current preferences and accepting responsibility for the changes. A client of mine named Carol made this struggle perfectly clear when she said, "If I make changes in my life that I know in my heart of hearts are right for me, I feel better about myself. On the other hand, people close to me may not agree with my decisions, won't support me, maybe will even withdraw or leave me. That would be too great a price to pay." Carol sees catastrophic results from her attempts to move in new directions, so she does what many of us do: stops thinking, stops dreaming. Unfortunately, that choice cuts off the process of growth and change much too soon.

Even when you are hesitant to *act*, you still owe it to yourself to *consider* the possibilities. No one will challenge your silent thoughts, wishes, hopes, dreams, or plans unless you tell what you're thinking. If you tell at this stage, you may be looking for someone to set you straight, say no, talk you out of it, and put the issue to rest. Sometimes the resistance you feel is really your own, but you attribute it to others. Your certainty of their disapproval may really be your own ambivalence or discomfort with a new idea. You may not be ready to act. You don't have to act; it's your choice. There's an alternative.

If you have the courage to *consider*, here are some necessary activities. They lead to self-growth, awareness of your reactions, and anticipation (fantasy, wishing). The following experiences are meant to be enjoyed, so if you begin to feel uncomfortable, feel free to skip around, but at least ask yourself why you want to avoid the opportunity:

This Is Your Life

Do you remember the TV show of long ago? You may recall that a person was selected, someone who had usually lived a good deal of her or his life. That person's past and present were paraded in front of her or him through a stream of significant people. All those who had meaningfully touched the honored guest's life were invited to participate. What an experience that must have been!

This exercise is called "This is Your Life," but it goes beyond the scope of the TV show.

Who have been the most influential people in your life? Who has helped define what you believe about yourself or the world? During which decade of your life did these people influence your development: before age ten? In your teens? In your twenties, thirties, or forties? Is that value or influence still significant? Is it currently meaningful in your life?

This exercise requires sorting that goes beyond the TV show. While the story of your life cycle unfolds, you can modify the present and future by setting aside those influences that no longer feel relevant or meaningful.

Person	Value Learned	Age	Retain?	Why?

As an example I'll use my own life. I grew up in a big city in the Northeast in a big apartment house and with little opportunity to learn about the beauty of the outdoors. In my community, the outdoors was seen as a way of getting from place to place and was mostly viewed as a nuisance in terms of the weather. Yet, as a midlife adult, I have a great appreciation of nature, and I find its effect on me to be very calming and nurturing. I used to wonder where this value came from and remembered my grandmother.

As a young child, I would sit with her by her window and watch the only tree in front of her apartment house. We watched that tree in every season and in every light. We watched and listened to the bird that called it home. It began as an experience I shared with her, but it took on a life of its own. It affects me still in profound ways, even though Grandma has been gone for many years. The comfort that nature then provided is still a powerful resource. It is one that I would never willingly part with. At the same time, other beliefs and values from the past no longer fit the "me" I've come to be.

One such belief comes to mind. As a child, I somehow learned that I should be uncomfortable with people who have a different ethnic or cultural background. It doesn't make sense to me now. Respectfully setting this and other beliefs aside, in a historical place in my life, was a necessary step in my further growth.

As I discussed this exercise with friends and colleagues, I began to accumulate others' experiences of values cherished and discarded. A friend of mine in her forties recently changed careers and became a writer. After years of writing in her spare time, she left her full-time paid job and committed herself to writing. Because of time and financial constraints, this was a decision that couldn't be reached until her kids were grown.

When we talked about her interest in writing, it seemed that it had always been with her. We wondered how far back she could trace this "calling." Her parents and siblings had not been writers, nor were others involved in her childhood world—except for her third-grade teacher. Even before she was ten years old, she had had a champion who encouraged her to write, valued her work, and inspired creative expression. She had not thought about Mrs. Van for many years, but now, as she did, she experienced a warm, comfortable feeling. As I watched her remembering, I could see the power of this early guidance in shaping the direction of her life. Clearly, this was a value she still embraced.

Tom grew up in a home that was a showplace. His parents felt that "a home reflects who you are to the outside world." He had lived his adulthood according to this rule, but without much conscious thought. In his late forties, when considering a move to another city, he was annoyed that none of the houses he saw were pleasing to him. Most of the houses met his needs for space and would hold his belongings. What was wrong?

He began to realize that he was trying to adhere to the rule that had been instilled by his parents many years before: "I can't believe that all these years I've lived the way I was supposed to, and it really didn't reflect me at all. I personally like modern things, and not the overstuffed chairs and ornate decorations that I let surround me because that's how my parents felt it should be." Fortunately, his wife did not have a big stake in the outcome. She agreed there was too much clutter. Tom felt excited and liberated by his value clarification.

When you have worked on this exercise so that you can identify at least one value or life lesson at each stage, look back over your uncensored reactions. The more you become aware of your own inner world, the more you can build on and shape it. If this exercise gave you an "Aha!" find someone supportive to share it with.

Fantasizing and Daydreaming

Fantasizing and daydreaming give you an opportunity to open up your thinking and give your dreams some freedom, even if only in your head. Remember, this step requires thinking (e.g., wondering, recalling, imagining, planning, and sorting ideas) and feeling (e.g., sensation, mood shift, excitement, heart throb, or a surge of energy), but not acting (carrying out a plan of action). You have a built-in safety net because, if your dreams scare you, they needn't be enacted.

Most of the theorists discussed earlier describe the search for a positive state of being. Erikson (1950) called it "integrity," while "self-actualization," the fulfillment of individual creative potential, was the term used by psychologist Abraham Maslow, who identified a hierarchy of human needs (1968). In essence, the need to create a whole, positive existence is never totally fulfilled. Still, it is something worth striving toward.

To get started with this exercise you will need to find a quiet time and a quiet place. Playing some music may help take your attention away from the distractions and stresses of everyday life. Complete the following statements spontaneously. Try not to get caught up in finding the "right" answer:

1. To become my most developed self, I would _____

_____.

2. To fulfill my life, it would be necessary for me to _____

_____.

3. In looking back at my life, to feel acceptance of myself I would have to _____.

4. To accomplish 1, 2, or 3, I would have to *do* or *change*

_____.

It may be helpful for you to know that the future is changed in very small, undramatic ways. Accomplishing one step gives you the courage to go on to the next. For example, if you felt a need to go back to school to complete your wished-for education, you might start with sending away for a college catalog. You can take this step without turning your life upside down. If you are finally ready to consider opening the boutique that has lived in your imagination for years, you might meet with a leasing agent to see some property.

Sometimes we get the first step confused with the final step, and so it becomes too scary to consider. The initial step marks playful fantasy, without any admonitions, whereas the last step is anchored in reality. Ordering a catalog or looking at shops for rent is a starting point. Worrying about how to support yourself, or your family, while going to school or being an entrepreneur is a step that is likely to stop you in your tracks at the beginning of your exploration. These are important considerations, but they are premature and will stifle your creativity at this point.

Your reactions are a natural starting point that will lead you closer to the self you value and wish to become. Remember, you need take only the first few steps toward change. Once begun, the process usually continues because of the satisfaction in taking control of your life and moving in your preferred direction.

The following exercise will help you identify the first few steps in the change process. Complete each of the following ideas by writing the first words that come to mind, without much censoring:

Spend more time _____.

Work _____.

Exercise by _____.

Live _____.

Eat or drink more (less) _____.

Believe in _____.

Focus my energy on _____.

Wear _____.

Relax by _____.

Contribute to the community by _____.

Develop an interest in _____.

Build relationships with _____.

Making Changes and Coping with Them:
A Double-Edged Sword

After taking stock of your present strengths and weaknesses, you may have initiated some changes that have altered your life course. You may be surprised to experience an increase in stress. After all, moving from automatic pilot to self-driving takes much more vigilance. Remaining conscious and questioning your roles and personal goals, as you go from day to day, take more energy.

Having made some changes you may notice one of the following effects:

1. *Your self-confidence has increased.* Having mastered a problem or challenged your long-held ideas about how things ought to be, you feel an inner strength. If this is your experience, then you're on your way, and your coping skills are probably good enough. At this point, you may require only some structure and support to continue making progress.

2. *The changes you are attempting to make cause anxiety or panic.* This might take the form of immobilization, that is, a fear of doing anything. In this case, you may be stopped by negative thinking (e.g., "This will never work," or "I'll fail and embarrass myself") or procrastination (e.g., "This project needs to wait until I have more money, time, courage, skill"). On the other hand, your fear could lead to impulsive behavior, acting too quickly with too little thought, to avoid discomfort. In such a situation, you respond before the anxiety or panic takes hold, but without the prerequisite steps that will ensure success. An example might be quitting a job prematurely or making a commitment without knowing the consequences. If this describes you, then you have the need for some additional coping skills or resources (sources are suggested in the next chapter).

Next, we need to identify the blocks that inhibit changing, whether they are internal (your own fears and doubts) or external (pressure or detours placed in your path by others).

As change takes place, the equilibrium needs to shift if you are to maintain balance. Again, imagine a scale, in which the weights on each side must balance. If you change one side, then you must also adjust the other to retain stability. For example, suppose your goal is to modify your eating habits because high cholesterol and middle age are natural enemies. You begin to shop and prepare food differently. The consequence may be that you feel better, look better, or are satisfied that you can carry through to your own goals. The balance is maintained. But what if the consequence of your change is resistance from your family to new ways of eating? Or what if you can't get yourself to stay away from burgers and shakes? The balance between your new behavior and its consequences won't be achieved and will create anxiety, maybe panic, and certainly frustration.

There are several ways to cope with change; some are more healthful than others:

1. *Avoid it, deny it, shut it out of your awareness.* For example, you may ignore your aging body's need for more rest and be surprised when an "all-nighter" leaves you feeling exhausted. I am reminded of a friend who is approaching fifty. He is proud of his softball skills, especially his ability to move quickly in the position he plays: shortstop. He likes playing in a league of young men, with "no one even close to being forty." In recent years, he has sustained a number of injuries following softball games, all attributable to lower back problems. His pain should alert him to the possible connection between his aging back and the way he pushes himself on the field. Sadly, he still needs to deny it. He is not yet ready to deal with this information.

2. *Overdose on it.* Allow so much change in a short time that it feels overwhelming and chaotic. You may want to change everything about yourself and your lifestyle at once: exploring a new interest, losing weight, remodeling your house, and being there less for your "helpless" adult-child. When this happens, there is little stability and no comfortable place for retreat. Change can be very exciting, but the human organism can handle only a limited amount of overload stress before symptoms develop.

3. *Maintain the equilibrium.* Compensate just enough for change to still have a sense of balance. For example, after thirty years on the job, Abe was looking forward to retirement but was worried about endless days of unstructured time. To reduce his fear of boredom or depression, he began to think about a new hobby, even before his retirement date. He channeled his energy in a new way, and his stability was maintained.

4. *Grow with the changes.* Incorporate new experiences and self-awareness in such a way that you actually expand and be-

come a more complex person over time. The change is then not seen as threatening. Psychologists call this process *successive approximation toward a goal*. You begin with small, tolerable changes, like making changes in your job description or requesting training in a new area, to increase your satisfaction at work. Though scary at first, the change soon may not seem challenging enough. With increased confidence, you might consider requesting a promotion or a move to another company, which *now* seems perfectly comfortable.

The moral of the story is: Gradual change results in your ability to tolerate the changes and to adapt still more, which is good for your body as well as your psyche. This point is made by Ernest Rossi, psychologist and author of *The Psychobiology of Mind-Body Healing* (1986). He is a pioneer in the field of psychobiology, which studies the mind–body connection in sickness and health.

In discussing change and the way in which people manage it, he notes:

> We struggle in vain to preserve our past way of thinking, feeling, and doing until a symptom or problem becomes manifest evidence of our lack of adaptation to the current and ongoing changes that are taking place. Our symptom or problem is then our best guide to where "inner work" needs to be done to readapt and recreate ourselves. (p. 70)

Noticing your discomfort or anxiety may be the best way for you to begin coping with change.

Life Planning: Skills and Techniques

Wouldn't it be nice if life planning had cruise control, like a car, to provide a smooth ride and prevent sudden speedups and slowdowns? Unfortunately, life takes on the guise of a car that needs periodic maintenance or a house that requires spring cleaning.

Short- and long-term planning, like your car, need periodic

tuning. Even the ten-year-old who knew that she had to be a lawyer or a veterinarian when she grew up and achieved that goal might have new needs or goals at forty-five. The belief that long-term planning is forever can produce a great deal of anxiety as you change and grow in ways that were unimaginable years ago. If life planning and goal setting were simply a matter of identifying your likes, preferences, and dreams and then acting on them, there wouldn't be a need for psychologists like me.

In addition to looking at short-term (immediate) and long-term goals (between one and five years), we need to consider the brick walls we run into along the way. Sometimes we place the brick walls there because we are afraid to go beyond the current ways—and to fail. Sometimes we're afraid to succeed because success will lead to increased responsibility—until failure finally results. When brick walls are set in place by others, by society, or by chance, they need to be worked around or removed. This is no small task, but it is possible to identify solutions or resources that can help you to find solutions.

Goal planning, in general, has two phases:

1. *Exploration*. This is broad and is meant to create possibilities. You look at all of the information, including your fantasies, interests, values, and any other information available. Then you narrow your focus to keep from being overwhelmed by so many possibilities, many of which are unrealistic.
2. *Crystallization*. This is a narrowing of your focus and leads to decision making or at least to planning your direction. This step is often a natural outcome of your exploration.

Goal planning begins where you are right now, and a career checkup is a good focal point. This should be a once-a-year activity. It provides a "barometric check" on your current satisfaction. No matter what your daily work, whether you are a manager, a tradesperson, or a homemaker, you can ask the following questions:

- Am I satisfied?
- Have my objectives changed over the years?
- Is my current "job" meeting my expectations?
- Are my strengths being exercised or acknowledged?
- How can I achieve greater satisfaction in this job?
- What else can I do?

Your honest answers should give you some useful information about the need to switch direction. You may enjoy the awareness that you are actually *in* a situation that is compatible with your current needs and skills.

Here is another exercise to get you thinking about the future:

1. Within the next year I want to become ——————————. I plan to achieve this by ——————————.
2. Within the next year I want to do ——————————. I plan to achieved this by ——————————.
3. Within the next five years I want to become ——————————. I plan to achieve this by ——————————.
4. Within the next five years I want to do ——————————. I plan to achieve this by ——————————.

To make this process more concrete here is a step by step analysis of a short-term goal.* Use one or more of the goals you have identified so far:

	Steps	*Anticipated blocks*	*Possible remedies*	*Resources*
1.				
2.				
3.				

Once again most goals that you haven't achieved on your own are probably blocked by an internal or external brick wall. By

*Based on material developed by Walsh (1983).

identifying these brick walls, you can face the issue head-on, which may give you a great deal more power. To sum up the strategy for change:

Gaining control over your life leads to having a positive attitude toward impending change ("I can"), which leads to actively and seriously planning short- and long-term goals.

For most of us, making life changes is extremely difficult and stressful. While there is no easy way to avoid stress, maintaining a balance between creating change and coping with it is necessary. Remember, small changes are more tolerable than large ones, and even these need to be offset by ways of reassuring yourself or getting support and reassurance from others. There is an ongoing dance between the emerging stresses and the developing strategies for coping with them. When you realize that you're *leading* this dance, you are likely to feel an appreciation of your evolving self.

Chapter 10

Identifying Community Resources

But I've Done So Well!

There is no easy road around the struggles of life. Reaching mid-life relatively unscathed should be celebrated simply because it's a major accomplishment. Arriving at age fifty with your self-esteem intact and with the remnants of a sense of humor should be acknowledged as a milestone worth noting. Keeping your sanity amidst the pulls, pushes, and changes that characterize mid-life is no small accomplishment. It may have been a challenge to accept your adult son, who is still searching to find himself, or your adult daughter, whose lifestyle is so different from yours. Actually, your coping skills may seem quite effective. Then, one day, there are too many emotional demands coming too quickly to sort through by yourself.

The lives of normal, healthy, and high-functioning people can benefit from consulting professional helpers when too many changes come about too fast or when obstacles seem insurmountable. These are the times that seem especially stressful or confusing, and a helping hand will make the difference between feeling overwhelmed and being able to go from day to day. There are all kinds of people to turn to for help, but sometimes a person unconnected with your everyday life is the right choice, someone you feel won't judge you or belittle your concerns. It is perfectly normal to feel the need for professional services in addition to the kind of self-help provided in a book.

This chapter describes what kinds of community resources are available, how to find them, who provides them, and how to get more information about them. It is intended to give you additional options for support and also to help you feel like a more knowledgeable consumer of these specialized services.

Therapeutic Resources

Therapeutic resources provide professional psychological assistance, usually on an ongoing basis or in some regular way, which allows time between sessions. The psychotherapist helps you to grow or change in whatever direction you choose or helps you to enhance your well-being or to resolve problems. Because he or she is an outsider to your life, the psychotherapist is unlikely to have a vested interest in the ways you change. In contrast, even well-intended family and friends have a stake in the outcome of the therapeutic process and are therefore less objective.

Sometimes, the support from friends and family reflects their own discomfort. They may try to close off your feelings prematurely because your sadness, frustration, anger, or other psychological pain is hard for them to tolerate. Typically, friends and family try to help by giving reassurances that "things will be okay." It is not unusual for such well-meaning people to offer support in the form of statements that justify the current situation: "It's better this way. When she realizes that you're her only mother, she'll miss you and want to repair things with you. Don't aggravate yourself. I hate to see you in all this pain." These statements are intended to hasten your recovery. They are not usually very helpful.

When such supportive statements do not work, there is a tendency to give advice of a more forceful nature, such as, "Snap out of it"; "It's time to get on with your life"; "Self-pity won't get you anywhere"; "You're stronger than that"; or "This isn't the end of the world."

Needless to say, this approach does not work very well either, except that it may serve to reduce the frustration and impatience of the helper. However, the one on the receiving end of the "help" may feel criticized and may even feel guilty and responsible for causing discomfort to others by not "getting better" faster.

As we have seen throughout this book, the process of change and healthy movement toward a new, or reconstructed, future is lengthy and slow. Professional helpers know this and do not show impatience. They also tend not to have a stake in the direction of growth. These ideas are reflected in the words of Sheldon Roth, a psychiatrist associated with Harvard Medical School and the author of *Psychotherapy: The Art of Wooing Nature* (1987). In his book, which discusses the therapist's experience in doing therapy, Roth says:

> To a great extent, therapy sets in motion an organic and self-directing process. We oversee this, comment on it, influence some of its momentum, pull and lean against its inertia this way or that, but for the most part, as Freud said, the patient does what "he can or what he wants." (p. 160)

The patient leads the way on this expedition. The therapist helps to clear away the brush and serves as an expert wilderness guide.

A middle-aged widow named Rose shared her experience, which underscores why a therapist may be helpful: "I knew that I needed to set off on my own course, away from my adult-children. My decision to move four hundred miles and go through job retraining was not an easy one. I had thought about this change for the past two years, and the time finally seemed right to act.

Now I can finally pursue my interest in floral arranging." Her decision was not made lightly, and she was ready to begin the process. Still, she knew that she was likely to experience a great deal of pressure to stay in the city from her family and friends, who would be adversely affected by her decision. They might offer her all kinds of valid reasons for not making a move, but their motivation would really be a twofold blend of valuable counsel and the wish to hold on to a cherished friend.

Rose said, "I was really disappointed in my children's reaction. They seemed to consider only their own needs. Sure they would lose a free and available baby-sitter. When money got tight, I wouldn't be right there to ask for help. Neither would there be a shoulder to cry on when needed. Still, what about my future, my goals? They didn't seem to care."

Rose confided these thoughts to her therapist, who did not have to struggle with a divided loyalty, so Rose was aware of feeling less defensive than when talking about her proposed life changes with family and friends: "I don't have to censor my thoughts or worry that someone will find out something they don't like or don't want to hear." Psychotherapists also maintain confidentiality, except where their client's behavior is dangerous to themselves or others. Therefore, you don't have to fear that what you say, however "bad" or "bizarre," will come back to haunt you through a slip of the tongue of a trusted friend. Therapists simply do not talk about their clients, except professionally with their colleagues, and then not by name.

Finally, a psychotherapist has a very specialized body of knowledge and expertise to foster your self-growth. Certainly, people who have experienced the heartache and disappointment of conflict with their adult-children can reduce their pain through the help of concerned friends and relatives or through their own self-analysis. Yet, a professional helper will often facilitate or speed this process. Rose summed it up when she said, "Unlike my family, my therapist is part of the solution, not part of the problem."

The Professional Helper

Finding the right professional helper is not an easy task. It is not a simple matter of choosing a pleasant-sounding name from the telephone directory. There is much information that a prudent consumer should be aware of before making a selection.

Anyone who provides psychotherapy can call himself or herself a psychotherapist. The term *psychotherapist* is a generic label. Without more information, you can't be sure of the person's professional qualifications or minimum level of expertise.

There are at least four groups of recognized professionals who provide psychotherapy. What is important to remember about these four professional groups is that they are all required to meet licensing (or certification) standards that attest to their minimum qualifications for independent practice. A license does not guarantee therapeutic ability as much as it acknowledges that a particular practitioner has good judgement, ethical standards, and basic knowledge.

Marriage, Family, and Child Counselors

The licensing and/or certification requirements for a marriage, family, and child counselor (MFCC) vary from state to state, but the minimum is a master's degree in counseling or psychology from a recognized university. Candidates for this license must accumulate a large number of supervised hours of counseling experience after receiving their degree and before being eligible for licensure. You know that if they are licensed, they have had a great deal of experience.

MFCCs have training in family and couple counseling. They usually provide counseling to the population of "normal" people who are going through a life crisis or a life change. This group includes individuals whose psychological adjustment has been basically good until about the time they have sought help with a specific problem. Like other professionals, MFCCs are required not to "practice beyond their area of expertise." They usually do not qualify for the licenses that follow.

Psychiatric Social Workers

A two-year master's degree program in social work is required to be eligible for licensure as a Clinical Social Worker (LCSW), which is a nationally recognized license. It is awarded to a social worker who has accumulated a large number of post-degree therapy hours, under the supervision of a licensed practitioner.

Psychiatric social workers tend to work with a broader population than marriage and family counselors. Their training generally includes more emphasis on "disturbed" populations, that is, people who have had less emotional stability in their past history. Social workers tend to provide more long-term counseling than marriage, family, and child counselors. This difference usually has to do with the orientation of their graduate school training.

Psychologists

Psychologists are divided up into a variety of subspecialties. Psychologists who work as psychotherapists must be licensed or certified by the appropriate state agency. To be eligible for licensure, a psychologist must have completed a lengthy graduate school program leading to a doctorate degree (usually a Ph.D. or a Psy.D.). In addition, they must complete a large number of supervised therapy hours before they take a written and oral exam, the successful completion of which leads to licensing.

Most licensed clinical or counseling psychologists have had training that allows them to deal with a broad range of problems and with a broad-based population of people, ranging from "normal" to "extremely disturbed." The methods used by psychologists are diverse and reflect the theoretical orientation of the practitioner more than the discipline of psychology itself.

Training as a psychologist usually includes "diagnostic evaluation" or "projective testing." Psychologists, as differentiated from the other therapy providers, are able to use these procedures to gain information about a person's psychological functioning that is often not directly available. This evaluation is only rarely needed by a person seeking psychotherapy because of the psychological pain of midlife transition or family conflict.

Psychiatrists

Psychiatrists are distinguished from the other three groups by medical training. A psychiatrist is a medical doctor who has completed a three-year residency in psychiatry. The advanced training, usually carried out in a hospital that provides psychiatric care, gives this group of practitioners extensive experience in working with the most psychologically disabled segment of society.

In addition to psychotherapy, psychiatrists may recommend medication. Patients who may not be able to profit from psychotherapy alone may concurrently receive psychotropic medication (sometimes more commonly known by their effect as antidepressants, antipsychotics, mood elevators, etc.). An individual who is acutely upset may benefit from medication before beginning psychotherapy or counseling or may receive or obtain them concurrently.

Psychiatrists are licensed as medical doctors. They are eligible for "board certification" if they have successfully completed a residency and an examination. Like other mental health specialists, however, they should be chosen on the basis of their individual competence or style, and not exclusively on the basis of their degree.

Choosing a Therapist

Assuming that a licensed therapist in any of the four groups meets your needs, the next step is to consider how a therapist views the process of therapy, the role of the therapist, the role of the client, the length of time required to allow change to take place, and so forth.

The simplest way to determine whether a particular therapist is compatible with you is to spend an hour with him or her. Ask some questions about how he or she sees psychological change taking place. Explore his or her philosophy of human nature. Ask about things that seem relevant to you, and be aware of how you feel in his or her presence. Clearly, this session won't be a comfortable time, but if your discomfort increases to the point where it interferes with the therapeutic process, this is an important sign of a potentially poor fit. Trust your instincts. Try another hour with another therapist, and evaluate your feelings before you proceed. In most cases, you will have spent only an hour's time and a consulting fee.

Remember, the therapist has the license, the status, and the expertise, but you have lived in your own body long enough to know when a shoe does not fit properly. Again, trust your instincts.

Finally, in your search for a therapist, keep in mind that a licensed professional should be a basic requirement. Each of the four professional groups described above maintains a referral list of qualified licensed individuals. (You will find the local phone number in the telephone directory's yellow pages under "Marriage and Family Counselor," "Social Worker," "Psychologist," and "Physician—Psychiatrist.")

A good fit between you and your therapist is essential. Much of what goes on in psychotherapy depends on the relationship between patient and therapist. This relationship is similar to others in that trust and mutual respect must exist before meaningful change can take place. Roth (1987) comments on this special relationship:

> The dedicated therapist is a nonfantasy flesh-and-blood figure, providing a consistent role and function not readily available in the daily course of human events. This real aspect of the therapist is not to be minimized as a strong

factor in helping a patient maintain and endure the pains of sadness and anxiety attendant on a meaningful therapy. That a therapist has shared these experiences with the patient creates a relationship special unto itself, and in that sense is real and a new event in the actual ongoing events of a patient's life. (p. 76)

Individual Therapy or Counseling

Individual therapy is probably the most familiar to you of all the therapeutic resources. Some of your associations with this type of help may be related to its popularization by famous people. Woody Allen talks about his "analyst." Other celebrities refer to their "shrinks." In some places, having a therapist is a sign of status. The reality is that individual psychotherapy or counseling is not an exotic contrivance for the rich and famous. At this point, it is a viable source of help for everyone.

Before discussing it, however, some of the popular myths about individual therapy should be debunked.

Myth 1: "Only crazy people see a shrink." This is simply not true. If people were foolish enough to ignore their psychological suffering and/or confusion until they became "crazy," individual psychotherapy would do them very little good.

Psychotherapy is most useful when the individuals seeking help are aware of their pain, believe that the source of some of that pain is within themselves, and are motivated to change how they feel, think, or behave.

Myth 2: "Individual therapy costs are prohibitive." While it is true that most professional services are costly, individual therapy costs also depend on other factors. Private practitioners generally charge higher fees than therapists in community-supported therapy programs. Many practitioners maintain a sliding fee scale for a certain percentage of their clientele. This is not specific to a particular geographical location. Wherever you live, it is appropriate for you to ask for a reduced fee if your budget is limited.

Some therapists also accept benefit payments such as Medicaid or Medicare. You may be able to get lists of these providers from your county health or mental health department.

Virtually all licensed therapists can accept third-party payments from insurance companies, so it is important for individuals considering therapy to check the mental health benefits included in their health insurance policy. Finally, consider whether the prohibitive cost of medical care would keep someone from consulting a physician if he or she were in physical pain.

Myth 3: "The unhappiness that I'm now feeling will go away by itself in due time." Research does support the idea that some forms of psychological problems do improve or disappear with the passage of time. The questions to consider are how much time needs to pass and how much discomfort can be tolerated without its having a disruptive effect on your everyday life.

Psychotherapy is not the only resource available to a troubled person, but it may be one of the most valuable resources. It can crystallize issues and speed recovery. It may also help to restore an individual's faltering sense of self-worth before it gets to rock bottom.

Individual therapy is the usual starting point for those seeking psychological assistance. The process usually begins when a person feels the need for help in unraveling the emotional web entangling him or her. Even when a person has been a paragon of mental health, the psychological impact of unrelenting conflicts within the family can be devastating. Somehow, you must go on with life, accept the pain, heal your own wounds, and continue to function more-or-less adequately. This is a gigantic strain when heaped upon the everyday stresses of contemporary life. The person who seeks the support of a therapist for guidance through these awful times has, at least, a modicum of self-kindness.

What actually happens in therapy? Most individual therapy is based on conversations between the counselor and the client. The goals, procedures, and projected outcomes of this process depend on many factors, such as the theoretical orientation of the therapist, the wishes of the client, and the time available for treatment. The course of therapy is a joint venture of the therapist and the client. No one else need be involved, unless she or he is brought into the discussion by the client during the therapy hour. Individual therapy is a private matter, and the professional counselor selected is the sole confidant. This fact alone may partially account for the satisfaction many people report with their therapeutic experience.

Counseling Groups

People learn about themselves in many ways. In addition to individual therapy, a second very effective way is through group counseling. The typical counseling or psychotherapy group is made up of between eight and fourteen individuals who have been brought together through their need for support, encouragement, and an opportunity to talk about the issues in their lives that are a source of unhappiness. Counseling groups offer their participants a chance to learn about themselves in some special ways. The superficial politeness and propriety that one finds in everyday transactions are the jumping-off point leading to a deeper level, where feelings, impressions, wishes, and candid observations are shared.

The group can provide a powerful support base for an individual making life changes. It can help a person identify and struggle with stumbling blocks and blind spots, and it does this in an environment that is encouraging. It offers a place where brand-new ideas, feelings, and behavior can be presented and then incorporated or modified with the help of other members' feedback.

The group is a community. Like a family that comes together on a regular basis, usually once a week, it takes care of the psychological needs of its members. Like a family, the group comes to know its members, with all of their strengths and weaknesses, through observation and interaction. Unlike a family, the group does not require that its members change or grow in any direction, except the one that is healthiest for that particular person. The direction in which a person grows or changes is a joint venture of the group member and the therapist or counselor who is there to guide the group.

There are as many kinds of counseling groups as there are psychological problems or individuals who are in emotional transition. Some groups are general, and a mixture of issues is explored by members of both sexes with a wide age range.

Some groups have a specific focus and therefore may be more tailor-made for you. Some communities provide life transition groups and support groups for the parents of gay or lesbian children, substance abusers, or adult-children with disabilities. The specific groups are very similar in size and format to the previously described groups. The major difference is in the focus and the composition of the group.

A group for the parents of disabled adult-children provides an opportunity for ventilation, discussion, emotional support, and clarification of the future for the participants. These are individuals who have firsthand experience in coping with a handicapped adult-child. The group might have a professional leader or be of the self-help variety (to be discussed later).

A special focus group offers the distinct advantage of shared experience. Everyone in the group would know intimately the struggle of setting limits, guilt, responsibility, and so on. According to one group member, "There is instant understanding. I don't have to spend much time outlining a problem or concern. As parents of disabled adults, we share a lot of the same experiences and feelings. It's so reassuring to see compassion and acceptance in someone's eyes and to know he's been there and will even share his wisdom."

Other kinds of specific focus groups are sometimes available in a community. A divorced woman trying to define her own place in the world, apart from her adult-children, felt safer in a group limited to women only. According to her, "I am concerned about not being taken seriously. My husband made me feel unimportant. It's not that I believe that all men will treat me the same way, but I don't feel that I would let myself be open and honest in a mixed group. Right now, I am more trusting of women."

A middle-aged person whose adult-child has severed her or his family ties might prefer the comfort of a group of other middle-aged people. Colin, who participates in such a group, feels that "there's a certain amount of shame involved. It would be hard for me to explain my situation to someone who has young children or no children. I am afraid of being blamed because they're too young to understand."

The variety of groups available is limited only by the size of a community and the creativity of the psychological practitioners who serve it. While rates are generally tied to the cost of living in a particular community, it is safe to say that group counseling is significantly less expensive than individual counseling. For a group that meets one-and-a-half or two hours a week, the cost per meeting will be less than half that of individual one-hour sessions.

Family Therapy

Family therapy focuses on the family as a system that is interdependent, and that is at the same time dependent on all of its components. Everyone in the family feels the stress of family changes and conflict, but different people express it in different ways. All of the family members need the opportunity to explore how the current situation affects their lives, and the family unit as a whole may need help in re-forming its structure to meet its future needs.

Family therapists are specialists who, through training and personal interest, work with the family system to stabilize it and help it shift. At the same time, the therapist pays close attention to the psychological issues of each family member and to his or her interactions within the family group. It is crucial that no one gets lost or becomes a scapegoat in the process.

To understand the usefulness of family therapy when, for example, an adult-child chooses an "unacceptable" lifestyle, imagine that the family is like a structure made of concrete blocks. Picture what will happen to this structure when a segment is wrenched out or no longer fits. If you see building blocks precariously balanced or toppled and the whole structure needing reinforcement or realignment, then you have a pretty good sense of what happens to the family during such turmoil.

Family counseling or therapy is a sister to group counseling. It may be ideally suited to a family that is itself divided, such as Jack's family discussed in Chapter 4. While Jack's parents were still immobilized, his siblings were much more tolerant and accepting. This difference in attitude could have caused additional conflict within the family if the parents had experienced increased distance from Jack's siblings as well as from Jack.

Family therapy might also be the treatment of choice where a family has been disrupted through the absence of an adult-child who has joined a cult or has otherwise disappeared. While the person is gone, a "ghost" is left behind, and the remaining family members must deal with the void created in their midst.

The cost for this style of treatment, depending on the size of the family, is similar to that of individual therapy.

Locating Therapeutic Services

The Private Sector

Psychotherapists in private practice and facilities that are not subsidized or controlled by government budgets or regulations make up the "private sector." The least effective way to locate the services of a licensed therapist in private practice is to use the yellow pages, looking under such labels as "Psychiatrist," "Psychologist," "Marriage and Family Counselor," or "Licensed Clinical Social Worker." Each listing will give the names of licensed practitioners, the degrees held, addresses, and phone numbers. You may be able to ascertain the sex of the therapist but little else. This method is chancy and should be avoided except as a last resort.

The ideal way to locate a therapist is through the recommendation of a close friend or a colleague, someone with values and attitudes similar to your own. The fit between therapist and client may still not be perfect, but a few potential problems can be eliminated.

The next best way to find a private therapist is through the local mental health association in your town, which probably maintains a referral service. Also, each professional discipline has a local organization or society that may publish a listing of therapists. Some organizations publish a pamphlet that includes much information about their therapists, such as their specialties, their degrees, the services provided, and their fees. There also may be a section on consumer rights and professional ethics.

National organizations also provide directories of qualified professionals (available in libraries). Many provide listings by city. The National Register of Health Service Providers in Psychology maintains a list of highly qualified psychologists throughout the United States.

An important point to remember about the private sector is that the person seeking therapy enters into a therapeutic relationship with the mental health professional and the fees for services are negotiated between the two of them. There are no outside agencies involved, and there is no substitution of therapists without the agreement of the client. Clearly, since the contract is with a particular therapist, changing therapists, for any reason, is the client's prerogative.

The Public Sector

The public sector includes psychotherapists and facilities supported by government funds or grants. It also includes community-based nonprofit agencies. In this category you can also find the grass-roots organizations and volunteer groups that provide quasi-professional services, generally without cost.

Community-based mental health facilities usually provide the full range of psychological and psychiatric services. Individual, family, and group therapy are usually available. Sometimes more specialized groups (e.g., for women or grieving) may be found. The professional qualifications of the therapists in these facilities are generally the same as those of private practitioners.

An advantage of public-sector professional services, compared with those of the private sector, is that the fees are usually on a sliding scale since government-subsidized care is available. This means that an individual with limited financial resources and no health insurance can generally get high-quality care.

One disadvantage is that, while there may be a number of mental health facilities from which to choose, picking a particular therapist may not be an option. A therapist may be assigned based on availability, appointment time, and so on. You are free to request a particular therapist, but she or he may take a while to become available.

Another potential disadvantage is the brevity of the treatment. Community-based services tend to be short-term; in some agencies, this means an eight-session limit. However, a great deal of help can be obtained during this time, especially when the psychological problem has been caused by a crisis or a family trauma.

Although communities differ in the precise kind or extent of the psychological services available, there is much commonality. Below is a list of typical community services. It may or may not accurately reflect your town.

Professional Facilities

1. *Community mental health services.* These services may be operated by the city or the county. There are usually a number of local clinics providing outpatient care. The full range of services is offered, including individual, group, and family therapy.

2. *Teaching hospitals.* These may be connected with a university medical school. Therapists may be full-fledged professionals or graduate interns under professional supervision. The full range of services is generally available.

3. *Nonprofit agencies.* These are agencies with financial support from a variety of nongovernmental sources, such as United

Way. They function in much the same way as community mental health services, with the same advantages and disadvantages. They tend to offer similar services and professionally trained therapists. An example of such an agency is the Family Service Agency found in most cities.

4. *Services operated by religious organizations.* Many houses of worship offer professional counseling services provided by therapists or clergy with specialized training. Three such programs, with service throughout the United States, are Catholic Social Services, Lutheran Social Services, and Jewish Family Services. Programs serving other denominations and faiths may be found in fair-sized cities. Also, these services are often available to the community at large and may not necessarily have a religious orientation. The nature of the services offered may vary greatly, depending on the location. Fees are generally on a sliding scale, or the services may be free to congregation members.

5. *Volunteer services.* Volunteer services are just that. The individuals who offer their help often receive training from professional consultants or more experienced helpers. However, these individuals, by and large, are not credentialed and could not offer their services privately for a fee. They are generally well meaning, sensitive, and concerned persons who do what they do because it is meaningful to them. There are generally no fees though donations may be accepted. In most communities, the local mental health association keeps a comprehensive listing of volunteer and self-help organizations. City and county government can also provide information about a variety of local programs.

Educational Resources

Therapeutic resources and counseling have their limits. While they provide growth, support, and nurturance, they tend to be time-limited. In addition, these services do not meet everyone's needs. Some individuals are simply not comfortable with this kind of help.

Educational resources offer information, an opportunity for the discussion of ideas, and an exchange between individuals with similar experiences. These tend to provide a less personal experience than the therapeutic resources. A book or a continuing-education class may be as useful as psychotherapy, but at a different point in the recovery process.

Three types of educational resources are discussed below. These are representative of what is generally available. The specifics may vary from area to area.

1. *Continuing-education classes (sometimes called extension or extended learning)*. These courses are not usually part of a college curriculum and therefore may not apply toward a college degree. They are designed to be practical and to meet the specific needs of the individuals who register for them. They may be taught by regular college faculty members, community experts, or local professionals.

Courses of this type may also be offered through secondary-school districts, local park and recreation departments, or community mental health agencies. In some cities, private organizations sponsor classes on topics of local interest. The Learning Exchange or the Learning Connection is an example of the latter found in many cities.

In considering the possibility of taking such a course, you may want to keep the following thoughts in mind. A course will expand what you know, but it may not answer any specific questions. It may allow you to see things differently, but that different view may not soften your pain. A course may acquaint you with others who have shared the same fate, but that sharing may, in fact, open new wounds for you. On the other hand, you can commit yourself to a course to the extent that you wish. Unlike in therapy, you can hold back your feelings if the content or the process of the class seems too threatening.

Courses on "midlife transitions" and "career change" seem to be the most commonly offered. Any course with the general theme of "letting go" may be appropriate. Check course descriptions and instructor credentials as well as titles.

2. *Discussion groups*. These tend to be less formally structured than continuing-education classes. They may or may not have professional leadership. More often than not, trained volunteers organize and facilitate the groups. The duration of discussion groups is variable. Some are arranged to meet continuously, monthly or bimonthly. Membership is generally open, and regular attendance is not required or even anticipated.

Often, there is a fine line between a continuing-education course and a discussion group. The latter are sometimes led by professionals, and the former sometimes include more discussion and interaction than lecture. For our purposes here, the distinction has to do with the facility offering the service. Noneducational institutions generally provide discussion groups. Such groups may be offered by the YMCA, the county mental health organization, hospitals, churches, community service organizations, and women's centers.

3. *Books*. The bookshelves are full of various self-help books for people seeking information, support, and encouragement. Reading, in contrast to continuing-education courses and discussion groups, is an entirely private experience. Unless you belong to a book discussion group, the way you assimilate what you have read is up to you. Reading allows you to maintain a self-determined pace. When you feel ready to move forward, you can, and when you've taken in all that you can possibly process at one time, you can quit.

The solitude of a person and a book may offer exactly the right environment for allowing you to express held-back feelings and emotions. You can cry with a book without embarrassment or the need to explain.

In searching for additional books at your local bookstore, the best place to start would be in the "self-help psychology" section. Remember to be as discriminating when you select a book as you are when you select a professional helper. Not all books are equally useful. Knowing something about the author's credentials and background experience may help you determine his or her expertise in writing a particular book.

Coming back to the starting point of this chapter, it's important to take care of yourself in as many ways as possible. There are times when no amount of thoughtful planning can get you started down the path you've chosen. There are times when the stress you've experienced is not matched by any useful way of coping. There are times when the brick wall that faces you is taller or wider than you first imagined, and you may feel hopeless or helpless in its presence.

Sometimes building a future beyond parenting requires the help of someone, or something, outside yourself. This chapter has provided you with some additional options for coping when your own well seems dry. The options are starting points only: ways to get you going when you feel stuck and directions to take when you feel that you've lost your way. My experience is that most people need this and little more. The best antidote for lethargy and depression is to *do* something. Hopefully, some of the ideas presented in this chapter will inspire you to act on your own behalf.

References

Alpaugh, P., & Haney, M., *Counseling the Older Adult: A Training Manual*, University of Southern California Press, Los Angeles, 1978.

Bardwick, J., "Where We Are and What We Want: A Psychological Model," in R. Nemiroff & C. Colarusso (Eds.), *New Dimensions in Adult Development*, Basic Books, New York, 1990.

Bombeck, Erma, *Motherhood: The Second Oldest Profession*, G. K. Hall, Boston, 1984.

Brans, J., & Smith M., *Mother, I Have Something to Tell You*, Doubleday, New York, 1987.

Colarusso, C., & Nemiroff, R., *Adult Development*, Plenum Press, New York, 1981.

Costa, P., & McCrae, R., "Personality Change and the Changes in Adult Life," in M. Storandt & G. VanderBos, *The Adult Years: Continuity and Change*, American Psychological Association, Washington, DC, 1989.

Donohugh, D., *The Middle Years*, W. B. Saunders, Philadelphia, 1981.

Ellis, A., *Reason and Emotion in Psychotherapy*, Lyle Stuart, New York, 1962.

Erikson, E., *Childhood and Society*, Norton, New York, 1950.

Fischer, L., *Linked Lives: Adult Daughters and Their Mothers*, Harper & Row, New York, 1986.

Fodor, I., & Franks, V., "Women in Midlife and Beyond: The New Prime of Life?" *Psychology of Women Quarterly*, 1990, 14(4).

Friday, N., *My Mother Myself*, Dell, New York, 1976.

Gerber, J., *Life Trends: Your Future for the Next 30 Years*, Avon, New York, 1991.

Ginott, H., *Between Parent and Child*, Macmillan, New York, 1965.

Gould, R., *Transformations*, Simon & Schuster, New York, 1978.

Gross, Z., *And You Thought It Was All Over: Mothers and Their Adult Children*, St. Martin's Press, New York, 1985.

Halpern, H., *Cutting Loose: An Adult Guide to Coming to Terms with Your Parents*, Simon & Schuster, New York, 1976.

Harris, T., *I'm O.K., You're O.K.*, Avon, New York, 1973.

Hoover, M. *The Responsive Parent*, Parents' Magazine Press, New York, 1972.

Hudson, F., *The Adult Years*, Jossey/Bass, San Francisco, 1991.

Hunter, S., & Sundel, M. (Eds.), *Midlife Myths: Issues, Findings and Practical Implications*, Sage, Newbury Park, CA, 1989.

Klass, D., "In the Midst of Years," in R. Kalish (Ed.), *Midlife Loss: Coping Strategies*, Sage, Newbury Park, CA, 1989.

Kübler-Ross, E., *On Death and Dying*, Macmillan, New York, 1969.

LaSorsa, V., & Fodor, I., "Adolescent Daughter/Midlife Mother Dyad: A New Look at Separation and Self-Definition," *Psychology of Women Quarterly*, 1990, 14(4).

Lerner, H., *The Dance of Intimacy*, Harper & Row, New York, 1989.

Levinson, D., Darrow, C., Klein, E., Levinson, M., & McBee, B. "Periods in the Adult Development of Men: Ages 18–45," *The Counseling Psychologist*, 1976, 6(1).

Levinson, D., *The Seasons of a Man's Life*, Knopf, New York, 1978.

Maslow, A., *Toward A Psychology of Being*, Van Nostrand, New York, 1968.

Mazor, A., & Enright, R., "Individuation: A Social-Cognitive Perspective," *Journal of Adolescence*, 1988, 11(1).

McGoldrick, M., & Gerson, R., *Genograms in Family Assessment*, Norton, New York, 1986.

Mitchell, A., & Helson, R., "Women's Prime of Life," *Psychology of Women Quarterly*, 1990, 14(4).

Morris, D., *The Human Zoo*, McGraw-Hill, New York, 1969.

Naisbitt, J., *Megatrends: Ten New Directions Transforming Our Lives*, Warner Books, New York, 1982.

Neugarten, B., "Adaptation and the Life Cycle," *The Counseling Psychologist*, 1976, 6(1).

References | 263

Neugarten, B., & Neugarten, D., "Policy Issues in an Aging Society," in M. Storandt & G. Vander Bos, *The Adult Years: Continuity and Change*, American Psychological Association, Washington, DC, 1989.

Oldham, J., "The Third Individuation: Middle Aged Children and Their Parents," in J. Oldham & R. Ciebirt (Eds.), *The Middle Years: Continuity and Change*, Yale University Press, New Haven, 1989.

Rossi, A., "Aging and Parenthhood in the Middle Years" in P. Baltes & O. Brim, *Life-Span Development and Behavior*, Academic Press, New York, 1980.

Rossi, E., *The Psychobiology of Mind-Body Healing*, Norton, New York, 1986.

Roth, S., *Psychotherapy: The Art of Wooing Nature*, Jason Aronson, Northvale, NJ, 1987.

Rotter, J., "Generalized Expectancies for Internal versus External Control of Reinforcement, *Psychological Monographs*, 1966, 80(609).

Rubin, L., *Women of a Certain Age: The Midlife Search for Self*, Harper & Row, New York, 1981.

Scarf, M., *Intimate Partners*, Random House, New York, 1987.

Schlossberg, N. & Troll, L., *Perspectives on Counseling Adults: Issues and Skills*, Brooks/Cole, Monterey, CA, 1978.

Sheehy, G., *Passages*, Dutton, New York, 1976.

Sheehy, G., *Pathfinders*, Morrow, New York, 1981.

Storandt, M., & VanderBos, G., *The Adult Years: Continuity and Change*, American Psychological Association, Washington, DC, 1989.

Toder, F., *When Your Child Is Gone: Learning to Live Again*, Ballantine Books, New York, 1987.

Thomas, R., *Counseling and Life-Span Development*, Sage, Newbury Park, CA, 1990.

Toffler, A., *Future Shock*, Random House, New York, 1970.

Toffler, A., *Previews and Premises*, Morrow, New York, 1983.

Troll, L., "Myths of Midlife: Intergenerational Relationships," in S. Hunter & M. Sundel (Eds.), *Midlife Myths: Issues, Findings and Practical Implications*, Sage, Newbury Park, CA, 1989.

U.S. Department of Commerce, *Statistical Abstract of the United States, 1992*, in *The National Data Book* (112th ed.), Washington, DC, 1992.

Vaillant, G., *Adaptation to Life*, Little Brown, Boston, 1977.

Van Hoose, W., *Midlife Myths and Realities*, Humanics, Atlanta, GA, 1985.

Wallerstein, J., & Blakeslee, S., *Second Chances: Men, Women and Children a Decade after Divorce*, Ticknor & Fields, New York, 1989.

Walsh, P., *Growing through Time: An Introduction to Adult Development*, Brooks/Cole, Monterey, CA, 1983.

Weick, A., "Patterns of Change and Processes of Power in Adulthood," in S. Hunter & M. Sundel (Eds.), *Midlife Myths: Issues, Findings and Practical Implications*, Sage, Newbury Park, CA, 1989.

Winnicott, D. W., *Psychoanalytic Explorations*, Harvard University Press, Cambridge, 1989.

Index